C000180402

The Book of

AXMINSTER WITH KILMINGTON

Portrait of a Devon Market Town

BY LES BERRY & GERALD GOSLING

HALSGROVE

First published in Great Britain in 2003

Copyright © 2003 Les Berry & Gerald Gosling

This book is dedicated to the people of Axminster, past, present and future.

All rights reserved. No part of this publication may be reproduced, stored in a retrieval system, or transmitted in any form or by any means without the prior permission of the copyright holder.

British Library Cataloguing-in-Publication Data
A CIP record for this title is available from the British Library

ISBN 1 84114 230 1

HALSGROVE

Halsgrove House
Lower Moor Way
Tiverton, Devon EX16 6SS
Tel: 01884 243242
Fax: 01884 243325
email: sales@halsgrove.com
website: www.halsgrove.com

Frontispiece photograph: *Axminster seen from the River Axe in 1900.*

Printed and bound by CPI Bath Press, Bath.

Whilst every care has been taken to ensure the accuracy of the information contained in this book, the publisher disclaims responsibility for any mistakes which may have been inadvertently included.

Contents

Top right: *Jack Soper, Axminster's town crier, outside Collard's jewellery store and Leslie & Bullard's drapery in West Street, c.1923.*

Below: *Floods at Axminster Bottom in 1970.*

ACKNOWLEDGEMENTS

We are grateful to the people who have kindly allowed us to use their pictures or other memorabilia, without which this book would not have been possible. First and foremost our thanks go to the Axminster Museum in Church Street, well worth a visit even if local history is not your strong point. Likewise, we are indebted to Jim Rowe, Axminster's lord of the manor in 2003, who generously allowed us access to the Rowe family collection.

In addition we must thank Philip Evans, Editor of *Pulman's Weekly News* – not just for his kind introduction but also for permission to use the back editions of that worthy paper for our research.

Thanks also to Axminster Library in South Street where the staff are so courteous (they can even make you feel good when being fined for a late book) and to Douglas Hull for his Postscript (page 156).

Others we must thank are: Chris Bolton, Colin Bowerman, Ron Cross, Pam Dowell, Steve and Brian Downton, Kathleen Gage, Sheila Hughes, Elaine Huxford, Kilmington Parish Council, David Lavender and Kilmington Cricket Club, May Lavender, the *Midweek Herald*, Shirley Moore (née Manley), Christopher James, John Nicholls Love, Chris Scott, the late Donald Thomas, Gordon Westcott of Alex R. Thirkettle, Dave Wheadon, Darren Windsor and Eileen Wittridge.

The staff of Pulman's Weekly News *outside their South Street office in 2002.*
Left to right: *James Coles, Michelle Williams, Steve Downton, Jackie Evans, Tony Woodman, Philip Evans, Michelle Taylor, Amanda Foster, Rose Siwek, Alex Alexander, Alexandra Phryce-Jones.*

Above: *A postcard dating from around 1910.*

Top right: *A receipt from Robert Snell, of Summerleaze Farm, Kilmington, an auctioneer and estate agent.*

Right: *A fine example of the Kilmington 'squared-circle' postmark used from the 1880s until the 1920s.*

Wally Fellender had been the Axminster and Lyme Regis area staff reporter for Pulman's Weekly News *for 40 years when he retired in 1972. At his retirement party in the Cedars Hotel he was presented with a tea trolley. Those present were,* left to right: *Mrs Martin Heale, Miss Jacqueline Williams, Martin Heale (news editor,* Western Gazette*), Les Toucher (*Chard & Ilminster News*), Dave King (photographer), Gerald Silverlock (photographer), Mrs Dave King, Frank Cole (staff reporter for the Sidmouth area), ?, Philip Evans, who succeeded Wally Fellender, Lindley Fellender, Olive Fellender, Wally Fellender, Ernie Day (Dorset area reporter), Mrs Fellender, Chloe Wheadon, Colin Hayball (staff reporter for Honiton area), Dave Wheadon (photographer), Mrs Hayball, Courtney Harris (photographer for Honiton area). The two men behind Wally Fellender have not been identified. Wally Fellender wrote his articles in longhand but, when he retired, the* Western Gazette*, the parent of* Pulman's Weekly News*, gave him a typewriter.*

INTRODUCTION

Axminster from the air in the late 1950s. Of interest are the gasometers at 'Chimney Corner' in Vale Lane, near the railway line on the left.

Axminster has always been the spiritual home of *Pulman's Weekly News*, first published by George Pulman, son of Axminster, and organist at the Parish Church, on 10 March 1857. In fact Pulman printed his first issues at his brother's printing works in Crewkerne and they were transported to Axminster, and other towns and villages throughout Devon, Somerset and Dorset by horse and cart and sold for three half pence. George Pulman, of course, went on to write the most famous local history book of them all – Pulman's *The Book of the Axe*.

In launching *Pulman's Weekly News*, Pulman wrote in his first editorial:

> *We shall endeavour to combine the ledger and the library, the abstractions of the closet, and the calculations of the counting house, the business of the market and the relaxation of fireside to form, in short that which every newspaper ought to form... a map of busy life, its fluctuations and its vast concerns.*

In the very first issue of *Pulman's*, news from Axminster included the appointment of parish constables at a Vestry meeting. There was also a report on the second monthly sale of horses and cattle conducted by Mr B. Gage, with the correspondent recording: 'Mr Gage as usual, gave entire satisfaction, both to the buyers and sellers, and there was a general expression of approbation in his regard for thus endeavouring to revive our market.' *Pulman's Weekly News* has faithfully recorded the history of Axminster ever since and much of the town's illustrious past has been recorded in our columns by Gerald Gosling and Les Berry.

I first worked for *Pulman's Weekly News* as a fresh-faced young man in the 1970s, succeeding the doyen of all local reporters, the late, great Wally Fellender. Wally was well respected. I can remember that during one difficult debate D.F. Baker, chairman of Axminster Rural District Council, turned to the press bench and said, 'Mr Fellender, what do you think?'

After several years in London, I returned to Axminster to work and as I walked into a meeting of the Axminster Parish Council one of the councillors looked up and asked, 'How are you Pip?' (my nickname). It was as though I had never been away. Nothing has changed very much during those 25 years – and that's part of the pleasure of editing Axminster's local newspaper. Axminster – made world famous through its link with the carpet industry – is a fascinating town with a fascinating history, and I believe George Pulman would have enjoyed reading it.

Philip Evans, Editor, *Pulman's Weekly News*,
June 2003.

Edwin Dawkins & Son Ltd's shop on the corner of Chard Street and Victoria Place, c.1908. At the time they sold furniture, clothing, boots and shoes, as well as ironmongery.

The first cattle auction held in Axminster after the Second World War, 1 July 1954.

1

EARLY HISTORY

Man left his mark around Axminster long before the narrow confines of recorded history. Such evidence can be found in the sandy soil at Broom Crossing, and on the hilltops that dot the Axe valley, the shared boundary of the Durotriges, who gave Dorset its name, and the Dumnonii, remembered to this day as the original Devonians.

The Romans passed Axminster by. Their Fosse Way, after approaching the modern-day town from the east, veers away and, via Stoney Lane, passes the town on its way to the sea near Seaton. The Fosse crossed the Icknield Way to the south of the town, somewhere in the region of what has become the modern-day Woodbury housing estate.

The Saxons arrived in the Axe valley at the start of the seventh century after winning the Battle of Beandun (AD614), which is said to have taken place at Bindon above Axmouth. With their lovable way of calling a spade a spade the Saxons named most of their new settlements after a geographical feature of that area. As such those rivers in England called Axe, Exe, Usk or even Avon are corruptions of the Saxon word for water. The name of Axminster was born after AD786 when Cyneheard founded his church there; it was literally the Minster by the River Axe. Down the centuries the name has appeared in many corrupted forms – one of the earliest forms dates from around AD900 when it can be found as Ascanmyster. It is Alseministre in Domesday (1086) and other forms include Aixeminstra, Asseminister, Exeminstre and Æxemenistre. Other Saxon place names that can be found in the parish include Smallridge (once smalrigge) from smael or narrow ridge. Weycroft (Wigacrosta) was probably 'Wiga's croft'; Undercleave Farm (Underclyne) was 'below the hillside'; Stammery Hill (Huverastamerlege) most likely stems

The Icknield Way ran to the south and east of Axminster and on towards Honiton via Gammons Hill and Kilmington. During the excavation work for the Axminster bypass, which was opened in 1991, part of the road was uncovered at the foot of Gammons Hill.

from Stan, mære and leah – the place lying on the parish boundary. Huver is for uver, in other words over or upper.

However, not all the place names come from our Saxon forebears. Bever Grange appears as Bewer and Bever in the thirteenth century and is probably from the Norman-French 'belvoir', or beautiful view, and almost certainly was named as such by the monks at Newenham Abbey. In addition, of course, there are a considerable number of farms and places that owe their name to a previous owner. Payne's Place speaks for itself and certainly can be found as such as early as 1550. The origins of Stoney Lane, Chard Road, Lyme Road, Castle Hill and Church Street are also fairly obvious.

There are some parts of the town whose names derive from a particular event. Ducking Stool Bridge was the bridge over the mill stream at the foot of Castle Hill. It owes its name to the ducking-stool that once stood beside it. Its primary purpose was for female scolds although, having said that, the last person to be ducked was a man called Butcher. As Davidson says, it seems he had applied the *Argumentum baculinum* to his offending *Cara sposa*, and his indignant female neighbours inflicted the humiliating punishment on him. The name lived on in later years when Frank Rowe, the lord of the manor of Axminster, jocularly gave Herbert Jeffery the nickname of Lord Jeff of Ducking Stool Bridge (because he lived in a house more or less opposite the site of the ducking-stool) and it stuck.

Bow Bridge, over the River Axe on the Kilmington Road and formerly known as Axe Bridge, is said to be named after a man called Jimmy Bow who sold his famous cure for snake bites at Axminster market and other places. He would take an adder out of a bag and let it bite his arm and then he would take a deep draught of his medicine. Needless to say he suffered no ill affects and, in an age when most people were engaged in agricultural work during which they often encountered adders, business was brisk. Sadly, for him if not the folklore of Axminster, on one occasion he reached for his medicine and found that he had left it at his home in Kilmington. He rushed away but, when he had got as far as the bridge, he died. Surely an occasion when taking one's own medicine would have been a good idea.

Axminster's recorded history begins in AD786 when Cyneheard founded a church there just before his death. It is one of the oldest churches in Devon. He was a shadowy figure, definitely a descendant of Cerdic, the founder of the Royal House of Wessex, but his line of descent is not certain. His reign was short, his death coming less than a year after he wrested the throne from Cynewulf (AD757–86) who had defeated and killed Cyneheard's brother Sigebert (AD756–57) at Merton. Tradition has it that it was Cyneheard's bones that were discovered in St Mary's Church, Axminster, in 1782.

The church and town remained in royal hands – passing through Alfred the Great to his grandson, Athelstan, who endowed the church with the manor of Prestaller to support the priests who were 'to pray for the souls of seven earls, and others, who fell in a great battle with the Danes outside the town.' Tradition also has it that this battle was at Brunanburh (AD937). George Pulman in his famous *The Book of the Axe*, along with James Davidson, other Victorian historians, and even a few modern ones, are firm on this point. Even modern-day civic authority has joined them by naming a housing estate on the edge of the town after the battle – and getting the spelling wrong (Brunenburg). That a battle took place in the lush water-meadows between Axminster and Kilmington is beyond doubt. A Charter from Henry VIII's time that is lodged in the British Museum tells us that:

> *The entrance to Otterford* [Otterton] *and Seton ryvers are londings and in the time of King Athelstan there entrid at Seton dyvurse strange nacions, who were slain at Axminster to the number of v kings, vii erles, a bushope* [bishop] *and ix score thousand in the hole* [whole], *as a book old written does testify.*

Nine score thousand is 180,000 and that does not include those who survived, which means that the Danish forces surely must have been in excess of at least 200,000. If one boat held 100 men, which few longships ever did, there would have been 2,000 boats in Seaton Bay. No doubt the local fishermen were grumbling.

The Battle of Brunanburh was between Athelstan's English forces and those of King Constantine III of Scotland, an old foe of the English King who had found that discretion was very much the better part of valour when confronted by Athelstan's vastly superior army. He went back home to Scotland where he gathered together a grand alliance of men with their own scores to settle with the English, including Anlaf Guthfrithson, an Irish prince, and many other Irish and Danish leaders. They landed in the Humber estuary and, with autumn and the end of the campaigning season fast approaching, would hardly have had time to reach as far south as East Devon, even if Athelstan had not stood in their way.

Colonel A.H. Bryne, in his excellent *More Battlefields of England*, claims that Brunanburh took place at Brinsworth where, like Axminster, there is a strong local tradition of a battle with the Danes. Brunanburh is said to have taken place at a fort on a hill called Weondun ('Holy Hill'). It is not possible to state with any certainty where this fort was but it is possible that it was one of the forts on Northumbria's southern border in the Don valley.

The invaders fled the field leaving behind them Constantine's son, Cellach, 'five other kings, including the Viking king of the Western Isles, Owain of the Cumbrians, and seven of Anlaf's earls.'

St Giles' Church, Kilmington.

Above: *Looking into Trinity Square from Victoria Place, c.1906. Nicholl's Bazaar on the left is Forbuoys in 2003; the private house with the balcony became part of the Dawkins' empire, and then Potter's furniture shop. Next to it was Chick's butcher's shop and then the Old Bell Hotel. The butcher's shop became part of Potter's, while the Old Bell has been converted into a small shopping precinct.*

Left: *Chard Road looking down to Millbrook Farm around 1900.*

Right: *Granny Rockett gave her name to the corner at the junction of Lyme Road and Sector Lane where she ran a sweet shop for many years in what was once the East Gate toll-house. Formerly a Miss Enticott, she married Hugh Ebdon, a quarry worker who was killed in a pit fall at Raymonds Hill. Her second husband was a Mr White and finally she married a Mr Rockett. She continued the business until at least the early 1940s. The shop and house behind her in this picture were demolished, but even in 2003, the older generation of Axminster still refers to this site as Granny Rockett's Corner.*

That the slain at Axminster's 'Brunanburh', according to the cartulary of Newenham Abbey, included 'seven [English] earls and many others', is a coincidence and may have led to all the confusion from which many later historians suffered. On the other hand there is an interesting supposition by Major W.H. Wilkin, in his excellent *Notes on Axminster Church and the Vicars Since 1602*. He says, 'If so [the battle taking place in the North], we must definitely reject the tradition that the Minster was founded here to commemorate the burial of his [Athelstan's] earls.' Now that is a thought.

That alarm apart, Axminster slept out most of the rest of the Saxon era, although it would have trembled like everyone else whenever there were Viking raids in the vicinity, such as at Charmouth in AD833 and AD837. The Vikings also marched up from Exmouth to sack Exeter in 1001.

Another Axminster tradition is the Saxon castle that, according to Watts in his *Book of Axminster*, was built in AD916. Although there is a Castle Hill, there is no proof that any fortification existed other than the discovery of large, underground stone works, which were, in fact, the cellars of the former Dolphin Inn. Watts' choice of AD916 is interesting; it was, of course, the year (in December) when Canute became King of all England.

The Battle of Hastings was too far away to bother Axminster. However, in its aftermath, when William the Conqueror wanted to give certain East Devon estates to the Abbot of Mont St Michel in Normandy as a show of thanks for his services rendered in preparation for the invasion of England, he had to send a large army westward because the Countess Gytha, Harold II's mother, refused to give up the manor of Otterton. That army would have been close enough to Axminster to cause some anxious moments.

Axminster fared badly during the Black Death; it suffered early because the plague arrived in England through the tiny port of Melcombe Regis, now part of Weymouth and less than 40 miles from Axminster. The cartulary of Newenham Abbey states that only the abbot himself and two other monks survived and that 20 monks and three lay brethren died between 1348–49. It also reports that 88 others perished, many of them being the townspeople of Axminster.

The town was not affected by the Wars of the Roses, took a distant interest in the Spanish Armada, after all Drake 'e wer a Devon man', and did not have too many worries during the times of the Henrican and Marian persecutions.

Axminster slumbered through a few centuries as a typical English rural community and was described by John Leland, the celebrated intinerist, who passed through in 1585 as:

> *Ax then rennith to Axminstre* [he was coming from Ford Abbey] *a pratie quik market toun of three miles lower, ripa citeriori* [on the bank on this side]; *this toun is in Devonshir. The personage of Axminstre, so I learned, is in impropriateto the chirch of York. The chirch of Axminstre is famous by the Sepultures of many noble Danes slain in King Athelstan's time at a batel on Brunes-doun thereby the Sepultures likewisesome Saxon lordes slain in the same Feld. Ax thens renneth through Axminstre bridge of stone about a quarter of a mile lower than Axminstre toun; Sumwhat lower than bridge entrith Artey* [Yarty] *river, being sumtyme a Raging Water into he river. There is a stone bridge of Artey. About half a mile from the place where it entrith into Ax; this Bridge of sum is called Kilmington bridge,* [after] *a village not very far it. About half a mile lower than Axminstre bridge is Newenham, sumtime an Abbay, of Bernadines, of the foundation of Mohun, Erle of Somerset. Ax rennith a mile lower through Ax Bridg of two archis of stone. This bridg servith not to pass overat High Tide, otherwise it doth. Then Ax rennith half a mile lower to Axmouth Town and a quarter of a mile lower, under White Clif into the ocean se, ther cullid Ax Bay.*

In 1822 Lyson visited Axminster and had this to say of the town:

> *Axminster, in the hundred of that name, and in the deaner of Honiton, is an ancient market town, twenty miles from Exeter on the road to London from which it is 147 miles distant. The market was confirmed in or about 1204 to William, Lord Brewer to be held on Sundays as had been accustomed. In the Cartulary of Newenham Abbey are two transcripts of two Charters of King John of later date. In the 11th and 17th year of his reign both confirming the Sunday markets. He former grants likewise that Axminster is a free borough, and that the burgesses should have a fair for eight days, but the time is not mentioned.*
>
> *The present market day is Saturday; the corn market is becoming inconsiderable; there are three cattle fairs, the first Tuesday after the 25th April, the first Tuesday after the 24th June and the first Wednesday after the 10th October. At this place is a celebrated manufactory of carpets; a considerable quantity of tape and fillettings are also made in Axminster. The carpet manufactory, which is conducted by Mr Ransome* [sic] *Whitty, was established in 1755 by his grandfather, Mr Thomas Whitty, to whom, in 1759, was adjudged a premium of thirty pounds from the Society of Arts for having made the largest Turkey carpet that had Been manufactured in this country. It was 26 feet 6 inches by 17 feet 6 inches.*
>
> *The number of inhabitants in this town and parish was, in 1801, 2,154; in 1811 2,387, according to the returns made to Parliament at those periods. The historic notices that I have Found relating to this town are the celebrated battle with the Danes, hereafter mentioned, and an action in the month of October 1644 between Sir Richard Cholmondledy, then stationed at Axminster with a party of the King's*

Left: *Looking up into Lyme Street from Victoria Place, c.1900. Much of that side of the George Hotel seen here was taken down when Lyme Street was widened for traffic safety purposes some time after 1960. Nicholl's Bazaar on the right became a newsagent and in 2003 the local branch of Forbuoys.*

horse and the Parliamentarian forces, in which Sir Richard received his death wound.

The abbey of Newenham in this parish, was founded for monks of the Cistercian order in the reign of Henry III (1216–1272) by Reginald de Mohun and his younger brother William. The Intention appears to have originated with the latter, who gave for the purpose his lands in Torr and Mariansleigh.

Axminster's experiences during the Civil War were mostly limited to skirmishes in the surrounding countryside although the fact that neighbouring Lyme Regis was a Parliamentarian stronghold (why was it not stripped of its Regis tag?), and that its garrison made frequent excursions almost as far as Exeter, eventually led to a force of 300 Royalist soldiers being garrisoned in the town.

Lady Drake, at Ashe House, supported Parliament, and her request for troops to be stationed at Ashe was granted in 1644. Lord Poulett heard about it and marched from his home at Hinton St George and drove them out. Half-naked, in her nightdress, Lady Drake fled with them to Lyme Regis. Before he left Lord Poulett burnt Ashe to the ground. The Roundhead guard at Ashe House had come from Lyme Regis and it was from that tiny port that Axminster was attacked twice in 1644 by a force under no less a person than Colonel Creeley, the commander of the Lyme forces.

Davidson states that 50 local people were being kept as hostages by Lord Poulett's Royalist troops and, almost certainly correctly, suggests this indicates that Lyme Regis was not the only town in the area to be rather lacking in its loyalty to the King.

The first attack, on 15 November, ended with the defending Royalist troops bottled up in St Mary's Church. The Royalist commander, Sir Richard Cholmondledy, was killed and the attackers also lost a man and had five wounded. However, after setting fire to part of the town, the Government troops returned to Lyme Regis. A few days later they were back in strength hoping to surprise the Royalists but found them still in the church, a substantial building to attack. The attackers also claimed that they 'thought it fit not to fall upon a church' so they torched most of the town instead.

Perhaps they lacked the courage to tackle armed men in the strongest building in Axminster but, whatever their motive, at this distance in time one can hardly accept that any follower of Cromwell, an even bigger iconoclast than Henry VIII, would be unduly upset at the thought of destroying a church. Whether in the first attack, or the second, it seems that at least one shot was fired at the church – later drawings show that a sizable chunk of the tower was missing. If the people of Axminster had been lukewarm to the King's cause, they would hardly have been filled with Republican fervour after their town had been destroyed, especially with winter fast approaching.

Charles I duly lost both the Civil War and his head (in 1649). In 1651 his son, later Charles II, fled from the

Looking up Castle Hill c.1905. The thatched cottages on the left have long-since gone. Note the 'parked' carts at the top of the hill.

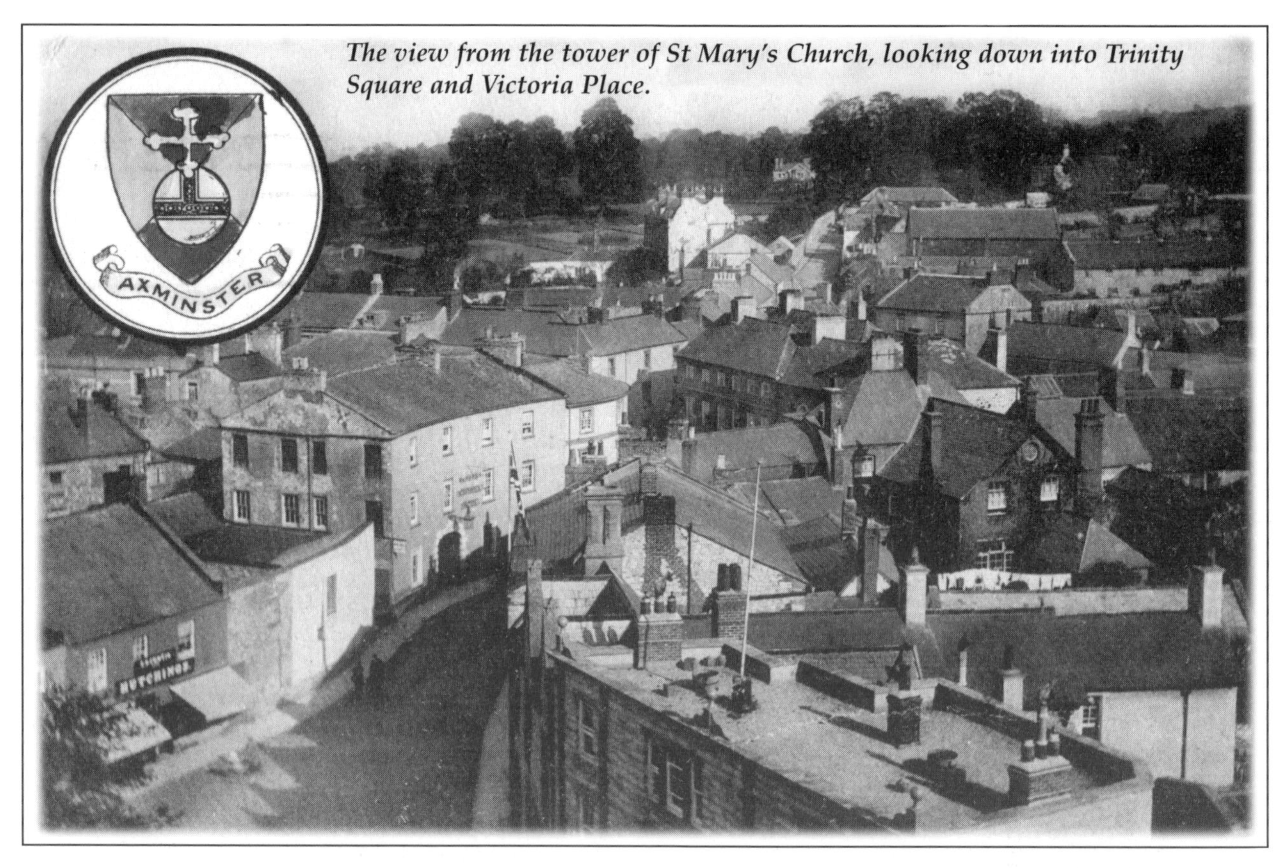

The view from the tower of St Mary's Church, looking down into Trinity Square and Victoria Place.

field after the Battle of Worcester and headed south-west in search of a boat to take him to France. He is said to have arrived in Axminster, closely followed by his pursuers. He sought refuge at Coaxden where, with his enemies virtually following him through the front door, he was forced to hide under the voluminous petticoats of a Mrs Cogan, the lady of the house. This story is unlikely to be true; it is told of so many places that it is a wonder that he ever found time to sail to France.

The next man to raise the dust on the streets of Axminster was Charles II's bastard son and pretender

IN ALL 78 AXMINSTER MEN WERE SAID TO HAVE STOOD TRIAL FOR THEIR PART IN THE DUKE OF MONMOUTH'S ILL-FATED REBELLION. C.W. BRACKEN, IN THE 1936 EDITION OF THE REPORT & TRANSACTIONS OF THE DEVONSHIRE ASSOCIATION, GIVES THESE NAMES:

John Bare
John Batts
George Blachford
William Blachford
Thomas Bobbett
Caleb Bragg
James Browne
John Bull
Robert Bull
Abraham Bunson
Richard Champ
Abraham Clarke
Robert Clarke
George Cleave (senr)
Robert Crosse
Richard Davy
Richard Denning
Henry Dittee
Robert Drower
John Edwards
James Enticott
George fford [sic]
William ffowler [sic]
William Gibbs
Robert Gold
John Gravidge
William Guppy
John Hamblen
Enoch Harvey
John Harvey
Samuel Harvey
Tristran Harvey
William Harvey
James Hill (senr)
James Hill (junr)
Nathaniel Hill
Samuel Hooper
Joseph Irish
Henry James (junr)
William Kelway
Robert Lincoln
John Long
John Love
Bernard Loveridge
John Lyddon
Malachi Mallack
Nicholas Matthew
Nicholas Moore
William Newton
John Olliver
Robert Olliver
Francis Perrick (junr)
Azariah Pinney
William Phippen
Luke Pyke
Samuel Ransome [sic]
David Reade
Philip Rockett
James Rowe
William Rowe
John Salisbury
George Searle
David Seward
Richard Seward
William Seward
Edward Slade
Richard Smith
Thomas Sprake (junr)
Robert Spurway
James Stroud
James Sweatland
James Taylor
Richard Thompson
Thomas Warren
John Williams
Robert Williams
John Wryard
William Wyatt

Left: *South Street, looking into Lyme Street, c.1900. The building on the left has long-since gone and in 2003 South Street car park stands in its place.*

Below: *Called Station Road on this Chapman postcard dating from around 1901, this is actually Anchor Hill, which has changed almost out of all recognition today. All the trees have gone, Shand's, and then Tesco, appeared on the left and only West House on the right remains.*

Right: *Tovey's jewellers' shop in West Street in 1915. Pictured in the doorway is Miss D.M. Tovey (presumably his daughter) who ran the business when Mr Tovey was serving in the Armed Forces during the First World War.*

to the throne, James Scott, Duke of Monmouth. The son of Lucy Walters, he passed through the town a few days after landing at Lyme Regis on 11 June 1685. The local militia moved to intercept his ragtag and bobtail army but quickly decided that discretion was a more preferable tactic and so allowed Monmouth to pass through Axminster unhindered. He picked up around 100 volunteers as he went on his way to Taunton (where he declared himself King), Sedgemoor (where James II's troops achieved a decisive victory) and, eventually, the block on Tower Hill.

Axminster's next connection with the rebellion was after the Battle of Sedgemoor, when James II sent Judge Jeffreys westward to deliver his bloody retribution.

C.W. Bracken states that the two men who were sentenced to death at the Dorchester Assizes by Judge Jeffreys on 10 September were John Bull, a husbandman of Uphay, and Malachi Mallack, an Axminster clothier. Bull was hanged at Bridport two days later. His widow survived him for 20 years, being buried at Axminster on 22 January 1706. Although he probably deserved his fate, Bull was unlucky in that Thomas Lane, an elder of his chapel (later the Congregational), and Stephen Towgood, two of the ringleaders, escaped punishment.

Malachi Mallack also escaped punishment receiving a pardon under the Great Seal dated 15 October 1685. He had turned King's evidence against Edmund Prideaux of Ford Abbey. Fortunately for Mr Prideaux there was no second witness and he was not tried. However, he was given as a present (by James II) to Judge Jeffreys, and only set free after paying the Judge £15,000. He could consider himself especially fortunate; his father had been Attorney General under Cromwell and was connected with the execution of James' father, Charles I. Mallack had five children baptised at Axminster. His wife was buried there on 22 September 1703 but he lived for another 29 years before being buried in the town in 1732.

Several men were transported to the West Indies; among them appear the names of Robert Clarke, Robert Drower, John Edwards, William Guppy, Samuel Harvey, Bernard Loveridge, William Phippen, Azariah Pinney, William Rowe and Robert Spurway, although these men may not necessarily be the Axminster men of those names. Azariah Pinney was the younger son of the Revd John Pinney, the intruder vicar of Broadwindsor during the Commonwealth. On arrival at Nevis he was ransomed for £65 and went on to play quite an important part in the life of the island. He later returned to England where he died in 1719. His son John became the Chief Justice of Nevis and his grandson, another John, represented Bridport in Parliament.

At the time Bracken was writing in 1936 he did not have the benefit of Robert Cornish's notes on the church accounts because his list omits at least one other man who we know to have been not only sentenced, but also executed in Axminster. The church accounts state that after laying out 11s. 'for when we went to take ye rebels', a further 16s. was paid 'for building ye gallows'. The unfortunate man was John Rose who, according to Mr Cornish (writing in 1896) was the only Axminster victim of Judge Jeffreys. Tradition always claims that the place of his death was in Stoney Lane.

Happily Robert Cornish went through the church accounts and noted much of what they contained. They give us many insights into life in Axminster during the seventeenth and eighteenth centuries. Sadly, however, they are prefaced with the remark:

These accounts dealing fully with the years 1660 to 1802 were formerly kept with the Church Registers in the Vestry but in 1896 they had to be handed over to the newly constituted Parish Council. Before this transfer I amused myself by taking some notes of some of the more interesting entries as detailed below. A few years later when given permission to consult them I was shown a heap of worthless pulp lying on the stone floor of a damp room. Happily I am still in possession of the rough notes taken 34 years ago, some of which may be of more than parochial interest.

Robert Cornish, Cedar House,
Axminster, Nov. 21 1930.

The notes began with a brief entry from 1660, 'Pd for outcomers – 6d.' There were many such entries and vagrants of all sorts were escorted to Penn, a mile over the Dorset border and left there, probably with a threat of what would happen to them if them came back.

In 1665 a warrant to 'out strangers' cost 6d. and two decades later 2s. were spent on 'whipping a man who threatened to burn our town and for a passport [warrant] for him.' Almost certainly the money went to the man who did the whipping but, although it was in 1685, the year of the Monmouth Rebellion, there is no evidence that the man was anyone other than a vagrant who was drunk and turned nasty when told to move on.

In 1677 'monies were paid for looking after a women which had a child born at the Swann.' The Swan was near the junction of Musbury Road and White Pot (Wide Post) Lane and was closed by 1817. The following year another unknown sum was paid for 'keeping and whipping ye papist'. The date of the whipping (1678) may be significant; it was during the summer of that year that the Popish Plot was uncovered. This was the so-called Jesuit plot concocted by Titus Oates and Israel Tonge to assassinate Charles II and put his Catholic brother, the Duke of York, on the throne. Whether the shock waves reached Axminster is unknown but Oates would later end up in the pillory himself.

The stocks in one corner of the churchyard (which can be seen in Axminster Museum) were often in use, a new pair being built in 1684 at a cost of £1.1s.6d. Among the early offenders to try them out for size was George Cleare who was 'kept one night in the Stocks'.

If a vagrant was too ill to be moved on it was the duty of the town to look after him, as was the case in 1693 when 'a sick traveller lay at the Angel' and the bill came to £1.5.7d. That same year 10s. was paid for 'carrying ye sick seaman to Penn'.

The end of the seventeenth century saw England engaged in William III's French wars and many wounded returned to England and sought charity as they walked to their home towns. In 1698 Axminster 'gave to poor prisoners who came out of France two shillings,' and a year later £3.1s.5d. was 'paid to 285 exchanged prisoners'. This works out at 2d. each.

There were also many references to payments made for ringing the bells at St Mary's, especially on grand occasions of State and military successes. The first to be found in the accounts was in 1666 but they would certainly have been rung six years earlier when Charles II returned from exile. Much of Charles' reign was spent at war with the Dutch and that 1666 entry was to 'Pay the ringers the thanksgiving day for the overthrow of the Hollanders the sum of fifteen shillings.' Later 5s. was spent on a ring on 'concluding ye peace with the Dutch'. In 1683 payments were made for the bells to be rung on Easter Day, an annual event of course, and on 5 November. Charles II was hardly likely to forget that Guy Fawkes had tried to blow up his grandfather some 80 years earlier. They were also rung 'for ye thanksgiving for ye discovery of the Plott.' This would have been the Rye House Plot at which the murder of King Charles II and his brother, the Duke of York (later James II), was planned. The cost of that ring was £1.15s.5d. The ring for James II's proclamation (1685) included an item of 6s. to build a stage from which to make the announcement.

In 1689 the parish stumped up 17s.6d. for a hogshead of cider for the bell-ringers on the occasion of the proclamation of William III and Mary II. A hogshead is 52 gallons, so 17s.6d. for a hogshead works out at ½d. per pint (happy days). Surely the ringers would have needed help to down 448 pints! In 1690 the ringers were paid 3s. (and no cider) for pealing at 'the news of the Irish being routed'. This was for William's victory at the Battle of the Boyne on 12 July.

In a similar vein a beacon was maintained on Trinity Hill along with a small building, probably for keeping a store of firewood dry. It is possible that its upkeep was shared by surrounding parishes because, in 1678, Axminster's churchwardens recorded that 'our share of Trinity Beacon and Beacon House' was £8.3s.6d. Robert Cornish, writing in 1896, tells us 'the beacon on Trinity Hill was last fired at Queen Victoria's Golden Jubilee in 1887.' It would almost certainly have been fired on her diamond jubilee in 1897, in 1902 for the coronation of Edward VII and in 1911, for George V's coronation. If it was still there, it may even have been fired in 1918 for the Armistice.

The stark poverty that stalked the land between the seventeenth and twentieth centuries can be easily traced in such records as those of Axminster's churchwardens, which contain many entries of payments to alleviate the suffering of the sick in the town, to help to cloth the poor and to pay for the burial of the destitute. In 1682 £2.16s.11d. was paid 'for shoes of several poor people and redeeming Joan Atkins' clothes and for a waistcoat for ye old Langbury.' It is interesting to note that the use of the word redeeming suggests that there was a pawnbroker in the town at the time and that, despite being poor, old Langbury warranted a waistcoat.

The great frost that occurred during the winter of 1683–84 led to many workers being laid off and it fell upon the churchwardens to pay 'several poor people in ye hard season and in the year in which [they] have not been in constant paye.' As much as £11.19s.3d. was paid out at that time.

In 1687, when 'Lincloth and money to the poor' was given, Robert Cornish suggests that it was from the rents from the parish land that had always been distributed in clothes. Among the payments that year were:

> *... one pair of shoes for Harmen's children, three and six... given old Joanes for his sons and families about him, three shillings... three pairs of shoes for Harmen's children, four and tuppence.*

In 1689 as much as £231 was spent on poor relief. The wardens paid John Pinney, an apothecary, 5s. for 'searching Enticott's wife's wounds'. Apparently she died and Enticott was tried at Exeter Assizes but no mention was made of the outcome. Of interest were the 2s. paid to Agnes Bearnes when her son had 'the evil'; another 10s. went to Mrs Elizabeth Mallack for 'curing the evil'; in 1724 6d. was paid for 'curing Clark's family of ye Ich'.

A payment of £1 for four yards of 'blew cloth' and 5s. for a couple of yards of red cloth to make some badges is recorded in 1697. There is no mention made at the time as to what purpose the badges would serve, although it was obviously for something that was so well known that the writer felt an explanation was not needed. Later, in 1727, another entry provides us with the explanation:

> *That the overseers, from hence forth, are not to pay any poor person their monthly or weekly pay unless they consent to wear their badges pursuant to an Act of Parliament, and we direct three officers to immediately make badges for that purpose, and if such poor persons do refuse to wear such badges in the weekdays their pay is to be cut back.*

People were not only poor; it was a matter of course that everyone knew it.

There was certainly an almshouse in Axminster in 1720, as records reveal that money was spent on its thatching at this time. It seems likely that there was a poorhouse of some kind that had fallen into

Trinity Square, Axminster, c.1905.

disrepair or become too crowded by 1737, when a meeting of the wardens agreed that a building be purchased or rented in order to construct a hospital or workhouse for the relief of the poor. Some of the leading citizens of the town, including Thomas Whitty, of Axminster Carpet fame, met to decide where to build (or convert) a workhouse. They leased a property in West Street at an annual rent of £8 from a Mrs Brooks. It was next to the parish house and the two were joined, thus forming a larger workhouse than that which had initially been envisaged. It needed to be; in 1747 there were 37 inmates who were supervised by a James Newton and Marjory Turner, governor and governess, with salaries of £6 and £4.10s. per annum respectively.

A map of 1770 shows that the parish workhouse had been moved; it was located at the bottom of the garden of the present Gamberlake House (although Gamberlake House itself was not constructed until about a century later). Whether this workhouse was still in use in 1770 is open to question.

The parish clink was, and still is, in Phoenix Lane (now Castle Street). At one stage, the parish constable was the licensee to a small house in Market Square as the tap to the Old Bell Hotel. Obviously the constable's salary was not enough to provide a decent living. In time the county constabulary was formed (in the 1850s) and, when the purpose-built police station followed, it had its own cells and the town clink became redundant.

Axminster was supplied with its water via a leat certainly as early as 1660, when it ran down Lyme Road and Lyme Street on the opposite side to the Catholic church. Drinking-water was later available from a sluice on the other side of the road in the wall at the side of what is now Lyme (once Lion) House. We do know that gutters took the surface water in the town because, in 1799, the trustees of Axminster's turnpike trust recorded that they had provided 'new Ham stone guttering to take the water through the town.' This was nothing to do with the leat. The trust, which was more than careful when it came to spending money, was only concerned with the condition of its road.

2

KILMINGTON'S HISTORY

Kilmington Cross around 1905 with the Old Inn in the background. The road vanishing up the hill towards Honiton, now the busy A35 part of the Folkestone–Exeter trunk road, was formerly part of the Icknield Way.

When and where the village of Kilmington came into being is not known, but it would almost certainly have been around the site of St Giles' Church, which, in all probability, was built on the site of an earlier and pagan place of worship. Tradition has it that the dead from the battle with the Danes in the water-meadows between Kilmington and Axminster during the reign of King Athelstan were brought to the church and buried there. It is also said that a yew tree was planted at the time to mark the spot. There is some conjecture that Kilmington's name stems from the burial of these dead warriors; it is believed to be a play on the words kili and mini – the place where the killed men were taken (buried). Dead soldiers and yew trees may be a myth; being called 'the place of the dead men' certainly is a myth. The study of English place names points an incontrovertible finger towards the fact that Kilmington's founding father was a Saxon with a name close to Coenhelm. The presence of 'inga', or a corruption thereof within a place name almost certainly indicates 'the home of the people of'. Kilmington is referred to as Chienenetona in the Exeter Domesday Book (1086), which makes it likely that the village was associated with a man called Coenhelm. In time Chienenetona was corrupted into Coenhelningston and, eventually Kilmington.

This theory suggests that Kilmington was settled early in the Saxon expansion into Devon, probably not long after their successful Battle of Beandun (said to be Bindon, near Axmouth) in AD614. There they would have found shelter, water and timber.

Before all that Roman Road marched up Gammons Hill on its way from Dorchester to Exeter. Kilmington, of course, like Axminster, did not exist at that time.

Once the alarms of the Viking era were in the past, Kilmington slumbered through the centuries in

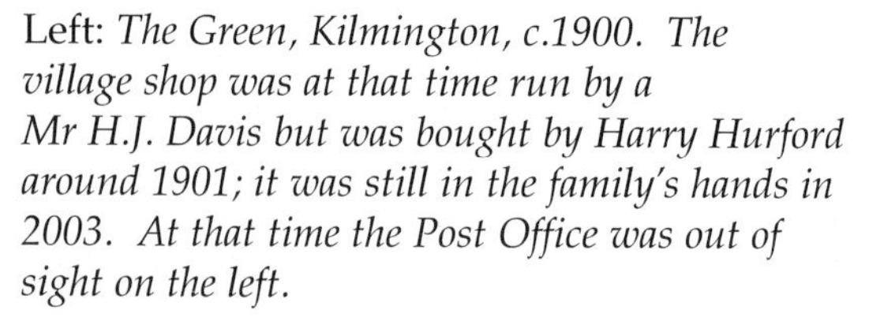

Left: *The Green, Kilmington, c.1900. The village shop was at that time run by a Mr H.J. Davis but was bought by Harry Hurford around 1901; it was still in the family's hands in 2003. At that time the Post Office was out of sight on the left.*

Right: *Brook House, The Green, Kilmington, c.1905. The Symonds family once occupied Brook House as a carpenter's shop.*

Left: *The Manse, Shute Road, Kilmington, c.1900. The thatched house was French's bakery.*

Right: *Loughwood meeting-house near Kilmington, built in 1643 by the Baptists, who were persecuted at the time. One of the oldest Baptist chapels in the country, it was originally thatched, then roofed in slate* (as picture), *and then rethatched. It is maintained by the National Trust in 2003.*

Looking down into All Saints from Smallridge, c.1910.

which the horizons of its ordinary folk were bounded no further than Axminster, Whitford or Dalwood. It would have suffered from the Black Death that decimated nearby Axminster and Newenham Abbey.

Neither the Wars of the Roses nor the Civil War would have bothered the village, apart from the passage of both Royalist and Roundhead soldiers making their way to and from the larger towns of the West Country.

However, Kilmington became involved in the religious upsets of the seventeenth century and, although it stands in Dalwood parish, Loughwood chapel was a direct outcome of those troubles. Before the Religious Toleration Act of 1869, Baptists were persecuted for their beliefs and were forced to hold their meetings in secret. Loughwood, which was built in 1643, served as one such meeting-place for the local Baptists and is one of the oldest Baptist meeting-places in the country. In 2003 it is the property of the National Trust and its interior has been restored to look just as it did in the seventeenth century, with its unvarnished-pine box pews, a plain wagon ceiling, simple white walls, a gallery, with a retiring room underneath, and a baptismal pool underneath the floor in front of the pulpit. The Baptists finally moved to Kilmington when they built their chapel there in 1832.

As far back as 1812 the schoolroom that had been built in Axminster had to provide education for two Kilmington children. Part of the money for this came from the will of local benefactress Penelope Saffin. Among the properties that helped provide for the education of the two children was a close of arable land of about two acres in the village. This land was said to be known as Stone's Ground and, at the time (1812) was let to John Stewart under a verbal agreement for a term of seven years at an annual rent of £16.

Kilmington's churchwardens' accounts are available in bound form between the years 1555–1608 and they cast some light on how the village ticked during the Elizabethan period. What is astonishing is the amount of money that was spent almost annually on repairing the church, which suggests that St Giles' at the time was not too grand a building. In 1556 for instance, Thomas Crandon was paid 12d. for riding after a prisoner and for performing repairs on the church and the parish house. The prisoner may have been sentenced to work on the church, the Elizabethan equivalent of community service, and absconded. Quite a bit of money was spent on fetching shyndels (rag slates used for roofing) from Seaton and sacks of 'Lyme' (lime), also for work on the church, the priest's house and the parish house. Other items that year included five ridge-tiles at 2d. each.

Of special interest in 1557 was that Robert Newton was paid 8d. for 'caryeng of a loode of stone to

Mr and Mrs Jim Newbery and family outside their Knapp Cottage home. The sign with the boot over the door indicates that Mr Newbery ran a boot- and shoemaking business there.

Left: *The Hill, behind the New Inn, around the 1950s. Balfour Terrace is on the left, Salisbury Cottages on the right.*

Above: *Members of Kilmington's Baptist church at an open-air meeting in 1913 near the common (Hillcrest has since been built on this site). Note the harmonium* (front) *and the cars* (background).

Kilmington Primary School in 1937. Left to right, back row: *Miss Willis, Joyce Young, Lily Atkins, Peggy Symonds, Stella Thatcher, Winifred Hutchings;* third row: *Stanley Harris, Bob Bazley, Peggy Thompson, Heather Cook, Doris Parsons, Peggy Purse, Peter Atkins, Stanley Madge;* second row: *Roy Cook, John Wareham, Maurice Wright, Betty Gater, Olive Newbery, Joan Newbury, Pete Hutchings, Bazil Gosling, Leslie Wilkinson;* front, seated: *Clarence Anning, Jim Hurford, Colin White.*

Above: *St Giles' Church Sunday school pictured in the cricket field at Kilmington, c.1977.*

Right: *The approach to Kilmington from Whitford Road showing Brook Vale, Rose Cottage and other buildings. Judging by the attire of ladies heading towards the village stores, the picture dates from around 1910.*

Above: *The Street, Kilmington, looking towards The Green in 1902.*

Right: *Fred Chard worked at Hills Farm and rang the bells at St Giles' Church for over 30 years. The mangolds he is proudly showing were grown on the farm; they weighed over 30lbs each.*

Kilmington Hill, 1907. The New Inn is in the background.

The Old Inn, Kilmington, c.1903. That part of the building on the right has been demolished and is now the entrance to the car park.

Axmynster Wall.' At that time there was no right of burial at Kilmington, as St Giles' was a chapel of ease where interments took place. For this the parishioners of Kilmington were bound to maintain 84 feet of the wall at Axminster churchyard. Payments to Kilmington parishioners for working on the wall were a regular occurrence at the time. For example, John Cook and Walter Tocke received 3s.9d. a day each.

Still with the church, in 1558 4d. was paid to Roger Loveryng for 'two days werke abowte the roodlaught' [rood loft]. A later payment of 4d. was made for carrying timber for the same purpose. Although there is no reason to believe that sixteenth-century Kilmington was in any way Republican, it is interesting to note that no payments appear to have been made for bell-ringing to mark the accession of either Elizabeth I (1558) or James I (1603). An entry in 1588 for 'drinks and other charges against the ringing day', was for 5s.10d., one of the largest sums found. In all probability this was in celebration of the defeat of the Spanish Armada. It might have been that the excess drink supplied led to lustier pulling – one of the more regular items in the accounts is money paid out for work on the bells and the replacement of bell ropes and bell wheels.

The two churchwardens were appointed biannually and it is nice to see that women's lib had arrived in Kilmington by 1559; the fairer sex, in the shape of Alsen (Alice) Dare and Alsen Waye, were appointed.

Right: *St Giles' Church choir in the 1890s.* Left to right, back row: *R. Snell, J.H. Snell, H. Tucker, John Symonds, Revd Bloxham, J.N. Symonds, J. Dampier, Elias Quick (organist);* front: *R. Banks, A. White, B. Newton, R. Styles, H. Symonds, H. Hurford, A. Symonds, E. Underdown, C. Snell, A. Sainsbury.*

Left: *Kilmington Cross, probably in the 1920s. The RAC patrolman with his box is in the background* (right). *The local cycle and shoe-repair shop is on the left.*

The hunt (probably the East Devon) meeting at Kilmington Cross in February 1908. Note the signpost in the middle of the road.

Right: *The Christmas club meeting in the New Inn skittle alley during the 1950s.*

Right: *A farewell tea party for Revd and Mrs Rogers from Kilmington Sunday school, August 1977.*

In addition, the Co-op movement might well have been working in the village long before its birth in Rochdale, church ale having been brewed there since the reign of Henry III (1216–72). The lord of the manor had given a house with half an acre of ground to the parish to sell ale for the maintenance of the chapel. The house, probably the parish house (separate to the priest's house), referred to regularly in the accounts, was still owned by the parish in George Pulman's time (the mid-1800s).

It is almost certain that there was a church at Kilmington during the reign of Edward I (1272–1307). Little is known of the building although it is thought that it consisted of a nave and chancel with a dividing screen with a rood over it. The lancet windows at today's church are said to have come from this original building. The tower, much the same as it was when built during the reign of Henry VII (1485–1509), has six bells that date from between 1672 and 1895. Around the beginning of the nineteenth century records indicate that four arches were removed from the nave.

In 1862 the dread hand of the Victorian restorers was laid on St Giles' but, at least, the acoustics were much improved at the time. The royal arms on the ceiling on the north aisle have to be among the oldest in the country, dating as they do from the reign of Charles II (1660–85). It was in 1660, immediately after the Restoration, that an Order in Council made it mandatory for every church to display such arms. They were probably originally placed over the chancel arch in the nave.

To supplement his job as manager of the Axe Vale Devon Dairy Supplies, James William 'Jack' Sanders ran a cycle shop, 1900–18. As this card suggests, he was an agent for Bramptons' cycle accessories.

The hatchment over the tower arch is a memorial to the Tucker family of Coryton Park. The Lady chapel that dates from 1958 is named the Tucker chapel and the family's coat of arms may be seen in the window there.

Curates and Vicars of Kilmington

Curates

Sir Colman, 1562–63
Sir Wyllyam Abbot, 1564–66
Sir Addis, 1571–72
Mr Cooke, 1580–82
Mr Slee, 1597
*Michael Downe**
Mr Tucker, 1799
Mr Ellard, 1802
Mr Steer, 1835
H.B. Sands, 1850
Revd Bloxham, c.1890
A.A. Slipper, 1905
J.T. Harris, 1906
J.H.H. Copleston, 1908

Vicars

C.K. Botwood, 1912–16
C.R. Bull, 1917–27
E.E. Benson, 1928–35
L.A. Dukeswell, 1936–43
Revd Stamp, 1944–49
Revd Quelch, 1950–55
Revd Mason, 1956–57
R.H. Callard, 1958–64
G. Rogers, 1965–78
David Moseley, 1978–95
Paul Wilson, 1995–2000
Nigel Freathy, 2001

*Revd Michael Downe, a teacher at Axminster School, was also the curate at Kilmington in 1712.

Right: *Kilmington bell-ringers after ringing the bells at the wedding of Jack Lavender and May Hurford.* Back row, left to right: *J. Newbury, C. Cook, S. Purse, Mr Paul;* front: *D. Swaine, Fred Chard, W. Fowler.*

Left: *The induction of Revd David Moseley to the Kilmington living in 1978.* Left to right: *Jack Lavender and Mrs Levett (Kilmington churchwardens), Ven. Arthur Ward (Archdeacon of Exeter), Right Revd Philip Pasterfield (Bishop of Crediton), Revd David Moseley, Revd Cyril Hope (vicar of Stockland and Dalwood), Revd Stuart Worth (rural dean and rector of Uplyme), Betty Budge and Francis Gardener (churchwardens of Shute).*

Young Helpers' League, Kilmington, c.1898. Mrs Braddick, (in black on the right) *invariably carried a cockatoo on her shoulder when she walked around the village.*

The dedication of the war memorial at Kilmington in 1921. The Revd John Way, the Baptist minister, is addressing the crowd and the Revd Charles Bull, Kilmington's vicar (1917–27), is standing to his right.

TO THE GLORY OF GOD AND IN HONOURABLE MEMORY OF THOSE MEN OF KILMINGTON WHO GAVE THEIR LIVES FOR THEIR KING AND COUNTRY IN THE FIRST WORLD WAR

E.H. Botwood, 1916
R.H. Bridges DSO, 1918
C.H. Chown (missing), 1917
L.F. Loveridge, 1916
R. Pound, 1918
W. Sansom, 1916
R.G. Wood, 1918
E.W. Woodman, 1915
F.W. Woodman, 1917
J.H. Woodman, 1915
C. Wright (missing), 1917

... AND THE MEN IN THE SECOND WORLD WAR

E.N. Lockwood (missing), 1943
A. Trott, 1943
R.J. Wilkinson, 1944

Kilmington Primary School, 1978.

IN THE PARISH OF

KILMINGTON, DEVON.

1½ Miles from Axminster Town and Station.

Important Sale of a choice

SMALL FREEHOLD FARM

with good old-fashioned FARM HOUSE, with mullioned Windows and Massive Carved Oak Beams and Panelling, (built 1629).

Containing :- 7 Bedrooms, Dining Room (20ft. x 17ft.), Drawing Room (17ft. x 16ft.), Breakfast Room, Kitchen, Dairy and necessary Offices, nice Lawn in front (70ft. x 68ft.), good walled Kitchen Garden, well stocked with Fruit Trees, Outbuildings comprise :- Motor House, 3 Stalled Stable, Trap House, Pound House, Root House, Stalling for 12 Cows, 4 good Pig Styes, and

ABOUT 55 ACRES

of very productive Meadow, Pasture, Orchard and Arable (19 acres) Land, which

R. & C. SNELL

Will offer for

SALE BY AUCTION, in one lot, at the George Hotel, Axminster,

ON THURSDAY, MAY 22ND, 1919,

at 3-30 o'clock in the afternoon.

and subject to the General Conditions of Sale of the Devon and Exeter Law Association, and to such Special Conditions as shall be then read.

The property is known as

"RUGG'S FARM"

and affords an exceptional opportunity to those seeking an excellent Residential Property in a good Sporting Neighbourhood, close to Church and Post Office. There is a good Well with Pump under Cover.

Possession at Michaelmas. Can be viewed Mondays and Thursdays only.

Further particulars may be obtained of

MR. LIONEL H. MORTIMER, SOLICITOR, COLYTON.

or of the Auctioneers, Axminster and Yeovil.

Dated, Auction Offices, Axminster and Yeovil, May 9th, 1919.

Edwin Snell, Printer, Axminster

KILMINGTON

Near Axminster, Devonshire.

To close two Trust Estates of Messrs. Benjamin and George Thorn, deceased.

TO BE SOLD BY AUCTION

BY

R. & C. SNELL

At the OLD BELL HOTEL, AXMINSTER, on

THURSDAY, MAY, 15th. 1902

AT 4 o'clock p.m. precisely, in two lots, subject, as to the major portion of the undermentioned property, to such Conditions of Sale as will be then and there read, and, as to the remainder of such property, to the General Conditions of the Devon & Exeter Law Association, and to such Special Conditions as will be read at the Auction, the following very

VALUABLE FREEHOLD

PROPERTY

VIZ :

LOT 1. All those excellent rich and productive closes of

GRAZING LAND

Comprising 22 acres or thereabouts, together with the Shed thereon, situate adjoining the River Axe near Yarty Bridge, in the parish of Kilmington aforesaid, and numbered respectively 311, 314, 316, 347, 348, 349, 350, and 354 on the Tithe Map for the said parish, which said Lands are now in the occupation of Mr. R. Snell, as yearly Ladyday tenant at the rental of £65.

This desirable Lot offers especial advantages for either accommodation land or as an investment. The Closes are in an excellent state of cultivation, and considered to be some of the best grazing land in the district; there is an abundant supply of water in every field the River Yarty runing through the property, and capital Trout and Salmon Fishing can be obtained in this River for about one-third of a mile.

The approach to the Lands is by way of a Road close to Yarty Bridge adjoining the Main Road from Kilmington to Axminster.

LOT 2. All those two undivided one-third parts or shares of and in those

CLOSES OF COMMON LANDS

Known as "Mount Hungary," situate at Kilmington Hill, containing 19 acres or thereabouts, and now in the respective occupations of Messrs. Wm. Adams and R. Snell as tenants thereof.

The Sporting Rights over the above Properties are let at £7 per annum.

To view Lot 1 apply at Summerleaze Farm, Kilmington aforesaid, and Lot 2 to the said Mr. William Adams, Builder, Kilmington.

Particulars may be obtained of the Auctioneers, or at the Offices of

W. E. PITFIELD CHAPPLE, Solicitor,

and Wm. FORWARD & SONS, Solicitors,

ALL OF AXMINSTER.

Where Plans of Lot 1, for the guidance of intending Purchasers only, may be seen 7 days prior to the Sale.

Dated Axminster, April 24th, 1902.

EDWIN SNELL, PRINTER, STATIONER, &c., AXMINSTER.

The Forge, Shute Road, Kilmington, c.1900. At the time the blacksmith was William Sanders.

HILL HOUSE, KILMINGTON

Saturday, August 6th, 1949

Attractive sale of a portion of the well-kept

Household Furniture

OUTDOOR and GARDEN EFFECTS

the property of Mr. R. J. Newbery, who is quitting, the Lots including:
a pinewood Chest of Drawers; Commode; 3ft. oak Combination Washstand: Toilet
Ware; Pedestal Cupboard; an antique CORNER CUPBOARD with glazed lattice
doors; 3ft. 3in. Chefoniere; Fireside Arm and other Easy Chairs; 6 single Windsor
Chairs and Arm ditto; Oak Umbrella Stand; Piano Stool;

A 4ft. Glazed Dresser

6ft. Dresser and Shelves; Two KITCHEN TABLES; Brass Fender Kerb; Linen
Basket; a Ripplingille 2-burner OIL COOKING STOVE with oven; a Valor
Heating Stove;

A 6ft. Enamelled Bath

with fittings; Deal Bath Top; Laundry Mangle, etc.

A Hebditch Portable Greenhouse

9ft. by 7ft. 6in. in good order with staging, etc.; an oil Greenhouse Heater; Steel
Water Barrel; Tubs; DOG KENNEL; a G.I. SHED, 9ft. x 9ft.; a metal WHEEL-
BARROW (rubber tyred); Garden Tools; Scythe; Beedle and 12 Wedges; Flower
Pots; Seed Boxes; 6ft. Garden Frame and Light; G.I. CORN BIN; Ferret
Hutch; Cross-cut and Hand Saws; a Porcelain Sink, Etc., Etc.,

Also for a Neighbour:
a brass-mtd Bedstead with spring mattress; 3ft. mahogany Drawer Chest; a 7-
piece SITTING ROOM SUITE; 2 Copper Urns; Electric Iron; small Electric
Cooker; 4½ doz. Dinner Plates; Mahogany Pedestal Round Table; a 3-50 x 19
TYRE with Inner Tube (both new); a G.I. PIG HUT and other items, which

Messrs. W. PALMER & Co. and R. & C. SNELL Ltd.

will sell by Auction as above

Commencing at 2-30 p.m.

Eland Brothers, Printers, Axminster.

Above: *Kilmington Players in 1954 before their presentation of their tenth annual pantomime* Beauty and the Beast. Included in the picture are, back row: *John Saunders, Vera Broom and Mrs Cook;* front: *Joan Boyland, Mary Rawlins, Betty Gage and Len Broom.*

Below: *Vealhayes, Kilmington, c.1910, with the entrance to Coryton Park in the background. Vealhayes, a private house in 2003, was originally a wheelwright and carpenter's shop.*

Kilmington's first Post Office was thought to have been in one of the village's inns. In the 1870s the Post Office was in the Old Inn with the landlord, John Chapple, as postmaster. At that time it was only a receiving house – in other words, an office where letters could be left and only stamps purchased. It was later moved to The Green and is seen here (top) *in the background between the two trees in 1906. Some time later it was moved to the top of The Street, before the council-houses were built* (above, in the background). *Later it was sited in the downstairs room of the house on the left* (above). *It stayed there until 2003 when it returned to The Green in Hurford's Stores opposite its old home.*

3

Getting About

Two Roman roads bypass Axminster. The first, the great Fosse Way, was built originally as a border road along which the Romans could move their legions rapidly in the event of trouble in Wales and the West Country. It comes into Axminster's story after running down from Windwhistle above Chard, through Perry Street, down Tytherleigh Hill and towards the town via what became the A358 as it runs along Chard Road. However, at the foot of Millbrook it ignores Axminster, turning slightly left to run up Stoney Lane, across Lyme Road and on towards the sea near Seaton. Although we may never know for certain whether Seaton was the lost Roman port of Moridunum, it does seem fairly clear that the Roman remains there are too big to warrant the mere title of a villa. Close at hand, was the stone at Beer that the Romans worked soon after their arrival in Devon. Flavius Vespasian (later Emperor) and his 2nd Legion were in Exeter not long before AD60 and a tile of that legion was found in Seaton during excavations of the Honeyditches site. It is therefore possible to surmise that Vespasian reached Seaton via the Fosse near Axminster.

The toll-house (right) *at the foot of Gammons Hill and looking towards Kilmington, c.1908, when the tolls were no longer in force. The building on the left belonged to the Axe Vale Devon Dairy Supplies.*

Following the course of the Celtic trackway, the other road, the Icknield Way, enters our story outside Hunters Lodge, where it forms the A35. Just below the entrance to Pigeon's Lane, the line of the road can be seen bearing away to the right across a field towards Symondsdown. There it turns to run along Woodbury Lane, skirt the edge of the modern Woodbury Park estate and, via Fairy Lane, cross Musbury Road (the A358) and the River Axe at the foot of Gammons Hill and on to Honiton. In 2003 Fairy Lane is a mere track. Its name has been corrupted from Farway Lane and a reference to it as Fairy Lane can be found in the minute books of Axminster's turnpike trust. At one time there were at least four cottages on the edge of Browhill facing the lane, but

Below: *The toll-house at the foot of Gammons Hill, c.1910. Formerly James and Clara Sanders occupied the toll-house. James was once the manager of the dairy that stood opposite and ran a cycle shop at the house. The young ladies with their new-looking bikes are posing specially for the occasion.*

Above: *Axminster Parish Council's water cart that was used for damping down the roads before tarmac was introduced in the early 1920s.*

they were demolished soon after the First World War.

In the early 1800s most English roads were muddy in winter and dusty in summer. Improvement was slow but, by the middle of that century, the establishment of turnpike trusts led to a big improvement. These trusts were set up to raise the money required to maintain the highways. Axminster's trust was one of the earliest in Devon, being set up in 1754. The term turnpike stems from a person having to turn the spike in a spiked road barrier and the name stuck when gates were used.

Axminster's turnpike trust was empowered by:

> *... an Act of Parliament passed in the 32nd year of his present Majesty King George III* [1792]*... for more effectively mending, widening and keeping the roads in repair... from Penn* [just over the county boundary in Dorset]*... as far as Shipley Lane in the parish of Honiton.*

In 2003, the minute book of this new trust, from its inception in 1792 until 1842, is held in the County Records Office in Exeter.

A total of 20 commissioners attended the trust's first meeting at the George Hotel on 15 June 1792. They were: the Revd Charles Buckland, Mr Isaac Tucker, the Revd John Rendell, Mr Peter Parmiter, Mr Thomas Taunton, Mr Samuel Forward, Mr John Bunton Liddon, Mr Francis Stevens, Mr Theodore Dunn, Mr George Tucker, Mr Nicholas Bragge, Mr William Wills, Mr Samuel Byshot, the Revd Charles Steers, the Revd Benjamin Symes, Mr Robert Hallett, Mr John Read, Mr Israel Harvey, Mr William Anning and the Revd William Trevelyan Cox. Several other members were later added to the trust.

It is surprising to find that on many occasions there were not enough commissioners present to form a quorum and the meetings were adjourned; indeed, seven in a row were ended in this manner in 1804. There was no regular chairman, a different one being chosen at each meeting. The meetings were held in the George Hotel at first, although later they were held in a loose form of rotation at the George, the Old Bell Hotel, the King's Arms and the Hotel Inn (which was in West Street).

At the first meeting the trust considered:

> *... the amending, widening and keeping in repair the road leading from Penn Inn in the parish of Whitchurch Canonicorum, through the town of Axminster to a distance of 100 yards past the entrance into Shipley Lane; also the road leading from Sector Lane end, at the east end of the town of Axminster as far as Quandoes Gate at the end of Hawkchurch Down and also the road leading from Quandoes Gate over Hawkchurch Down towards the Lyme Regis Turnpike Road in the parish of Hawkchurch and Whitchurch Canonicorum. And also the road leading from the house called the Old Inn in the parish of Kilmington, through the parish of Shute to the town of Colyton over Colyton Hill and Stoford* [Stafford] *Common to the Lyme Regis Turnpike Road at or near Bovey Gate within the parish of Colyton. And also from the White Hart Inn in the town of Axminster, through the several parishes of Axminster, Musbury and Axmouth to the Lyme Regis turnpike road at or near Boswell* [Bos Hill] *the turnpike gate. And also a line of communications for the said Axmouth road in the said parish of Musbury leading from Long Mead Lane to the place called Loud's Corner in the said parish of Shute consisting of not more than five furlongs.*

Those were the roads that Axminster's turnpike trust maintained and they can be followed with some accuracy, even in 2003. The Penn Inn was at the Charmouth end of the short dual carriageway, just below Greenway Head on the modern A35, and that stretch of road runs through Axminster and Kilmington and on to Mount Pleasant by the Offwell turning above Honiton. During the nineteenth century some re-routing took place, notably between Kilmington and Shute Pillars, Taunton Cross and Wilmington and Mount Pleasant and the top of Axminster Hill in Honiton, where Honiton's trust took over. From the bottom of Sector Lane to Hawkchurch Down was the road up Stammery Hill to Blackpool Corner on Crewkerne Road (the B3165); over Hawkchurch Down to the Lyme Regis turnpike road runs Crewkerne Road and Green Lane (the Raymonds Hill part of Crewkerne Road that joins the main road opposite the Hunters Lodge was not cut until later).

From the Old Inn in Kilmington to Bovey Gate on the Lyme Regis turnpike via Colyton and Shute speaks for itself, although the first part of the journey as far as Shute Pillars went along Roman Road in Kilmington rather than the modern A35 trunk road (the Kilmington–Taunton Cross part of which did not exist in 1792). The original section of road between the White Hart and Bos Hill is still used in 2003, and the Roman stretch from Musbury to Loud's Corner is the modern road from Musbury to Whitford. The Loud family have farmed at Pump Farm in Whitford for some three and a half centuries and it seems logical that the junction beside the farm would have been known as Loud's Corner.

The improvements envisaged by Axminster's turnpike trust, including the establishment of gates and a toll-house, had to be funded somehow. The trust borrowed money from several subscribers to whom interest was paid annually at four per cent. The amounts included £1,000 from Sir William de la Pole, £500 from John Rowe, £200 from John Stuckey and £100 each from Thomas Taunton, the Revd Richard Hothersall Hallett and Revd George Rhodow – a total of £2,000. Later, in 1805, the trust borrowed £1,050 from the Axminster Friendly Society and £200 from the Axminster Ladies' Friendly Society.

The trust's income was generated by the rent of the gates, which were offered at an annual auction

AXMINSTER TURNPIKE.
Colyton Gate.
day of 187

	No.	s.	d.
Horse, Mule or Ass not drawing ..			
Horse drawing ...			
Drove of Oxen or neat Cattle ...			
Drove of Calves, Swine, Sheep, or Lambs			

A full Toll at this Gate clears all the other Gates in the Trust.

AXMINSTER TURNPIKE.
Woodbury Toll Bar.
day of 187

	No.	s.	d.
Horse, Mule or Ass not drawing ..			
Horse drawing ...			
Drove of Oxen or neat Cattle ...			
Drove of Calves, Swine, Sheep, or Lambs			

A full Toll at this Gate clears all the other Gates in the Trust.

AXMINSTER TURNPIKE.
Mount Pleasant Gate.
day of 187

	No.	s.	d.
Horse, Mule or Ass not drawing ..			
Horse drawing ...			
Drove of Oxen or neat Cattle ...			
Drove of Calves, Swine, Sheep, or Lambs			

A full Toll at this Gate clears all the other Gates in the Trust.

Three unused toll-gate tickets for use at the Colyton Gate, the Woodbury Toll Bar and the Mount Pleasant Gate.

when the rights to collect the tolls were sold to the highest bidder. Each gate was auctioned separately but there was nothing to stop one person winning more than one lot. Sometimes the rents that were paid quarterly were in arrears and had to be chased.

There was a wonderful and bewildering scale of charges. For every horse or beast of draught drawing a coach, stagecoach, chariot, chaise, landau, etc., a charge of 6d. (2½p in modern money) was made. However, for a coach, chariot and chaise, etc., drawn behind or along with another such vehicle, it cost 6d. for four wheels and 3d. extra for each additional two wheels. A loose mule or ass, laden or unladen and not drawing, only cost 1d. A horse or beast of draught drawing any wagon, wain, cart, etc., with wheels of less than six inches in width cost 6d. It cost 6d. if four or less horses drew a cart with wheels of more than six inches in width. For some reason (probably a wider wheel caused less wear and tear on the road), if the cart had wheels of more than six inches in width and more than five horses it only cost 5d. A drove of oxen was charged at 10d. per score, a drove of calves, swine, sheep or lambs only 5d. a score. Later, damage to the roads by locked wheels led to a regulation being introduced that required skidpans or 'slippers' to be placed at the foot of the wheel.

Travellers were permitted to return through the toll-gate without charge as long as they did so by 9a.m. the following morning. However, travellers avoided payments at their peril; such a deception could result in a fine in the region of £5. Understandably the King and his family entered without charge, as did the Army, the local vicar going to church or visiting the sick, and other important people such as MPs. Free passage was also granted to those carrying hay, straw, wood, fruit etc., that was not destined for sale or market. Throughout England, the Royal Mail passed through toll-gates free of charge, except at Axminster, until 1811 when a bill was passed in Parliament exempting the mail coaches from paying tolls at any of the Axminster toll-gates, thereby bringing it into line with the rest of the country. Three mail coaches passed through the town on a daily basis; two were Royal Mail coaches (one from London, the other from the West) and the other was the auxiliary mail coach, which came from Salisbury along the A30 to Windwhistle and then passed through Perry Street to Axminster. There were other private coaches that carried mail once a week and the loss of this income was a serious blow to the trust and the improvements that they had planned.

Such income would have been useful in the winter of 1814 when heavy snowfalls in the Axminster area made the roads impassable and the trust had to pay casual labour to clear the highways. That year William Harris, one of the gatekeepers under the direction of trustee William Tucker, paid just over £11 for 49 labourers (at 1s.6d. a day) for clearing snow on the road to Honiton. In the town of Axminster itself, George Slyfield paid nearly £2 to 21 labourers for clearing the main road of snow. Slyfield, another trustee, was, for many years, the postmaster at Axminster and, as such, had an interest in keeping the mail coach running.

South Street after the 1881 blizzard. In 2003 the building behind the two men is the office of Pulman's Weekly News.

It was not only snow that led to a reduction in the volume of traffic through the gates. In 1825 John Wicker, the late tenant of the South Gate, who still owed £58 to the trustees, asked to be allowed some reduction, claiming that 'the great storm that damaged Axmouth Harbour led to the reduction in the number of carriages going in that direction.' They knocked off £32.

Of course, there were rules and regulations (when aren't there?). It was forbidden to sell liquor from a toll-house, breaking up or damaging the road was not allowed and no person living beside any of the turnpike roads was permitted to have a gate that opened outwards. No one could allow blood (from a slaughterhouse) to run on to the road, nor kill, slaughter or singe on it, nor have bonfires nor let off fireworks on it. In fact, no fires or fireworks were allowed within 80 feet of the road. Digging pits for timber sawing was not allowed (a timber pit was where two men sawed timber; the wood was placed over the pit, one man held the saw above and pulled up, then the man in the pit pulled the saw down – the latter of the two jobs was dusty and unpleasant, so the top man's job went to the senior of the two). In addition, no football or any other game was allowed on the roads and wagons or carts were not to be left longer than was necessary for loading or unloading. No tents, huts, dung, manure, timber or planks could be put alongside the road. There was a standard fine of £5 if any of these regulations were broken.

In 1792 the best bid for East Gate was £315.5s.0d. by William Cross. This gate was at the junction of Lyme Road and Sector Lane (or Granny Rockett's Corner). The name East Gate is retained even in 2003 in the name of a modern house on that site. The gate at Northcote and Mount Pleasant went to James Harris for £275.5s.0d.

In 1800 gatekeepers were given an annual allowance of one guinea (£1.05) for the oil needed for the lamp at each gate. At that time a 'weighing engine' was installed for £55 and placed near the north wall of the churchyard facing Phoenix Lane. Robert Hook was in charge and his duties included weighing all laden carriages passing through Axminster and taking the tolls for any vehicle that was overweight and, therefore, likely to damage the road. He was paid 1s. for weighing every wagon and 6d. for every cart. He also received 'the fourth part of said profit from said weighing engine.' In 1801 the engine was let out to tender and William Levis took it for £27 for the first year. It seems likely that he lost money, because there was no bidder the following year and later it went for as little as £10.

It also seems likely that the toll-gates were not the money-spinners they have sometimes been made out to be. On more than one occasion none of the gates attracted any bidders and the trustees were forced to put in their own temporary gatekeepers at a cost of half a guinea per week.

It was around this time that a Mr Benjamin Tucker put a window on the front of his house in Lyme Street, to 'the great annoyance of travellers on the said turnpike.' The affair was settled amicably when Mr Tucker bought some land opposite his house and gave it to the trust.

Over the years many alterations were made to the line of some of the trust's roads, mainly to avoid steep hills. The road at Hills Farm in Kilmington was considered to be too steep and a fresh line was taken which meant that a Mr William Tucker had to be compensated. A bridge had to be built at Gamberlake in 1802 at a spot where traffic for Musbury had previously forded the tiny stream. It was the steepness of Moorcox Hill that led to the re-routing of the road between Shute Piers (Pillars) and Ford Bridge at the entrance to Wilmington in 1828. Previously the turnpike road had left Kilmington via Roman Road and, when it reached Shute Piers, followed the line of Roman Road towards Stockland Hill before turning at Moorcox Cross and dropping down to Wilmington. The new road went through Deep Cut to Wilmington and cost £1,700 to build, the contractors having to maintain that stretch of the road for 18 months after its completion. Four years later what is now known as Crewkerne Road in Raymonds Hill was built at a cost of £260.

More straightening of the Honiton Road followed in 1837 when a new road was cut from Kilmington to Andrewshayes to link up with the already-completed stretch through Deep Cut. Apparently earlier work had been carried out on Anchor Hill in Axminster; indeed in 1832, the trustees recorded that 'Anchor Hill was lowered some years earlier and the causeway [pavement] was now dangerous.'

Axminster Ladies' Friendly Society on their annual outing to an unknown destination in around 1926. Left to right, standing: *Ada Manley, ?, Mrs Moss, landlady of the Commercial and, later, the Bell, Annie Burroughs, ?, Emmy Pincock, Marjorie Hill, her parents had a fish shop in Lyme Street;* seated: *Winnie Webb, Miss Harvey, Mrs Bonfield, ?, Miss Ellen Soper, ?, Nellie Box, May Powley, the daughter of the gateman at the level crossing at the bottom of Castle Hill, Miss Palmer, ?, Miss Gage, Mrs White, Mrs Harris, ?. Silver Cars of Beer supplied the charabanc, but the name of the driver is not known.*

Left: *The George Hotel, Axminster, on a postcard to a Driver Dare serving with the RASC in France during the First World War. Much of the building between the entrance and the right-hand side of the hotel, including part of the Adam Room, was taken down when Lyme Street was widened after the Second World War.*

Axe Vale Devon Dairy Supplies, Gammons Hill, Kilmington, c.1907. The building on the left is the old toll-house, the creamery on the right belonged to Mr E.H. Cuming who sold his produce from a shop in West Street, Axminster (the offices of Gribble, Booth and Taylor in 2003). The group standing on the right of the picture are about to load the cart. Left to right: *?, Vic Hurford, ?, Mr Cuming, James Sanders (the manager from 1896–1929), Ethel Sanders, Vera Snell from Summerleaze Farm (out of sight behind the toll-house), May Sanders, Olive Sanders. The identity of the boy on the cart is unknown. The buildings became derelict and the remains were finally destroyed during the construction of the Axminster bypass in 1991.*

More gates were planned, one at the three-cross way on the south side of Umborne Bridge at Colyton, another at Gamberlake. The latter site was considered too dangerous because of the steepness of the road at that point and a gate was erected at the junction of White Pot (Wide Post) Lane and Musbury Road. This gate was advertised at £100 per annum but there were no takers and a Richard Cloud was paid 5s. to collect the tolls, using his own house at that point for the purpose, until the trustees found a buyer.

In 1822 another toll-house was built at Kilmington 'opposite the George Inn [later George Farm] at the Yew Tree in Kilmington.' It was known as the Yew Tree Gate and was situated near the later site of Kilmington's war memorial. This toll-house cost £113 and in 1830 when a new one was built for £50, half a mile nearer Axminster at the foot of Gammons Hill, the low cost suggests that much of the material came from the older toll-house. The reason for the move was almost certainly that people were avoiding paying the tolls at Yew Tree Gate by going past the church, up The Street, and coming out on the main road a quarter of a mile past the gate. Other bolt-holes were closed. Gates were placed at the entrance to Woodbury Lane and at the road that led to Symonds Down Farm in 1826.

The main benefactors of the improved road system were the carriers and coach firms whose costs would have been considerably reduced by the steadily decreasing lengths of journey times; around 1760 it took a coach almost six days to reach Axminster from London – a century later the time was down to barely a day. Some of the savings would have been passed on to the tradesman and, through them, to their customers.

In 1824 the main excitement in Axminster was the daily departure at 11a.m. of the London mail coach from the George Hotel (called George Inn and placed in Castle Hill by *Pigot & Co.'s Devonshire Directory*). This coach travelled to the capital via Bridport, Dorchester, Blandford and Salisbury. An auxiliary mail coach left 90 minutes earlier and journeyed to London via what would become the A30 (through Yeovil and Shaftesbury to Salisbury). Some 20 years later the improved roads meant that journey times were reduced. Consequently the coach that had previously left in the morning did not depart until 3.15p.m.

Other coach owners complained bitterly that they had to pay toll charges but the Royal Mail did not. In 1839 such coaches included the 'Retaliator', that came through Axminster on its way from Taunton to Lyme Regis; the 'Vampire', that went to Bath every Monday, Wednesday and Friday and returned the next day, and the 'Red Rover', which left Axminster daily at 10a.m. for Southampton and returned the same evening.

Thanks in no small way to Christmas cards, the image in most people's minds when they think of the coaching era is that of the romantic mail coach speeding its way though the snow-covered country with horns blaring to warn the gatekeeper to open his toll-gates to help the King's mail continue on its way unhindered. However, such a notion reflects only a small part of England's coaching story. Before the advent of the railway network, that part of the nation's commerce which was not carried on the canals nor by the main coaching system was transported via the back roads and the carriers. These carriers, and their horse-drawn carts, were the lifeblood of rural England's commerce. They plodded out of towns such as Axminster until after the First World War when motorised transport finally killed them off. The countryside was criss-crossed by carriage routes that had evolved over the years. In this way, most towns were connected with their immediate neighbours and were consequently accessible on at least one long-distance route.

From the Bell Mr Edwards travelled twice a week to Bath and Bristol. The Bell was a popular departure point with (in 1839) Russell & Co. leaving there for London every Monday, Wednesday and Friday and returning a week later. This company also used the Bell as a departure point for Bridport and Dorchester on Wednesdays and Exeter three times a week. Mr Gill went to Beaminster once a week, leaving from West Street. Other departure points were the New Inn, Mr Chapple's house in South Street and other private premises.

Although it would possibly clash with the interests of Axminster's turnpike trust, there is no evidence to suggest that this organisation was among the many objectors to the several schemes that were floated between 1760 and 1830 to construct a canal to link the English and Bristol Channels. Such plans were brought up at regular intervals throughout the canal era and usually cited the lower valley of the Axe as the region most suitable for development; it was deemed ideal for the canal to bisect this area from Chard to the sea (at Seaton or Beer). The obvious route was from the mouth of the Parrett, near Bridgwater, through the Somerset wetlands, and then down the Axe valley to Seaton. Such a canal could have been a godsend to the tiny harbour at the mouth of the Axe which, after being silted up in Tudor times, was fighting a losing battle against increasing competition on the roads.

Mr Donald Newbery poses outside R. & C. Snell's old offices in Trinity Square, c.1910. The business is based on the opposite side of the Square in 2003.

The Lawns, Anchor Hill, c.1908, the home of Dr Langran. In later life it became a café and the stopping place for the Royal Blue coaches on the London–Exeter run. It was demolished in 1960 and replaced by three shops plus a garage and petrol station. Dr Langran played a prominent part in the life of the town including two spells as president of Axminster Town Football Club.

The first lorry bought by Reg Luff, the Axminster coal and builders' merchant, whose premises were in Woodmead Road. This picture was taken by local photographer Charles Humphries (1877–1959). Perhaps Mr Luff was cocking a snook – his lorry is parked outside the weighbridge office of his main business rivals, Bradford & Sons.

The advantages of such a canal were obvious. They included the saving of time on the long and dangerous passage along the Cornish coast, especially around Land's End, and the reduction in the cost of winter coal bills, said to be around £20 in the region around Axminster, Seaton and Bridport. It was estimated that a local canal would reduce this by half.

There were other suggested routes or schemes, including one that linked the Exe and the English Channel with the Parrett via Tiverton, which is outside the scope of this story.

Robert Whitworth, a well-known engineer at the time, was employed to check the possibilities of a canal from Langport to the Axe in 1769. It was envisaged that this canal would reach Seaton but not actually enter the sea. Whitworth came back in the 1790s for a second look at the idea. Bridgwater to Seaton seems to have been the most practical (and obvious) route. The great Thomas Telford was brought in to design a 15-foot deep canal between these two towns that could accommodate ships of up to 200 tons. A start was made but the canal was only built as far as Chard, where it was opened in 1834. It was known as the Chard Canal and traces of it still exist in 2003. It was only five miles from Axminster and 12 from Seaton and an extension to Axminster would have been a great boon to the town. However, the Chard Canal had been built far too late. The age of steam had already arrived at Chard and Axminster in 1860, so the canal quickly became redundant and closed in 1868, around the same time that the railway reached Seaton (17 March 1868) at, we suspect, the same spot that the proposed canal would have arrived in that town.

As late as 1906 a horse-drawn bus from the George Hotel still met all trains at Axminster Station but, by that time, the horseless carriage had appeared in the town. Who had the first motor car in Axminster is not known but, around 1909, Parsons Coach Builders in West Street announced above their entrance that they upholstered and painted motor cars and they were certainly selling them. Indeed, by 1914 a car was no longer the cause of excitement that it had been only a decade earlier. One of the possible claimants to having Axminster's first motor car has to be Captain A.C. Downes-Luttrell of Lea Combe House who often used it to collect Major Clive Morrison Bell, the Conservative MP for the Honiton constituency, from the railway station when he visited Axminster. He came there in 1910 to thank the voters for returning him after the general election. After lunch at Lea Combe House he switched to a landau which 'had been gaily bedecked with blue ribbon and flags and was drawn down into the town by his supporters, accompanied by cheers and much ringing of bells.'

Cheap lorries previously used by the War Department flooded the second-hand market after the Second World War, so mechanised road transport blossomed. Reg Luff, an Axminster coal and builders' merchant obtained the town's first such vehicle in 1920 and local photographer Charles Humphries, who covered the Axminster area, photographed its arrival. Charles worked from his house in West Street between 1900–25. In time he added to his mobility by the purchase of an Indian motorcycle and side-car, one of the first of its kind to be seen in the town.

At the start of the twenty-first century, when pollution by motor fuel is the cause of ever-increasing concern, the steam lorries of the early 1920s might well be considered to be a viable alternative to the juggernauts that pound our roads. One such lorry, certainly in use by the end of the First World War, was the Sentinel that belonged to the Devon Trading Company and used to haul material from Tolcis Quarry to Axminster Station, as well as deliver building materials around the area. George Morrish also purchased a Sentinel lorry in 1925 to deliver animal feed and flour out of Weycroft Mill. By the middle of the 1930s his five-strong horse-and-cart team had been entirely replaced by lorries. It was not only old War Department lorries that were coming on to the market; during the 1920s Donald McKay Ohm, headmaster of Colyton Grammar School, hired cars to overcome the bad railway connections that existed for pupils from Axminster who attended the school. One of the cars was a converted wartime ambulance, of which it was said that bullet holes could still be seen in its roof. The cars cost the school 15s. (75p) a day, so parents were charged 12s. a term per child.

Axminster's first motor ambulance did not arrive until 1932 when an Austin car, the Martha Pattie, was converted. It was a complicated task to get a patient inside. This involved opening the windscreen, placing the stretcher on a special stand and then sliding both the stretcher and the patient into the interior.

National Omnibus and Transport Company buses were running out of (and through) Axminster by the beginning of the 1920s. In 1923 the Parish Council discussed the nuisance they caused when they were parked in Trinity Square, especially on market days (nothing new there!). Membury man Stan Wakley changed from taxis to buses in 1933 when he bought his first 14-seater Ford bus for less than £60. He ran coach tours throughout the West Country and operated bus services from Membury to both Chard and Honiton, and to Axminster, via either Chardstock or Stockland. Prior to the start of these services small communities around Axminster, such as Membury, Holy City, Chardstock, Alston, Furley and Stockland, were very isolated. It is interesting for us in 2003, as we drive our family saloon from Stockland to Axminster, that Stan Wakley's Membury, Stockland and Axminster runs included a pick-up point at Beckford Bridge. A 14-seater could not cross that tiny packhorse bridge; instead would-be passengers from a wide area congregated on the Stockland–Kilmington road near the bridge.

Above: *A 33-seater AEC Regal coach seen here on delivery to Rambler Coaches in 1950.*

WAKLEYS

RAMBLER

BUS SERVICES

TIME TABLE

MEMBURY - CHARDSTOCK - AXMINSTER
MEMBURY - STOCKLAND - AXMINSTER
MEMBURY - STOCKLAND - HONITON
STOCKLAND - DALWOOD - SHUTE
AXMINSTER

MEMBURY - STOCKLAND AND HONITON

SATURDAYS ONLY.

		a.m.
Membury ...	dep.	9.40
Furley	„	9.50
Longbridge ...	„	9.55
Stockland ...	„	10. 0
Golden Square	„	10. 6
Cotleigh Bridge	„	10.10
Honiton ...	arr.	10.25
Three Mariners	dep.	10.40
Cotleigh Village	„	10.41
Honiton	„	10.50

		p.m.	p.m.
Honiton ...	dep.	12.30	3.15
Cotleigh Village	„	12.39	3.24
Cotleigh Bridge	„	12.44	3.29
Golden Square	„	12.49	3.34
Stockland ...	„	12.55	3.40
Longbridge ...	„	—	3.50
Furley	„	—	3.55
Membury ...	arr.	—	4.05

STOCKLAND - HONITON

TUESDAYS ONLY

		p.m.
Stockland	dep.	10.00
Golden Square ...	„	10.06
Cotleigh Bridge ...		10.11
Cotleigh Village ...	„	10.16
Honiton	arr.	10.25

		p.m.
Honiton	dep.	12.30
Cotleigh Village ...	„	12.39
Cotleigh Bridge ...	„	12.44
Golden Square ...	„	12.49
Stockland	arr.	12.55

STOCKLAND - DALWOOD SHUTE - AXMINSTER

		Tuesdays only	Thursdays only		Saturdays only
		a.m.	a.m.	p.m.	p.m.
Stockland ...	dep.	10.58	—	—	1.15
Cokers Elm ...	„	11.00	11.00	—	1.17
Marlpit Cross ...	„	11.03	11.03	—	1.20
Broadhayes ...	„	11.08	11.08	—	1.25
Ridge	„	11.12	11.12	—	1.29
Ham	„	11.14	11.14	2.00	1.31
Carters Cross ...	„	11.19	11.19	2.05	1.36
Dickens Marsh ...	„	11.23	11.23	2.09	1.40
Shute P.O. ...	„	11.28	11.28	2.14	1.45
Haddon Corner	„	11.33	11.33	2.19	1.50
Axminster ...	arr.	11.43	11.43	2.29	2.00
		p.m.	p.m.	p.m.	p.m.
Axminster ...	dep.	1.30	1.30	4.50	6.00
Haddon Corner	„	1.40	1.40	5.00	6.10
Chute P.O. ...	„	1.45	1.45	5.05	6.15
Dickens Marsh ...	„	1.50	1.50	5.10	6.20
Carters Cross ...	„	1.54	1.54	5.14	6.24
Ham	„	1.59	1.59	5.19	6.29
Ridge	„	2.01	—	5.21	6.31
Broadhayes ...	„	2.05	—	5.25	6.35
Marlpit Cross ...	„	2.10	—	5.30	6.40
Cokers Elm ...	„	2.13	—	5.33	6.43
Stockland ...	arr.	2.15	—	—	6.45

Axminster Fair Days to be run as Thursdays.

RAMBLER COACHES
(Proprietor: S. J. WAKLEY)
Coach Tours
to all Places of Interest
in the West Country
PRIVATE PARTIES CATERED FOR. MOST MODERN AND UP-TO-DATE COACHES
Local Bus Services connecting Chardstock, Membury, Stockland and Axminster.
MEMBURY
Telephone: STOCKLAND 235
and
Trinity Square, AXMINSTER

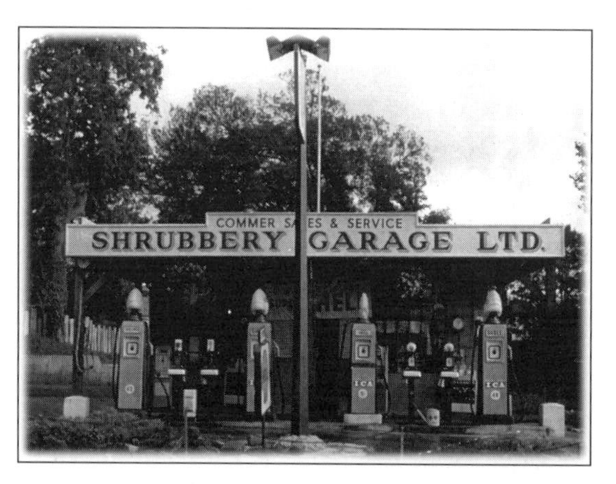

Shrubbery Garage, Anchor Hill, Axminster, soon after it was opened in 1946 by Stan Wakley, a Membury man, who ran his coach services from there until 1960. Three years later the garage was sold to the Blue Star Garage chain.

Trinity Square, Axminster, c.1948. The Taunton (via Chard and Ilminster) bus is about to depart. Having two bus-stops opposite one another in the Square has often been a bone of contention in the town, especially on market days.

Axminster had not had a resident coach operator since the 1920s and Stan Wakley, looking to expand, opened an office in Trinity Square after the Second World War. With a presence in Axminster it was not long before Stan moved his depot from Membury into Axminster where he purchased the Shrubbery in Anchor Hill at a cost of £6,000. There he built the Shrubbery Garage. In 1946 he bought two Bedford OWB Duplex coaches; in 1957 he bought his twentieth, and last bus, a 41-seater Commer TS3. The award of a contract to transport children from the villages to Axminster School was a shot in the arm to the business but, by 1960, the increasing number of private motor cars on the roads led to the Rambler Coaches being sold to Wessex Coaches of Bristol. The Shrubbery Garage was retained for three more years before being bought by the Blue Star Garage chain. In 2003 the site is the entrance to the West Street car park and the Co-op superstore. Stan Wakley retired and at the time of writing is still pottering around the district in his car at the grand old age of 93.

His first employee was Len 'Whip' Cornish. Among the others were: Arthur Boyland, Peter Crichard, Reg Denslow, Jack French, Stan Fifer, David Heighwey, Mick Mainwood, Buckie Mear, Michael Davis, Pete Muir, Charlie Parkhouse, Arthur Pring, Stan Reynolds, Fred Spiller, Les Smallwood, Charlie Swain, Bert Thomas, Stan Turner, Fred Willey and Nesta Densham. The conductresses were: Lily Fowler, Jean Gould, Esme Hann, Mary Harvey and Dorothy Pearce.

Other familiar sights in the town were the charabancs and omnibuses belonging to Herb Vincent of Thorncombe who started running a bus service from Thorncombe to Axminster on market days in 1926. By 1934 the return fare to Axminster was 1s.9d. (8¾p in modern money). Later the service ran four days a week. Vincent's also had the contract to bus pupils to Axminster School from certain outlying areas as late as 1982. Like Stan Wakley, Vincent's finally fell foul of the private motor car and closed in the 1970s. Earlier, in the late 1920s and early 1930s, Axminster Town Football Club travelled to away matches in one of the Vincent fleet – a charabanc that soon enjoyed the nickname of the Tiger after the footballers' yellow-and-black-striped shirts.

It is said that the arrival of the railway in Axminster in 1860 was a shot in the arm for a town dying on its feet after the failure of the carpet industry in 1828. But is this really true? It is interesting to look at the census returns for the town since they were introduced in 1801 (see above).

CENSUS RETURNS, 1801–2001

1801: 2,154	*1901: 2,906*
1811: 2,387	*1911: 2,854*
1821: 2,742	*1921: 2,868*
1831: 2,719	*1931: 3,320*
1841: 2,861	*1941: no census*
1851: 2,769	*1951: 3,676*
1861: 2,918	*1961: 3,650*
1871: 2,861	*1981: 4,954*
1881: 2,872	*1991: 5,180*
1891: 2,809	*2001: 5,751 (projected).*

Between 1821 and 1921 the population of the town increased by only 126, although it might be fair to say that had it not been for the railway there may possibly have been a decrease between 1860 and 1900.

The arrival of the railway in Axminster was initially delayed by the controversy over which way the westward line should run. It had long been accepted that rail connections between Plymouth and other South Coast Naval ports were needed. The Parliamentary committee that sat on the subject did so for 53 days at a cost of £300,000. There were three possibilities: Dorchester, Honiton or Taunton, although the first two would certainly have passed through Axminster in any case. As early as 1843 the town had petitioned Parliament that the line should run through Axminster. Some 17 years later their dreams were realised when the London & South Western Railway arrived on the edge of the town.

However, it was not greeted with pleasure by everyone. Sir Edmund de la Pole of Shute House only allowed the line to cross his land after considerable argument – and only then as long as it was not visible from his home. In complete contrast, and some 40 years later, Sir Wilfred Peek welcomed the Lyme Regis branch line on his ground at Rousdon and Combpyne – but only if a station was built that he could use. What a pity Sir Wilfred was not around when Dr Beeching decided to close the line.

Axminster Station was designed by the Victorian architect Sir William Tite and built in 1859 in the rather heavy and ugly style which was the trademark of our Victorian forebears. Sir Williams' tall chimneys soon gave cause for alarm and were eventually replaced. The official opening of the line at Axminster was on 15 July 1860 amidst the usual jollifications that were held in every town in England when the iron horse arrived. Axminster declared a public holiday and there was a sumptuous banquet at the George Hotel for the important people who dined on the best cuts and wines. The *hoi polloi* (they included the navvies who did the actual work) were not forgotten, although they were not allowed near the aforementioned banquet. Instead they dined on roast beef, potatoes and plum duff pudding. The workhouse inmates also tucked in.

One of the last branch lines to be built in England was the Lyme Regis line that starts from Axminster. The line was finally opened on 24 August 1903 amid celebrations held at both Axminster and Lyme Regis Stations. At 12.30p.m. the Axminster Parish Council, under its chairman Mr Pitfield Chapple, assembled at the Council Room and, headed by the Pride of the Axe Band, marched in state to the railway station to receive the civil representatives of Lyme Regis, who

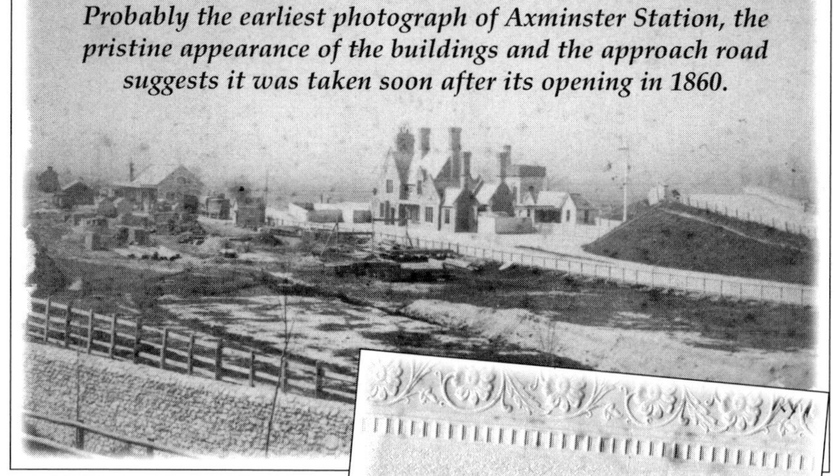

Probably the earliest photograph of Axminster Station, the pristine appearance of the buildings and the approach road suggests it was taken soon after its opening in 1860.

OPENING OF THE
Axminster and Lyme Regis Light Railway
MONDAY. AUG. 24. 1903.

12-30 p.m. Axminster Parish Council meet at the Council Room and proceed to Railway Station to meet Lyme Regis Town Council.

Reception of Lyme Regis Town Council.

1-18 p.m. Both Councils proceed to Lyme Regis by train.

2-0 p.m. Councils lunch together at invitation of the Mayor of Lyme Regis.

200 Lyme Regis Children journey to Axminster and back to Lyme Regis for tea.

Sports at Lyme Regis (on the Sands).

Below: *Axminster Station, c.1900. The tall chimneys were later taken down, presumably on safety grounds. Otherwise, apart from the removal of the paint on the bricks, the building is much the same. Jack Maeer and the George Hotel's horse-drawn bus waits outside for passengers.*

Axminster Station, c.1908. The George Hotel's horse-drawn bus is the central one of the three vehicles in front of the station.

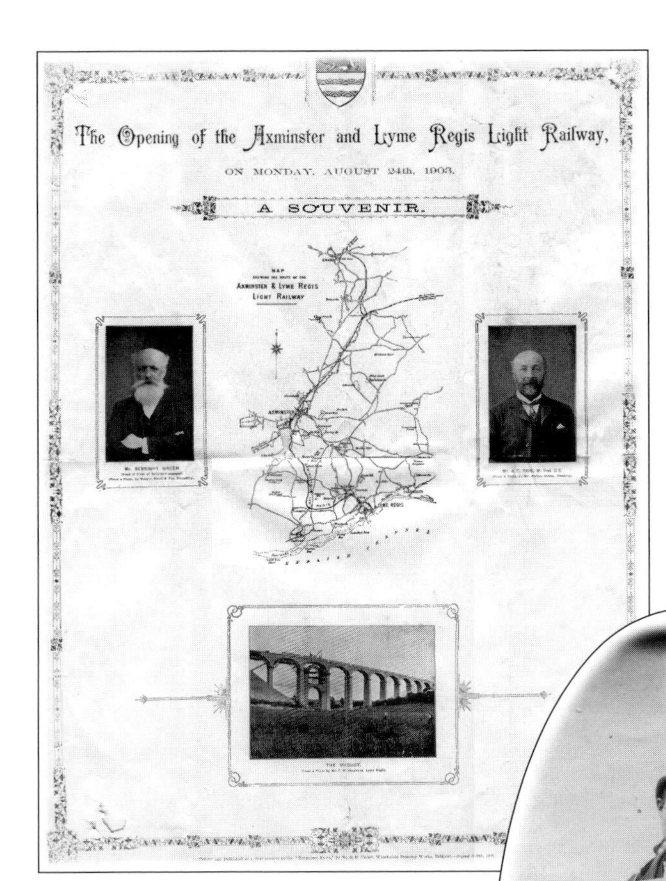

had arrived by the second passenger-carrying train to leave the Lyme terminus, at 12.25p.m., that day. As a taste of things to come, what with leaves and the wrong kind of snow, it was late.

The previous Friday Major Druitt, RE, one of the Board of Trade inspectors, had carried out the final inspection of the line for which he had left Lyme Regis station at 10a.m. His party travelled in an inspection coach with two engines (734 and 735). The gallant Major inspected every point and bridge, and especially the viaduct, the safety of which had been much doubted, and about which so much gossip had been spoken. For nearly an hour it was severely tested and examined and found to be safe. The inspecting party then left to arrive at the Axminster end of the line just before 2p.m. Major Druitt announced that the entire line was to his satisfaction.

Pulman's Weekly News told its readers that the opening of the line by the Lyme Regis Light Railway Company would be:

> *A distinct boon to the little borough of Lyme Regis, which has hitherto not been connected with the outside world by any railway, and to the villages of Uplyme, Rousdon and Combpyne. Previously the nearest station had been at Axminster, some 5½ miles distant, which was reached by a bus service* [horse-drawn], *several buses going to and fro each day.*

At first the six trains travelled the line daily but it was not long before Lyme Regis Town Council demanded more. The third-class fare to Combpyne from Axminster was 4½d. (barely 2p) and from Axminster to Lyme 6½d. A ticket from Lyme Regis to Waterloo cost 12s.7d. (63p).

Lyme's civic party was wise to travel on the second train; the first had left at 9.40a.m. in pouring rain that had left the bunting, flags and flowers looking a little the worse for wear. The train, its engine also decorated with flags and bunting, consisted of seven coaches and was in the charge of Inspector Chamberlain of Exeter. It was seen off by the new stationmaster, Mr Ely from Poole; the stationmaster at Combpyne being Mr Greenslade of Exeter.

The driver of the first train out of Lyme Regis was Mr S. Dwyer of Yeovil and it was crowded with passengers. Many others hoping for their own little niche in the town's history, that of being able to tell their grandchildren, 'I rode on the first train out of Lyme Regis', were unable to get a seat and had to watch those more fortunate folk depart to the sound of much cheering and exploding fog signals. The train reached the prettily decorated Axminster Station dead on time at 10.05a.m., where it was greeted by more fog signals and hundreds more cheering people. Again packed with passengers, it started its return journey to Lyme Regis at 10.45a.m.

After the civic parties clasped hands on Axminster Station's up platform when train number two arrived, they were entertained in the waiting-room by Mr Ball, the stationmaster. Both parties then took the train back to Lyme Regis for the official celebrations which were held at the Royal Lion Hotel. A total of 150 of the great and good of Axminster, Lyme Regis and the Lyme Regis Light Railway Company, not to forget Colonel Williams (MP for West Dorset) and Sir John Kennaway (MP for Honiton) tucked in with gusto.

The children were not forgotten. After their elders had junketed at The Royal Lion they were entertained with sports on the sands and then enjoyed their own tea.

The first breakdown followed four days later. The 1.18p.m. train left Axminster as usual but, when just a couple of miles out, one of the cylinders of the engine broke and the train had to return to Axminster. Another light engine was quickly

Above: *Axminster's (unknown) town crier inviting the inhabitants of the town to a public meeting in the school (then in West Street) on 26 January 1899 in support of the Axminster & Lyme Regis Light Railway.*

brought up from Exmouth Junction and, after a slight delay while the engines were changed at Axminster, the train set out again.

That first train to Lyme Regis carried 137 passengers, or at least 137 tickets were sold, according to the company's half-yearly meeting. However, the second train attracted around 350 paying customers plus, of course, the civic parties of both towns.

The meeting dwelt, at some length, on the delay in the opening of the line, much of which had been caused by heavy rains that hindered the progress of the workmen. Indeed, at one stage the work was delayed to such an extent that 250 extra workers were drafted in as part of an unsuccessful attempt to get back on schedule.

The line's most prominent feature is the 230-yard long viaduct that carries it over the steep Cannington valley to the south of Uplyme. It is one of the earliest examples of a major concrete construction in the south of England (the Axe Bridge between Seaton and Axmouth that was built in 1877 is said to be the first in the entire country). It was the cause for considerable concern soon after it was built as its extreme weight led to the number one pier and west abutment sinking into the sandy foundations. A jack arch had to be built to prop it up and prevent any further sinking. Flag men were posted at each end of the viaduct to watch for any movement when trains crossed over (with only a dozen a day it must have been a boring sort of life) but no movement was ever recorded and, when the L&SWR took over the line, the men were removed. However, Sid Baker, an Uplyme man, was retained to measure (check) the height of that particular arch for many years to ensure there was no more sinkage.

The main Waterloo–Exeter line was blocked for days following this derailment near Weycroft of a goods train on 22 February 1973.

Sadly Dr Beeching removed much of the rest of the line when his infamous 'axe' changed our English railways for ever. The line was closed to goods traffic in February 1964 and to all other traffic 13 months later. In 1967 the track was lifted and, apart from the odd bridge, all that remains of the famous old Bluebell Line is the lonely viaduct with its jack arch. Even that received the final insult when British Rail offered it for sale for just £1. There were no takers. A recent move to restart the line attracted many enthusiastic supporters to a meeting in Axminster. Predictably nothing has come of the idea as yet.

The 'Axminster'.

Immediately following the Second World War the Southern Railway named many West Country Class locomotives after towns that the company served including Axminster, Lyme Regis, Seaton and Sidmouth. Built at Brighton in 1945 the 'Axminster' locomotive, which weighed 128 tons 12cwt, was brought to Axminster for its naming ceremony by Harry Cawley, the chairman of the Town Council. Mr Cawley was presented with a coffee table at the time, which in 2003 is displayed in Axminster Museum.

4

The Post Office

In the early 1600s Axminster was not a post-town (a town with an official Post Office). Rather, it was a sub-office of Crewkerne from where its mail arrived by horse. There were early difficulties. In 1673 the Crewkerne postmaster, Mr John Bonnhill, was instructed to arrange for Axminster's mail to be taken by a rider. No reason is known why he acted thus, but Bonnhill refused to do this on a regular basis (perhaps for economic reasons). Consequently, it was not until his resignation that the new postmaster at Crewkerne, a Mr Greenway, began sending mail to Axminster on a regular basis.

However, the service was still far from satisfactory but, after pressure from merchants and the upper classes, a move was made to take the London–Exeter mail through Axminster. At that time such mail went via Salisbury, Crewkerne, Chard and Honiton. Axminster continued to receive its mail from the Crewkerne postmaster until October 1785 when the London–Exeter mail coach made its first run via Axminster.

Although the Royal Mail ran its coach from Axminster to Exeter via Honiton, by the closing years of the eighteenth century there was also a horse post to Exeter that went via Colyton, Sidmouth, Budleigh, Exmouth and Topsham. Axminster's postmaster, Jonathan Bilke, was paid £7.16s.0d. per annum to pay a man to make local deliveries on foot to Kilmington, Colyton, Seaton and Beer. The outgoing mail from those villages was handed in at a receiving house.

Since the eighteenth century, there had been a charge of 1d. to cover the cost of the journey to the Post Office and the letter was usually, but not always, hand-stamped to show that this fee had been paid. Not surprisingly, this system was called the Axminster Penny Post. It was not unique to Axminster, however, as almost every small town that had a Post Office served its smaller neighbours. Consequently, there was an Ashford Penny Post, plus an Ashburton Penny Post and so on.

Above: *Letter posted at Axminster in 1781 to Brighthelmstone (Brighton). The person sending the letter was of such importance, an MP or State official, that his mail was carried without charge.*

Mail either reached or left Axminster by four different categories of post: London letters, country letters, cross-post letters and bye-letters. The first group is self explanatory – letters that went directly to or from the capital. Country letters passed through London on their way to their final destination, such as Axminster to Norwich. As the name suggests, a cross post was one that went 'across country' and did not visit London on its way from one provincial town to another, such as letters from Dorchester to Bristol, or Exeter to Cardiff. Bye-letters travelled along the main coach runs without getting as far as London, from Axminster, say, to Salisbury or Andover. Once the letter arrived at Axminster from the receiving houses, the number of miles it had to travel dictated the cost of conveying it to its final destination. Before the introduction of the Universal Penny Post and the postage stamp in 1840 the charges were considerable, although the rate tended to be incrementally lowered for longer

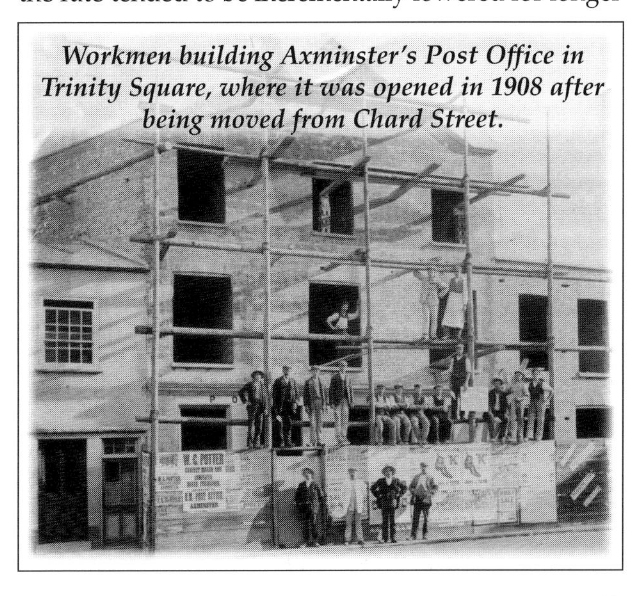

Workmen building Axminster's Post Office in Trinity Square, where it was opened in 1908 after being moved from Chard Street.

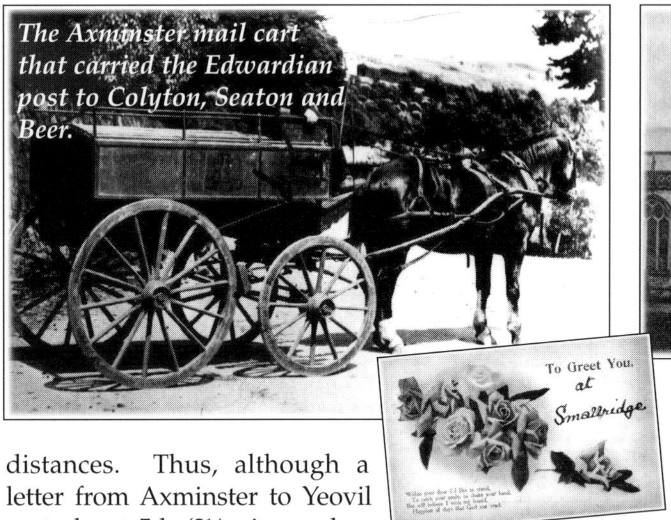

The Axminster mail cart that carried the Edwardian post to Colyton, Seaton and Beer.

distances. Thus, although a letter from Axminster to Yeovil cost about 5d. (2¼p in modern money), one to London cost only 10d.

The first known Post Office in Axminster was in Castle Hill when George Slyfield was the postmaster between 1822 and 1844. He was also a maltster and common brewer. (A George Slyfield junr in the town, who was a professor of music, was almost certainly his son.) At that time the mail coach left the George Hotel for London daily at 11a.m. The mail from London to Exeter and the West Country stopped at Axminster and left the George at 2.30p.m. By 1830 both types of mail left the town at 1p.m. and by 1838, when considerable improvements had been made to the roads and coach journey times reduced, mail left the George Hotel at 3.15p.m.

George Slyfield senr's son, William, who by 1850 had moved to Chard Street, probably in what would one day become the Town Club, followed George as postmaster at Castle Hill. By 1870 William Henry Tapshott was postmaster, a job that went well with his position of deputy registrar of marriages. By that time the first postbox had arrived in the town, being situated in the wall at Chard Street; others soon followed in Lyme Road, Trinity Square and the railway station. It is possible that the Post Office was moved to Victoria Place for a few years (where Forbuoys is located in 2003), but it was back in Chard Street by 1889. The selection of Chard Street and Victoria Place was obviously dictated by their close proximity to the George Hotel. A third move in 1908 saw the Post Office in Trinity Square, in what is the premises of Boots the chemists in 2003. There was no rear entrance to these premises and the danger posed by the combination of the increasing motor traffic and Post Office vans loading and unloading in the main street led to a move to South Street in 1937.

When the Millwey Rise housing estate was built a sub-Post Office was opened there and, for some years (from 1919 until around 1988), there was another sub-Post Office in a small grocer's shop (once a branch of W.J. Harris & Son, the Trinity Square grocer) in Musbury Road in Axminster. When Axminster's main Post Office was downgraded to a sub-office and

West Street, Axminster, c.1905. The tall building on the right became the fire station. Next door was once the National School, later the Church Rooms and, in 2003, the Post Office. This card is addressed to Mr W.E. Pitfield Chapple, Axminster's fire chief at that time.

also became a shop, the premises were thought to be too small, so it was moved to West Street, where it remains in 2003. The sorting office, which is still run by the postal authorities, however, remained in South Street. There was also a sub-Post Office at Smallridge where Sarah Elizabeth Richbell was postmistress for 25 years at the start of the twentieth century.

Receiving houses were found in a variety of places. Among those covered by Axminster post were a grocer's shop (Beer), a baker and stationer (Branscombe), a boot- and shoemaker (Colyford), a lace manufacturer (Colyton – where, later, the headmaster of Colyton Grammar School had a licence to sell stamps), a wheelwright (Chardstock), a schoolmaster and librarian (Rousdon and Combpyne), three successive shoemakers (Farway) and, best of all from the point of view of the foot post that covered the village of Kilmington, was John Chapple, a sub-postmaster who was also the landlord of the Old Inn. In time the increased volume of letters and parcels led to the introduction of the horse-drawn mail carts or, in the case of Hawkchurch, a donkey-drawn cart.

At the turn of the nineteenth century, the Uplyme haulier, Mr Stapleforth, had the contract to supply the Post Office at Axminster with the horses for its delivery vans. In 1903, when the Axminster and Lyme Regis mail from the Chard area still arrived by mail cart, one of his horses pulled up lame at Coaxden Cross. An examination revealed that the poor horse had a broken leg and had to be put down. Mr Stapleforth was told about his horse's mishap and rushed to Axminster Post Office, then still in Chard Street. While he was inside his own horse bolted, dragging the cart with it for some distance before the cart overturned. Happily the horse was unscathed; the only damage done was a broken wing on the cart.

A later breed of Uplyme residents will remember Henry Stapleforth, probably a son of the above-mentioned Mr Stapleforth. By his time the horse and carts in the family transport business had changed into taxis. Henry was one of Uplyme's characters whose driving often gave cause for concern to his passengers!

5

SCHOOLS

Axminster Council School, 1928.

The first mention of schooling in Axminster comes from Diocesan Records that list a John Guppy as being licensed in 1662 to teach the three Rs – reading, writing and 'rithmatic. Those Diocesan Records, strictly speaking the accounts of Axminster's churchwardens, make several references to monies paid out to the school during the seventeenth and eighteenth centuries. In 1665 an unspecified amount was paid for 'Iron, Iron Stuffs and nails, material and labour about healing [roofing] the School House.' A year later 5s.6d. (27½p) was spent again when 'the School House had healing'.

Daniel House was a teacher in Axminster in 1669 when £31.3s.10d. was paid for 'rebuilding the School House'. Six years later the church register states that the Church Room was 'used as a school room and for the parochial meetings...' Other teachers mentioned include Robert Smith (1673), Thomas Smith (1674), the Revd William Keate (1704) and the Revd Michael Downe, the curate at Kilmington (1712).

The school stood beside the Parish Church; in 1679, the registers mention 'the new door of the church which is before the school house.' It had heating and the registers also say that 2d. was paid for 'sweeping the school house chimney'. Davidson, in his *History of Axminster* places it in the ground floor of a building that stood in the churchyard on the north side of the church (near the junction of Silver Street and Trinity Square). He adds that it was referred to as a chapel.

By 1744 the school was becoming overcrowded, one report saying that '40 children were taught grammar, reading and writing there.' However, it was not until 1796 that teaching in a new school commenced. The earlier school may have already been condemned – in 1792 it was recorded that £2.12s.6d. was 'paid for rent of a room for a school'.

The new school was in West Street in premises facing the church. It was probably sited in an existing building because, staying with Davidson, we are told that a new two-storeyed school was built on this site in 1825, the upper room of which was a girls' Sunday school.

Back to 1746 when the school was still on the north side of the church; it was then that Thomas Courtenay, in consideration of a sum of £160, conveyed:

> *... a message* [sic] *and tenement in the parish of Kilmington, in trust to lease the said premises for the best rent, either for years or at will, without taking any fine, out of rents to pay all rates and taxes, expenses of trustees, and of repairing the premises, and of collecting the rents; and upon further trust to apply the residue to educating and instructing of poor child, inhabitants of Axminster, in reading and writing, at the discretion of the trustees, at the schoolhouse in Axminster, or some convenient place at that town, such children to be taught by a school master, to be provided by the trustees at a public meeting, which school master might also be removed at a public meeting, by a majority of the trustees, and a new one elected, and at such a meeting, our by direction in writing of the major part of the trustees, the children to be removed from the school that others of the parish might be placed there, so that the headmaster might have always under his care twelve such children.*

Of that £160, £100 was bequeathed in the will of Penelope Saffin of Exeter on 28 September 1742. The source of the other £60 is not known. With the monies an estate was purchased consisting of an orchard of just over an acre, a meadow of just over a couple of acres, another on an acre and a field of an acre, making half a dozen acres in all.

Vacancies at the school were filled on the recommendation of the trustees who were only allowed to nominate one child at a time. The age limits were between 6 and 11 years and no child could attend the school for more than four years. Attendance at Divine Service in the Parish Church on Sundays, as well as on holidays, was compulsory.

In 1849 John Austen was paid £45 per annum as head teacher at Axminster where he had two pupil-teacher assistants. His discipline was considered good by HM Inspector who also found that his teaching method was fair and that he 'took much pains, but there was still room for improvement.' He had trained at Exeter and was 'intelligent, pleasant and doing much good work in the school.'

A mistress and two pupil-teacher candidates taught the girls, but the infants were under an assistant. The inspector thought that the girls' 'discipline might be improved', but it was also admitted that 'the mistress had only just taken charge of the school that had been left by a late teacher in a very unsatisfactory state.' The new mistress was Anne Webster who joined the school on 29 September (Michaelmas Day) 1849. She rendered faithful service there for 27 years.

By 1863 the aptly named George Clouting was the headmaster of the Boys' School (believed to have been on the upper floor of the school in West Street) and his first entry in the oldest existing logbook is on 24 April of that year when he wrote:

> *This week I gave the teacher of the third class* [one of the pupil-teachers] *a week to show some improvement in writing... the week was used to some purpose.*

That Clouting was a kindly man is plainly evident from the logbooks. In later years teachers at the school (and at most other schools in the county) tended to disparage the school they had just taken over. It was done to impress the inspectors, no doubt, and they would take the credit when their school was found to be in good order at a subsequent inspection. Clouting was not that sort of a man; his decency and fair-mindedness stares out from every page of the logbooks. In 1863 he found a boy writing a naughty word on his slate and wrote, 'somehow it is an almost unheard of offence at this school... the lad seemed very penitent and begged most piteously to be forgiven.' He also found a broken window and 'appealed to the honour of the boys... found the offender at once... an accident... exhorted the lads to come and tell when an accident occurs.' In June 1863 the HM Inspectors arrived to find that Axminster School was 'doing well throughout, the writing is very good; the reading might improve, for it is very fair. Mr Clouting is working heartily and well.'

Absence might make the heart grow fonder. As far as the boys of Axminster were concerned in 1863, it also served to make them forgetful, Mr Clouting bemoaning the fact that 'there were 92 boys present for the start of the term in July but... they had lost much [ability] during the three weeks holiday.' He had admitted a 14-year-old boy but found him to be so behind in his learning that he had to put him with the 9 and 10 year olds in order to get him up to standard in three months.

Throughout the remainder of the school's Victorian years it did not take much for a parent to keep a boy away from school. Clouting often refers to a 'thin' school, one with far less than a full complement of pupils. Among the reasons he mentioned for absences were helping with the garden at busy times of the year, such as picking potatoes, club days, the circus being in town, the passing of military formations through the town, and harvest time on the farms.

He was also worried, with good reason, in 1865 that 'the factory in Axminster, after being closed for some time, has reopened.' His fears that some of his pupils would be encouraged by their parents to leave school early and bring a wage into the household were well founded. Four weeks later he mentioned that there had been pupil losses to the factory.

Clouting left Axminster on 21 June 1867 taking his son, a pupil-teacher, with him. His last words in the logbook were: 'I took leave of the dear Axminster boys after eight and a half years most pleasant labour... [it is] certainly the most happy part of my life so far.'

His last report was a good one. That April the inspector found that:

... this is a very good school. I think it has done better this year in the subjects of its standards than in any preceding year. Geography and Grammar very fairly taught and Religious Instruction is carefully and thoughtfully given.

Clouting was followed by Brice Bennett from Piggott School at Wargrave, Berks. He took up his appointment on 22 July that year. He found the Devonian accent hard to understand and wrote in the logbook that he was trying to improve the reading because all the boys read in a 'peculiar tone'.

He left the school in less than a year to take up an appointment as headmaster at the Reading and Wokingham School. He may have been wise to go – his only inspection found that:

... this school has fallen off in numbers and efficiency since last year. To do himself justice Mr Bennett must work very hard to bring the school up to its former efficient start... my Lords will require a better report from the Boys School next year as the condition of an unreduced grant.

Brice Bennett gave little notice of his departure and the authorities had to appoint George Hoare, a pupil-teacher, as a temporary master at the Boys' School until a permanent master could be found. Hoare found both the standards and the attendance levels low. On 1 May 1868, only 51 pupils were present and, five days later, he wrote, 'with many of the younger boys coming late to school, I have found it necessary to introduce more stringent rules with regards to punctuality.' Given the age this has to be a euphemism for caning. If so it was an instant success with attendances quickly improving.

Hoare had little support; one of the monitors, Henry Paul, whom he was unable to trust with even a small class, showed not the slightest interest in the boys' education, joining in their games instead. He was often late himself and, on one occasion, went off on a Sunday school treat without permission. That September he left the school (he was probably forced to), but the logbook is blank with regards the circumstances of his leaving. He was not the only one absent when a circus visited Axminster and most of the children attended the afternoon penny performance. A few weeks later Wormell's Menagerie was back in town and only 38 boys attended school that day.

George Hoare left on 1 October 1868 and the following day Mr F. Gower took up his duties as master. In keeping with what seems to be the tradition at Axminster he wrote disparagingly about what he had found: 'Children are extremely backward... no books in the school... many late... very small attendance (55).' A month later he resigned and in his letter he told the authorities: 'The school is far behind the representations made to me as to numbers [of pupils].' This, of course, affected his stipend. In the interregnum another pupil-teacher, George Hoskins, was in charge until February 1869 when Mr George Arnold arrived at the school.

Numbers improved, rising to between 80 and 90, and more punishments for bad behaviour appear in the logbook. His demands for books and equipment were met and, when HM Inspector arrived, we learn that:

From frequent change of masters, this school had fallen off from its former standards of efficiency. The present master appears to be active and intelligent. I trust that he may be able to raise the school again. The portfolio now in use ought to be replaced.

By May 1869 attendances had reached around 100 but in July he was forced to caution the boys about getting behind in the payment of fees and asked that arrears be paid before the holidays. Attendances showed a significant improvement when, in August, the annual tea party was imminent. Indeed, many former scholars put in an appearance.

In 1870 the numbers (approximately) were: Standard One, 24; Two, 20; Three, 14; Four, 10; Five, 8; Six, 3; Seven, 4. Obviously as children got older the more likely it became that they would be taken away from school in order to contribute to the family budget. Truancy (as opposed to being kept away by parents) increased in the summer months. So much so that Mr Arnold noted that 'this evil has been spreading of late... and I am resolved to adopt strict measures for its removal' (another euphemism for caning). Despite this the problem did not go away.

George Arnold did not stay long at the school but he left a permanent legacy in the shape of the lending library that he had started. By charging pupils ½d. a book, he raised around £1.10s.0d. (£1.50), with which he was able to purchase another 22 books for the library.

His successor was Mr Catford who became the new master on 28 August 1871. It was to prove a long reign; he finally retired in 1901 after 30 years' dedicated and successful service to the community.

The logbook for the Girls' School is in existence from 1863 when, on 18 May, Miss Anne Webster wrote, 'It was Ascension Day and the children went to church in the morning. It was a nice full school but the children are all so young.' There were around 150 pupils under her care, including the under-seven boys. Following the visit of a gentleman from Exeter (possibly a HM Inspector) who was 'pleased with... the writing and the arithmetic', she wrote that the boys were 'quite interested and a pleasure to teach'.

The summer holidays were usually around three weeks long and ended in mid-July when, like Mr Clouting, Miss Webster found that her girls had gone backwards during their absence. They were, she noted, 'rather careless after their holiday'. Perhaps they had other things on their minds; the annual school feast was looming on 26 August and the children were 'thinking of nothing else... very busy making flags'. It proved to be a disappointment. It rained and the children had to have their food indoors, which brought extra work for the staff who had to clean up the mess in the classrooms afterwards. The girls were soon forgiven; Miss Webster sent them home early on Michaelmas Day, the 14th anniversary of her arrival at Axminster.

Apart from the three Rs, great emphasis was placed on knitting and needlework for the girls, most of whom would finish up in service where sewing skills were a necessity. Anne Webster realised this, as evidenced by her entry in the logbook which said that it was important that the girls be taught knitting and needlework as they were obliged to be taken from school so young. It was an age when poverty was rife and, as soon as possible, a child's potential as a wage-earner had to be realised. A child, however young, who was out working, was bringing some money into the home; one at school was not but still needed feeding and clothing. In addition, to the parents' minds, reading and writing was not important; rather a girl needed to know about housework and needlework to get both a job and a husband.

However, education was taken seriously by HM Inspector whose visit in 1864 kept the staff on tenterhooks, especially as many of the great (elder) girls, generally reckoned to be able to give a good impression, were absent.

In the 1860s, problems undreamt of by today's teachers had to be faced, including the lack of good lighting in the classrooms, a point underlined one winter by Miss Webster who said 'children industrious but afternoons so short... very little needlework can be done.' On 15 January 1864, she wrote:

> *Thin school, many had gone and four of my best, first-class girls not at school this week. Fear they have left altogether and several of the girls have gone to service and others are obliged to be kept at home to help mothers. Parents are anxious for their girls to do as much needlework as they can.*

She said that there were eight children absent all that week which she found 'very trying after taking great pains with them all year.'

Obviously more than one person was needed to teach over 150 pupils but, apart from a reference to a pupil-teacher, Lucy, being away when her father was ill, the first real indication of staffing levels came in March 1864 when it was recorded that Anne Webster had the assistance of Elizabeth Victoria Northam, a pupil-teacher at the end of her third year, and Lucy Patterson, a pupil-teacher at the end of her second year. Even three teachers could not cope and monitors supervised some of the classes, even if, as was more than once recorded in the logbook, they were more in need of teaching than some of the children they were supervising. One monitor, H. Chick, received £10 per annum, while two others, Rhoda Harris and A. Webster (Anne's daughter?) received 9d. (3¾p) a week, and M.A. Chaffey half of that.

We have said that HM Inspectors took education seriously but, in a church-orientated education system, they also knew the place of religion and which branch of the Christian Church was the 'right' one. Miss Webster wrote in 1864 that 'not much done in reading and arithmetic, this being Passion Week, much time being spent in questioning the children in our Lord's suffering and death.' Later she mentions that she was 'obliged to close a little earlier every afternoon to enable us to get to church every night at five o'clock during Lent.' School was often disrupted by visits from the vicar or church 'bigwigs', such as Mr McKenzie, the Diocesan Inspector who was 'very pleased with the children... they had done very nicely indeed.' Not unnaturally, Miss Webster thought that the children and the teachers were all the better for 'a little praise'.

Illness and death were never very far away in the mid-nineteenth century, especially for the children. In 1866 an epidemic of measles swept Axminster. Children were especially at risk and, on 9 March, Miss Webster recorded that 17 children under six years of age were absent with the disease. Two weeks later such entries begin to appear in the logbook as:

> *... scarcely any children here today... many were ill... one of our infants died* [22 March]... *never had such a small school, 62 present out of a nominal roll call of 160–170... one more of our infants died* [25 March]... *one more of our infants died today* [27 March]... *another of our little boys died today* [28 March]... *another of our small children died* [2 April].

By 9 April the epidemic had passed over but most of the children looked 'very poorly' after their illnesses and dinners were provided in an attempt to strengthen them. More than 100 partook and, a week later, the children were:

> *... in high spirits about the soup and puddings... they had thoroughly enjoyed their dinners and are looking much better... there were a great number of children present.*

She did not mention that the good attendances were because of the dinners, but we suspect that that may have been the case. The dinners ended on 4 May when 'some of the big boys said they must eat enough for two days and kept us waiting for a very long time on them.' The food was provided by Mr and Mrs Tate who were presumably local benefactors, although no other mention is made of them.

Despite the measles, which also affected the Boys' School of course, HM Inspectors arrived that June to find that the school continued to improve, especially in writing and arithmetic, and that the personal influence of the mistress on her girls was very good. Sewing was also good but religious knowledge was very fair.

The County Council School off Chard Street, c.1909. Much of the building was retained when the school was considerably enlarged. The houses behind, however, were demolished.

Below: *Once a private school, Oak House on Chard Street is seen here c.1903. It was a boys' prep school between the 1880s and the Second World War. In turn it became a dormitory and canteen for the employees of Edwin Dawkins & Son Ltd. In 1945 it was taken over as an office by Axminster Rural District Council, and, in 2003, it is a retirement home. Like the Parish Church, it lost its railings during a Second World War salvage drive.*

Outside distractions continued to vie with the school for the childrens' attention. Thin (poorly attended) schools were still frequently mentioned, along with the causes. They included a cherry fair and another visit of Wormell's Menagerie to Axminster.

It was not only the children who were ill; Miss Webster was away from school for four months with 'the fever' between September 1867 and January 1868. During that time many parents, for fear of infection, kept their children away. The authorities were not very kind during her absence – no grant was allowed for the Girls' School during the time when an uncertified teacher taught the pupils.

Uncertified or not, the temporary teacher seems to have known her job because, that summer, HM Inspector was back at Axminster where he found that:

This school has passed an examination which, under the circumstances, reflects much credit on all the teachers. Reading, writing and arithmetic, especially in the lower classes, show much care on the part of the teachers. Religious Knowledge is weak in the higher classes. Sewing good, but the admission book should be carefully kept.

Measles and tragedy were back in 1869 when several children were very poorly with the disease. The log mentions:

... one of [the] *small children died this morning of measles... several more children absent in measles and several others very ill indeed... another of our little ones died in measles.*

This outbreak of measles continued to claim victims – a small girl on 11 June and others on the 14 and 21 of that month. That June several children were sent home with the mumps. Later, in January 1870, 'after a bout of fever had carried off one child, there were many staying at home due to chilblains.'

Tragedy of a different kind hit one Axminster family in the middle of the measles epidemic, when 'a poor man was burnt to death... some of his poor children come to this school... the whole school is in great sorrow.'

In 1871 the fever was back again and carried off two children, one from the Boys' School and one from the Girls'.

The following year consumption killed one girl as well as F. Chick, who had been a pupil-teacher at the school for many years. Measles came back in 1873 when 40 girls were reported as being absent, but no deaths were mentioned.

Anne Webster left the school on 14 July 1876, after 27 years as headmistress. She was much missed; her devotion to her charges is much in evidence throughout her entries in the logbook.

She was replaced by Miss Ellen Gibbs who, only four days after she arrived at Axminster, followed the habit of incoming teachers by denigrating the work of her predecessors by writing in the school logbook:

School is in a very disorderly state... children have a habit of coming in late... was occupied all week in getting order and method in school... had to reprove several children for want of cleanliness... examining children found they were in a very backward state.

Actually she was very lucky to arrive at Axminster when she did. Despite her disparaging remarks about Anne Webster, she had taken over a school that, for the time, was in very good heart. Also, it was 1870 when the new education bill, known as Foster's Act after the Education Minister in Gladstone's Government, was introduced. This act allowed school boards to take over in areas where the voluntary schools were not able to educate all the local children.

At Axminster a decision had to be made about how to finance the two schools which were, by this time, far too small to house all the children in the town. In March 1873 a meeting was held in the church vestry to consider the future of Axminster's parochial schools. A second meeting in April saw supporters of the voluntary system of education winning the day on the grounds of expense, a decision that was approved at a ratepayers' meeting six months later.

Somewhat tartly the managers at the National Schools not only pointed out that they did not have the money to run the schools, but added that the ratepayers made no contribution at all towards the schools. They claimed that the only way forward was a Board School; one was formed in March 1874 and a rate was levied for the new school (The Council School, *see page 45*) and its upkeep.

The first chairman of the new board was Captain E.C. Forward, the vice-chairman Mr William Pulman and the clerk was William Forward (a whiff of nepotism there?). Costing £3,600 and built to accommodate 425 children, the new school opened on a site just off Chard Street on 1 September 1876. It consisted of two buildings and two teachers' houses. One of the school buildings survives in 2003.

On the day that the children moved into the new buildings Miss Gibbs recorded that there was a great improvement in personal cleanliness and she added that she was going to make sure that it stayed that way by examining her charges before school each morning.

For all her self-praise Miss Gibbs had not improved the standard of arithmetic at the Girls' School. Anne Webster's last inspection had brought the comment from HMI that, 'arithmetic is very weak throughout the school.' Miss Gibbs had been told, a year later, that her pupils had, done 'fairly in reading and writing but arithmetic was weak in all classes.'

Miss Gibbs enlisted the help of the school board in her fight to improve punctuality by asking for prizes for the better children. It bore fruit; in her second report the inspector stated, 'the school has passed a creditable examination in reading, writing and arithmetic and punctuality was better.'

Punctuality may have improved, but not even Miss Gibbs was able to compete with the outside interests that still kept her charges away from school for an entire day. Indeed, on 2 May 1879 she closed the school on account of the local cattle fair and, in the months ahead, her school was closed for a circus, an animal show, the Mens' Club Day and another cattle fair. Between January and February 1880, attendances were very poor 'because of the fever'.

Miss Gibbs never seems to have made allowances for the long journeys some of her pupils had to make across fields, in all winds and weathers, in order to attend school and get home in the afternoon. In the winter months school work often had to be marked as early as 2p.m. to enable the girls to make the journey home before darkness set in. The quality of the school work does not appear to have been affected because, out of the 34 girls who sat the annual grammar examination in 1881, as many as 29 passed. That year the inspector recorded that 'this school has done more than commonly well in reading, writing and arithmetic, singing is very fair.' The exam results were: grammar, 29 passes out of 34; needlework, 35 out of 44. Edith Loaring, a pupil-teacher in her third year, was said to have 'passed fairly but should attend to history'. This was Miss Gibbs' last report; she left on 15 July 1881 and was replaced by Miss Margaret Meek. She began her life there by belittling the achievements of her predecessor, her opening remarks in the logbook being that:

> *... the children have been much neglected and left entirely to Edith Loaring... hardly any teaching of the present year's subjects have been given and lessons that have been given are forgotten.*

On 22 September that year Miss Meek punished several children for being late. *Pour les encouragement les autres* in reverse it seems – many children stayed away for the next few days.

Mr Catford, the headmaster of the Boys' School who arrived in August 1871 when the old school in West Street had already started to decline, agreed with HM Inspector who, on his first visit, claimed that 'the buildings are generally out of repair, and the offices [toilets] are in bad order.' This, no doubt, played a part in the low attendances, but there were other attractions that included old friends such as the visit of the Volunteer Artillery, the September harvest and obligations to pick the cherry, potato and apple yields. Soon after this came the Christmas Great Market Day – a red-letter day in Axminster's calendar.

Fever returned to Axminster in January 1880 when two of Mr Catford's boys died. Heavy snowfalls followed and attendances plummeted towards the zero mark. Despite all this, and the inevitable external attractions, the school was closed on 9 April 1880 when it was used as a polling-station for the general election when Disraeli's Conservative administration was replaced by William Gladstone's second Liberal Government.

Not even Mr Catford could complain on 18 June 1897 when an extra week was tacked onto the summer holiday so that the children (and the teachers) could enjoy the celebrations for Queen Victoria's diamond jubilee. Before they left, the children sat down to a celebratory meal and, without a shadow of doubt, there were no absentees that day.

In 1901 the school flag was lowered to half-mast as a mark of respect on the occasion of the death of American President Mr McKinley. Oddly enough, although it would certainly have been lowered on 22 January of that year, no mention is made in the logbook of the passing of Queen Victoria.

It was that year that Mr Catford retired and Mr Collard began his 28-year stint as headmaster. He, more than anyone, would leave his mark on the school by dragging it into the twentieth century. He had to contend with the war years, as did another of Axminster's great heads, his successor Herbie Tolchard.

The First World War left its mark on Axminster and its school. Many of those whose names are recorded on the war memorial in the churchyard would have been taught at the school. In 1917 the pupils sent 2,000 bunches of primroses to Exeter for sale on behalf of Red Cross funds and sphagnum moss was collected and packed for dispatch to the field hospitals (for use as wound dressings). Eggs, potatoes and other vegetables were also sent to the Armed Forces and all children were encouraged to save their pocket money for War Funds.

By the early 1920s Axminster children were also attending the grammar schools at Colyton and Lyme Regis, travelling there by train, the close proximity of the station to the latter school being an added bonus.

On 4 June 1923 the school opened a 'senior mixed' department for 79 boys and 68 girls under Mr Collard, with Mr S.J. Squance as his assistant. Three years later HM Inspector found that the change had been 'beneficial'.

In 1929 Mr Collard retired and Mr H.J. 'Herbie' Tolchard began what would be 33 years of great service to Axminster and its school. Among the many milestones of his early years was the provision of hot meals for the children in 1933. On Mondays, Thursdays and Fridays they were provided by two senior girls; on Tuesdays and Wednesdays the domestic science classes took over. The meals cost 3d. At first only six pupils availed themselves of the meal – many, of course, lived within a minute or two of the school and, at the time, 3d. was a lot of money. This fact was underlined the following year (1934) when the charge for a third of a pint of milk was reduced from 1d. to ½d. and the numbers of pupils taking milk rose from 25 to 93.

Radio had reached the school by 1934 when lessons were interrupted for half an hour to allow the pupils to listen to the launching ceremony of Cunard's new liner, the *Queen Mary*. The following year the education committee, to allow the children to familiarise themselves with its use, loaned a telephone to the school.

Two weddings and a funeral followed. First, in 1934, Axminster School was closed for the day when HRH Prince George of Kent and Princess Marina of Greece were married. The following year the wedding of the Duke of Gloucester and Lady Alice Scott brought another day's holiday. Early in 1936 the school again closed for a day, this time as a mark of respect when George V (whose silver jubilee had been marked only a year or so earlier) died.

One of the reddest of red-letter days in over 200 years of Axminster School's fascinating story arrived in February 1936 when Messrs Pratt of Clyst St Mary started work on a new school. On 15 March 1937, the work having been completed, the school moved into its new home. The move took two days with the new caretaker, Mr John Goddard, an Axminster footballer of some repute, being heavily involved in the work.

The Second World War obviously brought its problems to the school. Within days of the outbreak of hostilities the school greeted the arrival of evacuees and their teachers from the Faunce Street School in Kensington and Friern Road Central Selective School in Dulwich. They stayed throughout the war. The teachers were Mr Tiller, Mr Hooper and Mr Lancaster. In 1941 just over 100 children from Bristol joined them and, in 1944 when the German V1 and V2 attacks began on London, a total of 320 children from Kent were evacuated to the town.

A Luftwaffe aeroplane, that was said to have jettisoned its incendiary bombs on the way to raiding Bristol or Yeovil, attacked the school and other parts of the town. Lea Combe House was partially destroyed and never rebuilt, Dawkins' boot factory was destroyed and at least one other house (in North Street) was hit. Czechoslovakian soldiers stationed in the town prevented serious damage to the school. They climbed onto the roof, tore off the tiles and extinguished the flames. Mr Tolchard was soon on the scene and played a prominent part in fighting the fire. Two incendiary bombs were found in a field belonging to Uphay Farm and in 2003 can be seen in Axminster Museum.

As late as 1943, when the real threat of any gas attack had virtually ended, gas-mask inspections were still regularly held and air-raid warnings continued to play havoc with lessons.

Mr Tolchard and his staff coped with the extra burden on their time. In 1944 the Butler Education Act led to a change in name – the school became Axminster Secondary Modern School.

By 1947, when the evacuees had returned home, the school's population had dropped to 177. Pupils ranged in age from 11 to 15 years. The catchment area was the Urban District of Axminster as well as the primary schools of Axminster, Axminster Hamlets, Uplyme, Hawkchurch, Chardstock, All Saints, Membury, Dalwood, Kilmington, Axmouth and Musbury. By 1948 the senior children from Beer and Seaton had also been transferred to Axminster.

With such a widespread catchment area, the school canteen was more than needed. In 1947 a cook and a staff of four provided over 300 meals a day, which included those for the nearby primary school. At that time the school staff consisted of: Mr Tolchard, of course, Mr S.J. Squance (in his 40th year at the school in 1947), Mr C.A. Stock, Mr A.E. Denham, Mr F.J. Hall, Mrs M.E. Baker, Miss C.M. Wood, Miss G.M. Jennings and Miss A. Biggs.

One change not connected with the war was the forming of the school into four separate houses, Balmoral, Caernarvon, Powderham and Windsor. At least they picked one Devon castle!

The school had its own supply of fresh eggs as poultry was kept, along with pigs and bees, next to the school buildings. Doubtless the scraps from the school kitchens were put to good use. The boys continued to grow vegetables in the school gardens and they also played their part with the potato harvest – as many as 40 of them spent a week picking potatoes under the Devon War Agricultural Committee's arrangements at nearby, but unspecified, farms.

That the school was cramped was beyond dispute. However, one of Mr Tolchard's suggested measures, that of building a new school at Millwey Rise, where the old wartime American Army hospital was housing 'squatters', never got off the ground. He had also envisaged that the Axminster branch of the County Library could be included on the Millwey Rise site. The idea behind the Millwey move was that the retention of the old school as a Primary School would obviate the necessity of building a new one as was planned. In the event the Secondary Modern School stayed put and the new Primary School was built towards the top of Stoney Lane.

Transport, or rather the lack of it, continued to be a problem, but not for the children from Axmouth and Musbury who, rather than travelling on the hired school buses, came to school on the Seaton–Taunton regular bus service using season tickets that were provided by the County Education Authority. It was around this time that, because of a lack of alternative transport, the Hawkchurch pupils were reduced to travelling to school sitting on sacking on the floor of a Ford V8 van. Mr Tolchard, rather acidly, wrote in the school log, 'I feel that this arrangement would not meet with the approval of the education committee.'

In 1947 the entire country was gripped by one of the worst winters of the century. On one occasion only 126 out of a school population of over 300 arrived – and almost all of those lived in the town itself. The following day only 19 town children arrived and the school was closed for the day.

This is something of a mystery picture. The people (and their clothes) appear to be very similar to those present at the laying of the foundation-stone at the Cottage Hospital in 1911 (see page 62). However, the old Dawkins' boot factory in the background (the only known picture of a building that was destroyed by incendiary bombs during the Second World War) suggests that the picture was taken from the opposite side of Chard Street to the hospital. Therefore, it is highly likely that the photograph is a record of the dedication of some work at the Axminster School around the same time.

By July 1961, when the pupils of Colyton All Age School arrived at Axminster, there were 480 pupils on the roll. A wrench came the following year when Herbie Tolchard laid down his cane after 33 years' devoted service. He was the last of three successive headmasters whose combined service spanned 91 years – Mr Catford (1871–1901), Mr Collard (1901–29) and Mr Tolchard (1929–62).

Axminster has had many good teachers. Few were more popular in the twentieth century than Bryan Steane who retired in July 1997 after 21 years as headmaster. When he left the school the number of pupils there had risen to over 500. When he joined the staff at Axminster in 1978 he had done so as a replacement for Clifford Stock, the deputy head, and later he succeeded John White as headmaster. Of his last day at the school, 'one I will remember for the rest of my life,' he later said:

> *Children kept coming up to me with gifts and cards and I had an invitation* [from the senior pupils, one hopes], *'Come and get drunk with us at the George Hotel, Sir.'*

Away from the school Mr Steane received the Bill Knapman Award from the Rotary Club for 'his services to the youth of the town'.

Liz Pinfield who, on her arrival, said 'I'm tremendously proud to be here', succeeded Bryan Steane as head. Shortly after her arrival the Axe Valley School and Community College (as it has become known) was the first educational establishment in Devon to open a state-of-the-art computer department to enable both children and adults to improve their literacy. In 2003 pupils of all ages have access to a computer course called 'Touch-Type, Read and Spell'. It is housed in the newly constructed building, the Bryan Steane Literacy Centre. Another red-letter day arrived for the school in February 1999 when it was granted post-16 (sixth-form) status.

Oak House, 1907.

Axminster Roman Catholic School in Lyme Road was a gift of the Knight family who had built a Catholic church (1860) on the site of a church constructed in 1830. Henry Knight's school was behind the church in 1862 when it consisted of just one small classroom. Later, in 1865, cloakrooms and a tiny infants' classroom were added. The 1902 Education Act saw the school become a Voluntary Church School under the Local Education Authority and, in 1946, its senior pupils were transferred to Axminster Secondary Modern School and it became the Junior School.

Not far from the Catholic church, Lady Tullock had a school built in Woodbury Lane in 1875 with a teacher's house included. It was known as Axminster Hamlets School. She not only provided the school, she also gave £660 to the National Society towards its maintenance so long as it remained a Church school. She also paid for the construction of the Chapel of St Mary next door to the school. Later, around 1887, more land was obtained and another classroom added. The 1902 Act brought the Hamlets School under the wing of the LEA when it became a Voluntary Church School and was eventually given controlled status in 1952. The senior pupils had been removed to Axminster School as far back as 1937, the resulting Junior School continuing until it was closed in 1960.

Near the tiny hamlet of Smallridge, to the north-west of Axminster, and, until recent times when it became a separate entity, All Saints was part of the parish of Chardstock. A small church was built there in 1840 and a separate ecclesiastical parish was created in 1881 out of parts of Chardstock and Axminster parishes. In 1870 a National School was built next to the church, complete with a teacher's house. It consisted of a classroom with a much smaller infants' classroom. Later another classroom was added at the back of the school. In 1937 the senior pupils from this school were transferred to Axminster.

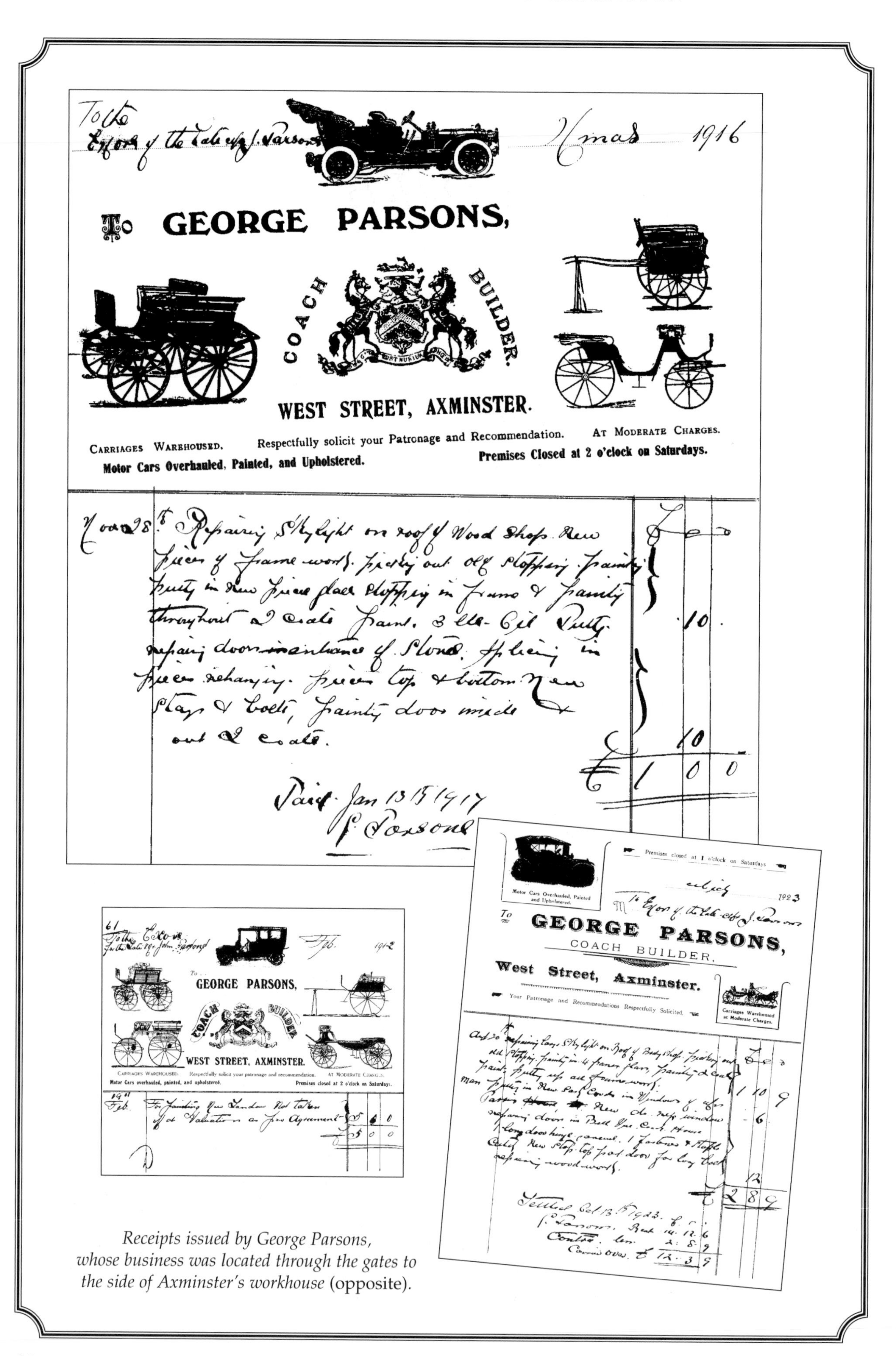

To the Exors of the Late Mr J. Parsons — Xmas 1916

To GEORGE PARSONS, COACH BUILDER.

WEST STREET, AXMINSTER.

CARRIAGES WAREHOUSED. Respectfully solicit your Patronage and Recommendation. AT MODERATE CHARGES.

Motor Cars Overhauled, Painted, and Upholstered. **Premises Closed at 2 o'clock on Saturdays.**

Nov 28th To Repairing Skylight on roof of Wood Shop New pieces of frame work. picking out old stopping painting putty in new pieces place stopping in frame & painting throughout 2 coats paint. 3 lbs Oil Putty. repairing door maintenance of Stores. Splicing in pieces rehanging pieces top & bottom New plates & bolts, painting door inside & out 2 coats. — 10. — 10 — £1 0 0

Paid Jan 13th 1917 G. Parsons

To the Exors of the late Mr John Parsons — Feb. 1912

To GEORGE PARSONS, COACH BUILDER

WEST STREET, AXMINSTER.

CARRIAGES WAREHOUSED. Respectfully solicit your patronage and recommendation. AT MODERATE CHARGES.

Motor Cars overhauled, painted, and upholstered. Premises closed at 2 o'clock on Saturdays.

1901 Feb. For Painting Your Landau Not taken of at Valuation as per Agreement £5 0 0 — £5 0 0

Premises closed at 1 o'clock on Saturdays

Motor Cars Overhauled, Painted and Upholstered.

July 1923

M To Exors of the Late Mr J. Parsons

To GEORGE PARSONS, COACH BUILDER,

West Street, Axminster.

Your Patronage and Recommendations Respectfully Solicited.

Carriages Warehoused at Moderate Charges.

Aug 30th repairing large Skylight on Roof of Body Shop picking out old stopping painting in 4 panes glass, painting 2 coats paint putty ... all frame work ... Panes in New Sash ... in Window ... repairing door in ... [illegible] ... New ... Settled Oct 13th 1923 G. Parsons — £1 10 9 — 6 — 12 — £2 8 9

Receipts issued by George Parsons, whose business was located through the gates to the side of Axminster's workhouse (opposite).

6

THE WORKHOUSE

The workhouse opened its doors in Axminster in 1738 in response to the 1723 Act that enabled parishes to make provision for their poor if they felt the need to do so. It was situated in an existing building on the north side of West Street and was soon joined to the old parish house that stood next door. In 1789 the building was destroyed by fire and new a stone-built workhouse took its place. Among the prominent members of the community who took an interest in the running of the workhouse were Thomas Whitty, of Axminster Carpets fame, and William Tucker, a local magistrate.

The Provision of the Poor Law Act was amended in 1834. This compelled adjoining parishes to form unions served by a single large workhouse. A total of 17 parishes joined forces to form the Axminster Union whose new workhouse was promptly built at Foxhill near Musbury Road. It was run by a board of guardians, elected from the ratepayers of the member parishes.

Known sometimes as Box House, the workhouse later became a home for the mentally handicapped and went by the name of St Mary's. The movement towards the mentally handicapped living in smaller communities led to St Mary's being demolished near the end of the twentieth century; the site was developed for housing.

Although claims were often made that it was 'a good life' for the inmates, in reality the labouring classes, partially because of pride, lived in dread of having to inhabit the workhouse. That said, there were nevertheless good times as well. Coronations, jubilees and other festive occasions saw inmates having better than normal fare although, more often than not, away from the rest of the community.

Christmas 1910 was highly enjoyable at the workhouse. The previous night Mr Robert Cornish visited the house and distributed gifts to the children. Those of a school age received 6d.; the younger ones had sweets and Christmas cards. On Christmas morning the children sang carols before Divine Service. The Christmas dinner, however, was served on Boxing Day in the main day room by Revd and Mrs Newman, Revd R. Bastaple, Revd P.L. Nicholas and Mr Hutchings of Kilmington. A large quantity of seasonable gifts sent to the workhouse included picture books, oranges and bananas, tobacco, magazines, sweets and crackers. Two days later the children were treated to tea by two guardians, Mrs Luttrell and Mrs Paine. They provided a huge Christmas tree, which was covered with toys. Entertainment followed in the evening.

It should not be forgotten that the other side of the coin was rather unpleasant. Two years earlier a female inmate was packed off to Exeter Prison for 14 days' hard labour for refusing to help with the washing-up.

Axminster's workhouse is the tall building on the right. To the left of the building are gates which, in 2003, lead to modern flats and Tesco's Walk.

Below: *Looking into Trinity Square from West Street. Although the exact date for this photograph is unknown, as it depicts men erecting hurdles for the market it must have been taken before 1912, the year that the market was moved to South Street. W.J. Harris & Son, Axminster's leading grocery shop at the time can be seen on the left.*

Above: *An 1890s market in Trinity Square.*

Market day in Axminster's Trinity Square, c.1900. Note the entrance for the stables at the rear of the Old Bell Hotel in the background.

A street market in Trinity Square in the 1950s.

7

TRINITY SQUARE

On Trinity Sunday 1834 the fire that gave Trinity Square its name consumed much of the town between the top of Phoenix Lane and the Old Bell Hotel. A total of 24 houses were destroyed. The Axminster turnpike trustees seized the chance to 'widen the road between the Bell Inn and the north-west corner of the churchyard,' thus forming the open square which modern authority seem determined to make narrower again. The houses were still in ruins as late as June 1836, when the trustees purchased the site at a cost of 2s. (10p in modern money) per square foot with the intention of taking 300 feet in all.

The owners of Axminster's market and fair tolls requested permission to erect sheep pens at the Axminster Fair following its purchase by the trustees. Permission was given on payment of 1s.

The fountain arrived in 1897 to mark Queen Victoria's diamond jubilee. It replaced an earlier fenced pump that was put in place in 1837, the year of the Queen's accession to the throne (it is not known whether this was a coincidence or if it was put there to mark that occasion).

Plans in 1997 to renovate and restart the drinking fountain have yet to realise fruition at the time of writing, but that same year, and after 30 years of 'darkness', three lights were placed on the top of the fountain in time to contribute to Axminster's Christmas illuminations. They are intended to be a permanent feature.

Left: *Trinity Square in the 1990s. Although the names above the shops have changed over the years the buildings around Axminster's centre are much the same as they were 100 years earlier.*

Looking out of Trinity Square towards the George Hotel, c.1900. Hutchings' shoe shop on the left became first the Post Office and then a branch of Boots the chemists. It was occupied by the Ministry of Food during the Second World War.

Axminster market, c.1905. Mr Gage, the auctioneer, is disposing of the cattle from Bulmoor Farm near Musbury.

Left: *Sheppard's grocery shop in Lyme Street, c.1895. In 2003 the South Street car park stands on this site.*

Restorick's butcher's shop in Lyme Street with its Christmas meat and poultry on display, c.1900.

8

The Twentieth Century

Axminster's Town Hall

The need for a Town Hall had troubled the minds of Axminster's Victorian councils for many years. The problem was still unresolved when a Mens' Institute was started in the old Gospel Hall on Castle Hill and officially opened in January 1909 by Mr Ramsay, the president. He was supported on the platform by Messrs Howard Dawkins, F.R. Heath, W. Tapscott and H. Clarke.

It was, for the time, a well-appointed place with various games and there were hopes that a billiard table would soon be forthcoming, along with a library. The rooms were heated by means of an 'apparatus', which suggests gas, and the rooms were quite large. The Institute was run on non-political and non-sectarian lines.

During his speech Mr Ramsay mentioned that there was a possibility of a Town Hall for Axminster, with promises of around £500 already to hand towards its estimated £1,000 cost. Previously the Victoria Hall (presumably in Victoria Place) had served as the town's gathering place for public meetings and entertainment, but this had been taken over by an unnamed religious body as their meeting-place.

That left Axminster without a meeting-place, a fact lamented by weekly columnist, 'Onlooker', in *Pulman's Weekly News* of 19 January 1909 when he said:

That a town hall is very much needed here there can be no possible doubt, as anyone who has visited neighbouring towns (smaller than Axminster) must have been struck with the absence of a such a public building in so important a centre as Axminster. I suppose it would be difficult to find a town, of the size, and importance, and antiquity of Axminster without its own proper building for a town hall. In many towns the hire to concert and entertainment companies pays annually a very large proportion of the current expenses of such public edifices.

Whether it was because the promises of financial support failed to get very far above the £500 already promised, or there was not a suitable site near to the centre of the town to be attractive enough for the proposed hall, is not known. Axminster did not get its Town Hall in Edwardian times – indeed, it is still waiting for it in 2003.

The Market-place

Axminster was granted its Charter in 1210 by King John, the right of a weekly market being included:

John by the Grace of God King of England lord of Ireland Duke of Normandy and Earl of Acquitane. To the Archbishops, Abbots, Earls, Barons, Justices, Sheriffs Prepositi and to all Bailiffs and his faithful people, greetings.

Know ye that we have given and granted and by this our present Charter confirmed to our chosen and faithful William Brewer at Axminster be a free

Judging by the stalls this is a sheep fair day rather than a market day. Although the increase of traffic may have led to the market moving away from the town centre, its actual move in 1912 was dictated by Parliament on health and cleanliness grounds.

Borough and that there be [a] *free market there once every seven days for one day and one fair in every year for a spece of eight days that is to say from the day of the Nativity of St John the Baptist to eight days with toll for page passage lastage stallage and all other liberties and free customs to a free Burough and to a Market and Fair pertaining*

We have granted also to the aforesaid William that his Burgesses of the aforesaid Borough be free Burgesses and be free of toll for page, pantage, passage lastage stallage and have all liberties and free customs and acquittance which belong to us through all this our Realm and through all the Ports thereof (except the City of London)

Therefore it [is] *our will and command that the aforesaid William and his heirs after him have and hold all the aforesaid Well and in peace liberty and quiet uninterruptedly fully and in an honorary manner with all his liberties and free customs as aforesaid.*

By Direction of Mr. A. S. Newbery

On the outskirts of the thriving Market Town of

AXMINSTER

Particulars of the

Attractive and Interesting Sale of

SEVEN LOTS OF FREEHOLD PROPERTY

forming part of

CASTLE FARM

IMMEDIATE VACANT POSSESSION

with the exception of Two Cottages

which

Messrs. R. & C. SNELL

are favoured with instructions to submit to Auction in Lots (unless any or the whole are sold previously by Private Treaty)

at the

George Hotel, Axminster

on

Thursday, 16th June, 1960 at 3.30 p.m.

Auctioneers :

R. & C. SNELL, Trinity Square, Axminster (Tel. 3122/3) and at Bridport and Chard

Solicitors :

SCOTT ROWE, Chard Street, Axminster (Tel. 2345/6) and at Lyme Regis

Despite the absence of punctuation marks it is fairly easy to follow the gist of this document.

Axminster's markets were held in Market Square until after the fire on Trinity Sunday 1834, when the middle of the town was gutted. The owners of Axminster's market and fair tolls recognised that the open space could be useful to them and asked for and received permission to erect sheep pens on the following Wednesday.

Like some of their modern counterparts, local Edwardian politicians dwelt over-long on many issues, none more so than on the subject of the relocation of Axminster's market from Trinity Square and the surrounding streets to its present purpose-built site off South Street. Many meetings were held, many words spoken, but the local council did nothing and, in the end, the initiative to provide Axminster with a new market-place came from two local firms of auctioneers, Messrs B. & J. Gage and Messrs R. & C. Snell, who bought the site and had the premises built themselves for around £2,000. Previously a large house and garden occupied the site. This action brought them much praise from the good people of Axminster but not, it seems, from the council.

Many think that the move came about because of the obstruction that the market caused to the fast-growing motor traffic in Trinity Square at the time. Indeed, this problem was beginning to become an issue, but the real reason that street markets such as Axminster's were being forced to move was that new regulations had been introduced by the Board of Agriculture, which wanted street markets moved to premises with hard floors that could be hosed down and cleaned, unlike the rolled-earth roads that went through most towns, including Axminster.

Despite King John's Charter, the street cattle market in the town only began (or restarted) in 1857 when Mr Benjamin Gage started holding a monthly market in Trinity Square. By the time of the move to South Street the market was being held fortnightly and, at the time, 'it was acknowledged to be one of the most important to be held between Yeovil and Exeter.'

Work on the new site began around June 1912. Once the project got under way it was soon finished and a grand opening took place on 6 October that year. Half an acre in extent, the new premises had concrete floors with

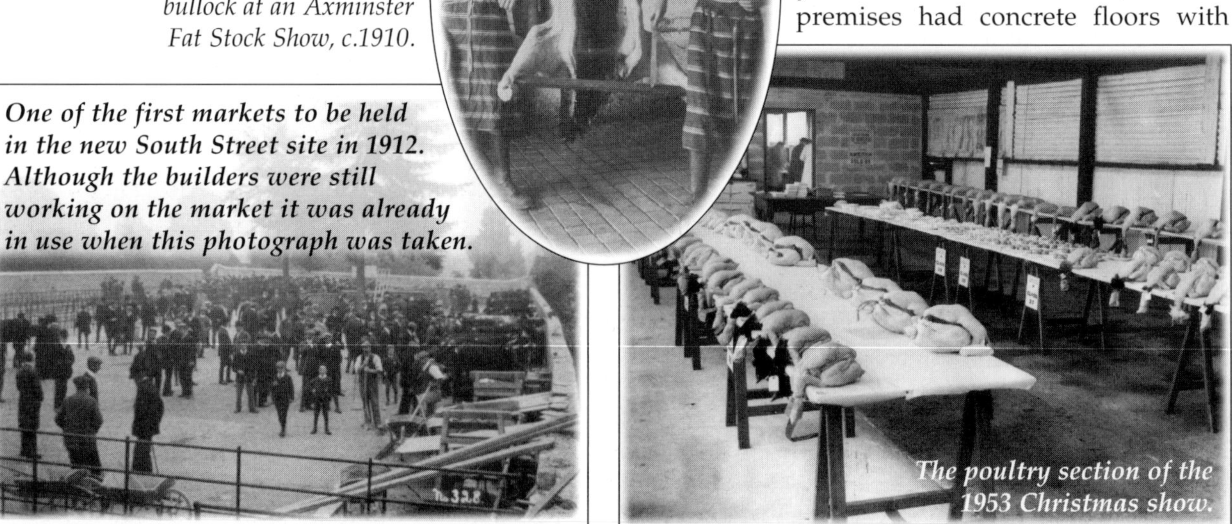

Right: *Richard Bull of Blackhakes Farm, Membury Road, and William Stuart with the carcass of a prizewinning bullock at an Axminster Fat Stock Show, c.1910.*

One of the first markets to be held in the new South Street site in 1912. Although the builders were still working on the market it was already in use when this photograph was taken.

The poultry section of the 1953 Christmas show.

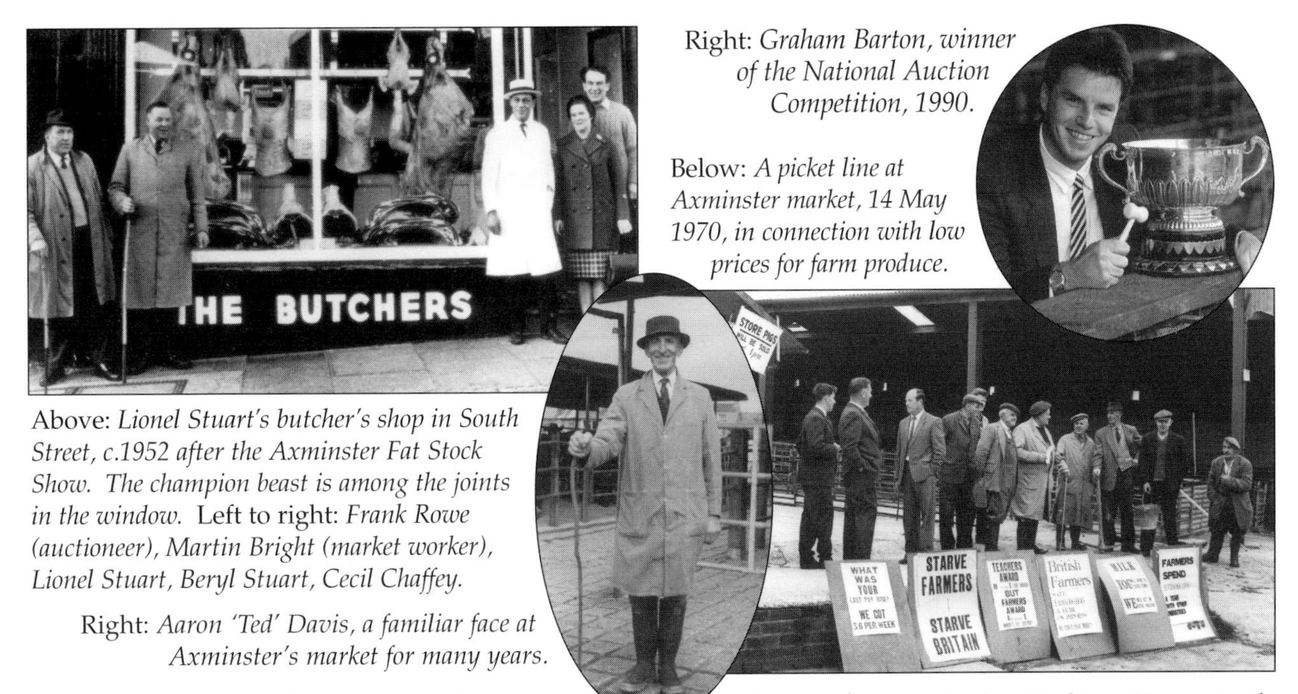

Right: *Graham Barton, winner of the National Auction Competition, 1990.*

Below: *A picket line at Axminster market, 14 May 1970, in connection with low prices for farm produce.*

Above: *Lionel Stuart's butcher's shop in South Street, c.1952 after the Axminster Fat Stock Show. The champion beast is among the joints in the window.* Left to right: *Frank Rowe (auctioneer), Martin Bright (market worker), Lionel Stuart, Beryl Stuart, Cecil Chaffey.*

Right: *Aaron 'Ted' Davis, a familiar face at Axminster's market for many years.*

accommodation for about 400 head of cattle, 2,000 sheep, 300 calves and 500 pigs. Brick pens were provided for store cattle, tie-ups (tethering places) for fat beasts, cows and calves, and pens, enclosed by metal hurdles, for sheep and pigs. A separate entrance was provided for the animals to be sold.

Water was supplied, by a force pump, from a well in the market-place, the water being used both for animal drinking purposes and cleaning after each market. One important change brought about by the auctioneers was that in time the market was held weekly. At first there were conflicting opinions on the matter. Some felt that it would benefit the farming industry to have a weekly sale, others wondered if the dealers would want to attend every week. In time the once-a-week school won.

The first animals to be sold at the new market were a cow and calf, offered by Messrs Snell, which fetched £23. At the same time Messrs Gage obtained 'highly satisfactory prices for some sheep they first brought under the hammer.' The two auctioneers obviously operated at opposite ends of the market-place because both started their selling at 11a.m.; it would have been awkward to have them shouting out within a few feet of one another.

At the time both firms of auctioneers regularly advertised all their market-place sales as well as their property and farmyard sales on the front page of *Pulman's Weekly News*. From the 4 October 1912 edition we learn that Messrs Benjamin and John Gage were offering for sale at Axminster Great Market at 'the new Market Place in South Street' ten cows and heifers with calves; two barreners and two fat Devon heifers (one maiden) for Mr Trott. Also on offer were a plated double harness; a brass single harness; 5 calves and 200 sheep, including 12 rare, fat Down wethers, for Mr Harris. In addition, 10 fat Down ewes for Mr Cunningham, plus 25 rare Down wether lambs and 4 ewes were on offer for Mr Crawford. Finally, '25 Down wether lambs; 25 ditto; 18 two-teeth Down ewes; 13 fat lambs; a gent's saddle; a lady's saddle' and a quantity of cheese were also on offer.

On the same page Messrs R. & C. Snell offered 14 cows and heifers with calves; 10 fat and store calves; two barreners; 20 Down lambs; 15 Down ewes; two barreners; 4 two-year-old Devon steers; 10 fat Down ewes; two Aylesbury ducks and a drake, all prizewinners; and several stag birds of various strains.

Axminster's Autumn Fair on Wednesday 12 October was also well advertised.

An unexpected bonus from the move was that there was only a remote possibility of a reoccurrence of a famous incident in 1895 when a cow of previous exemplary character escaped and ended up in Mr Gage's confectionery shop. It entered via the large plate-glass window, knocked over most of the stands of sweets and charged a large mirror at the rear of the shop. It was assumed that the animal saw its reflection and thought it was a rival. Axminster's version of a bull in a china shop!

Axminster's market has been blessed with more than its fair share of characters. In the later Victorian years, and down to around the time of the transfer of the market to South Street, the bewhiskered 'Old' Gage was a character who, it was claimed, would sell his wife if he got a good enough offer for her!

Probably the best known was Frank Rowe, who is discussed further in Chapter 19. Under Frank, Graham Barton quickly made a name for himself. Born in 1961, he joined R. & C. Snell (now Symonds & Sampson) in 1979. Among his many achievements while with the Trinity Square firm was winning titles at the UK National Auction Competitions in 1984, 1987, 1990, 1992 and 1996, including the overall championship in 1990. Widely considered in the trade as one of the most entertaining auctioneers of his generation, Graham, unusually for someone who spends his life selling livestock, is a vegetarian.

The Cottage Hospital

The laying of the foundation-stone for Axminster's new cottage hospital in Chard Street took place in September 1911. However, that statement does not tell of the hard work and dedication by the building sub-committee that was formed to oversee the 101 things that required a decision, including where to build it. Several locations had been considered before the decision was taken to build in Chard Road, at a site that had been purchased for £120.

A flurry of fund-raising activities took place to meet the accepted tender of £1,725 from Chard builders, R.G. Spiller. A donation list had already been started and nearly £2,000 had been received by August 1911. Among the biggest contributors were Mrs Emily Conybeare Craven, Mrs and Miss Stafford of Chattan House, Mrs W. Forward, Mr Minifie from Kilmington and Mr Pane of Wootton Fitzpaine, all of whom gave £100. In addition, Major H. Knight gave £50, and Mr Edwin Dawkins, Mr and Hope Hall (Kilmington) and Captain and Mrs Buckle (Membury) each gave £25. The proceeds from Axminster's carnivals for many years were donated to the hospital.

The architect for the project, London-based Mr T. Leslie Moore of Gray's Inn, was present when the foundation-stone was laid on 6 September and, with only 200 people present, it suggests that attendance was by invitation only with most of Axminster's great and good on parade. It included, naturally, the Church in the shape of Revd E. Adams, Axminster's vicar designate who opened the proceedings with a prayer and a short service. Supporting him were Revd F.B. Wyatt, the Congregational minister, Revd A.V. Cox, vicar of Stockland, and Revd A.W. Bull, rector of All Saints. Among the others in the front rows were Dr W. Langran, Mrs Cornish, Mrs Hope Hall from Kilmington, J. Gerrish, a former Axminster cricketer of some repute, Mrs W. Forward and Mr J. Overmass.

Axminster Cottage Hospital, c.1910. Thomas Whitty started his carpet industry in a building on this site that was later destroyed by fire. Today the building is back in the hands of the modern Axminster Carpets Ltd and is known as Thomas Whitty House.

The stone was laid by Robert Cornish, a former secretary and the first president of the Hospital Committee. The silver trowel bore the inscription:

Presented to Robert Cornish, Esq., JP Devon, on the occasion of the laying of the foundation-stone of the new building of Cottage Hospital, Axminster, September 6th, 1911.

Afterwards, the company sang the Doxology. Mr Cornish said that he was:

Deeply touched by the kindness shown me both in electing me as the first president of the Hospital Committee, and then in asking me to lay the foundation-stone of what promised to be a splendid building. I take it as a good omen that the ceremony coincides with the arrival of our new vicar whom, on your behalf, I venture to offer a most hearty welcome.

Mr Cornish (above, wearing glasses) *in his capacity as president of the Hospital Committee, lays the foundation-stone of the new Axminster Cottage Hospital on 6 September 1911. The hospital had largely been the work of Mrs Emily Conybeare Craven who is seen* (right, in front of the second window from the left) *at the new hospital's official opening on 18 June 1912.*

Axminster Cottage Hospital, Chard Street, c.1935. Both doors have been removed and in 2003 the entrance is located at the rear.

He went on to congratulate the building committee and, most of all, the retiring secretary Mr Hacon, on the great success of the venture. It was less than a year previously that they had started thinking in terms of a new hospital and now, springing before their eyes, was the proof of their success.

When the building was completed it contained two public wards, each containing four beds, a private ward, an accident room and well-appointed operating room. There were also the usual domestic offices and a boardroom, bedrooms for the hospital staff and the matron's apartments. Outside there were well laid out and enclosed gardens for the use of convalescent patients.

The Regent Cinema

The old Market House has led a varied life, being once the centre of business in the butchering trade; people in the 1930s recalled Mr Hiram Baker and Messrs Dare occupying weekly stalls there on certain days. The building was also used for public meetings. However, Axminster's first cinema, the Regent, was situated at the top of Castle Hill in Market House (also known as Regent Hall, and part of Potter's premises in 2003). Permission to change the use of the building to a cinema was granted at the Axminster Petty Sessions when Police Superintendent Braddell told the bench that it was a new cinema. He stated:

> *It complies, as far as possible, with the regulations. In view of the interest the Justices had evinced in the cinemas in their district, with the object of assuring themselves that the regulations were being complied with, I would like you to inspect the Regent Hall at the rising of the Court.*

The Justices, accordingly, adjourned to Market Square to inspect the new cinema and, being happy with what they saw, granted a licence until the next Brewster's Sessions in February 1931. *Pulman's Weekly News* of 19 August tells us that:

> *... the old Market House had undergone extensive structural alterations to provide the town with what is*

Left: *Lyme Road, Axminster, c.1935.*

Right: ***Newport and Lanherne Houses on Anchor Hill. A derelict eyesore for many years, it was finally demolished in 1985 when the car park behind was enlarged.***

The top of Castle Hill looking into Victoria Place, c.1901. The Market House on the right became the Regent Cinema and in 2003 is part of Potter's furniture business.

Above: *Edwin Dawkins & Son Ltd in the late 1980s.*

Left: *Nicholl's Bazaar, c.1908.*

now a commodious and admirably equipped cinema hall, where, the opening performance was given last Monday evening.

The first film shown there is not now known but from 16 September *Pulman's Weekly News* began carrying a weekly advertisement that gave details of the coming week's shows. The first films to be mentioned were: *The Wagon Master* (Monday and Tuesday with a newsreel, serial and comedy) and *Behind Closed Doors* and *Object Alimony* (a double-featured programme on Friday and Saturday with a super newsreel). Programmes commenced at 8p.m. each evening and there was a Saturday matinée at 2.30p.m. Admission, including tax, was 6d. (2½p in modern money), 8d., 1s. (5p), 1s.3d. and 1s.6d. with no charge for advanced bookings.

Axminster resident Ken Sansom recalls:

I remember my first visit to the cinema at the age of five. It was in 1920 at the Regent in Market Square where my uncle took me. The film was Charlie Chaplin and Jackie Coogan in The Kid. *That was of course in the days of the old silent films when the films were always accompanied by a piano player who, at the time, was a Mrs Wench, who lived in a cottage at Penny's Terrace. Saturday afternoons was always a matinée for the children when the admission was 2d. There was always a mad rush to get a seat in the front row.*

A Mr Walford, who had a wooden leg, ran the cinema. There was a ladder to get up to the projection box but how he got up there I don't know. Once a year the cinema was taken over by a travelling company who put on shows for that week, the leading light was a gentleman named Alf Beverlee. Then came the 'talkies', the first one at the Regent was The White Hell of Piz Palu, *which was a mountain drama.*

Mountain dramas were popular in the German cinema at this period and, not surprisingly, *The White Hell of Piz Palu* did not make it into the list of the 'Best 100 Films of the Twentieth Century' that was compiled in the UK media in 2002.

In the late 1920s a purpose-built cinema, the Plaza, was built on Anchor Hill by a consortium of local businessmen including Mr Sid Gill. It was the death-knell of the old Regent, which closed soon afterwards. Later, a dance hall at the rear was added to the Plaza and many a 'May I have this dance?' ended with an 'I do' before the altar. The Plaza became a victim of the decline in cinema audiences, caused in no small way by the arrival of television; it

Looking into Victoria Place from the top of Castle Hill with the George Hotel in the background, c.1920.

Melody House, Graham Newbery's wireless shop in King Edward Road, 1934. Later it became a grocery and at the time of writing is the shop and offices of Courtesy Care.

closed in the early 1960s. In 1963 the entire building was bought by public subscription and renamed the Guildhall. It was used for public and private functions and Axminster Town Council used the Churchill Room (upstairs) for their meetings.

Axminster in the Mid-1900s

On 24 November 1928 Samuel Nicholls, chairman of Axminster Parish Council and proprietor of Nicholl's Bazaar in Victoria Place, switched on Axminster's electricity supply 102 years after the town's streets had first been lit by gas (1826).

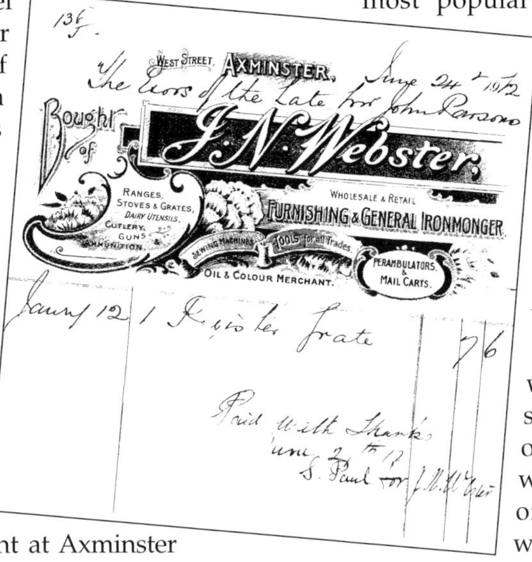
West Street, Axminster, June 24th 1912
The Exors of the Late Mr John Parsons
Bought of J. N. Webster
Ranges, Stoves & Grates, Dairy Utensils, Cutlery, Guns & Ammunition
Wholesale & Retail Furnishing & General Ironmonger
Sewing Machines. Tools for all Trades
Perambulators & Mail Carts
Oil & Colour Merchant
Jany 12 1 Register Grate 7/6
Paid with thanks June 27th 12 S. Paul for J. N. Webster

There was much expansion in Axminster during the 1930s, including the Gamberlake estate, the first house built there being Brookfield on land costing only £75. It was the home of Mr Gilbert Love and his bride, Irene Seager, who had been educated at Colyton Grammar School and had taught at Axminster Junior School before her marriage.

After the Second World War, Axminster settled down to doing what it does best, leading a quiet life as a sleepy Devonshire market town. In 2003, barely half a century later, not one shop remains in the same family's hands as in 1945.

The late Donald Thomas, who worked for Edwin Dawkins & Son Ltd in 1945, once put his memories of the town at the time down on paper. We were fortunate to receive a copy from him. His memories began in Victoria Place with the International Stores that had once been a branch of the Sidmouth-based shopping chain known as Trumps Stores.

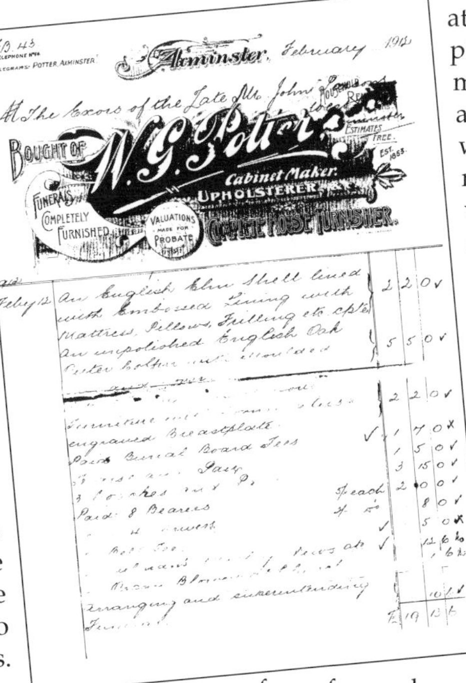
Telegrams: Potter Axminster
Axminster, February 1912
The Exors of the Late Mr John Parsons
Bought of W. G. Potter
Cabinet Maker, Upholsterer &c.
Funerals Completely Furnished
Valuations made for Probate
Estimates Free
Feby 12 An English Elm Shell lined with Embossed Lining with Mattress, Pillows, Frilling etc 2 2 0
An unpolished English Oak 5 5 0

Trumps was probably the blue riband of East Devon grocers with branches at Seaton, Beer and Ottery St Mary as well as Axminster and Sidmouth. The emphasis was always on service and the stores had assistants to serve and advise the customers. Delivery of purchases was a matter of course and everyone smiled.

On the opposite side of the street to Trumps was Dawkins' shoe department, managed by Sammy Wench, a great personality who knew all his customers' sizes and preferences. All that he needed to be told was whether the shoes (or boots) were for market or day-to-day wear. Then he would select either Holdfast boots, with their great studded soles with Holdfast (leather) leggings to match, or the brown kid market boots with matching leggings. The surface of the leggings, with the usual spit and polish, would come to such a sheen that you could positively see your face in them.

In Dawkins' outfitter's department, one of the most popular purchases was the Oxford shirt (a white, collarless shirt that sometimes had blue stripes and was often worn with a white soft collar for church or market). However, the real old-timers preferred a striped flannel shirt that, when it was wet, was said to weigh as much as a small bullock!

An article of 'clothing' that was obtainable in any drapers' shop was the ubiquitous 'West of England Sack', which was widely considered capable of keeping out any sort of weather. It was either fastened around the waist or put over the head and shoulders and hitched up with binder twine. It was much in evidence on market days.

One of the big differences between the Axminster of 1945 and that of 2003 was the handsome display of tidy flower-beds at the railway station and on the platforms in 1945. The stationmaster was Mr Grayer who could always be seen in a smart uniform with the Southern Railway's requisite timepiece complete with its Albert (chain) slung across the waistcoat from the right-hand pocket to the left. Not that it was really needed – the trains ran to time in those days! He met all the trains and knew most of the local passengers by name.

The 8.08a.m. train was a popular choice for a day in London. Just before its departure, the Lyme Billy slid into the Lyme Regis branch-line siding on the far side of the station, beside the up platform, from where the London trains departed.

A footpath was constructed during the war, from the main road beside the bridge to the up platform, to enable the American wounded from the hospital at Millwey Rise to be taken straight to the platform when they were moved to another military hospital. It was also used to convey coffins that were carried in

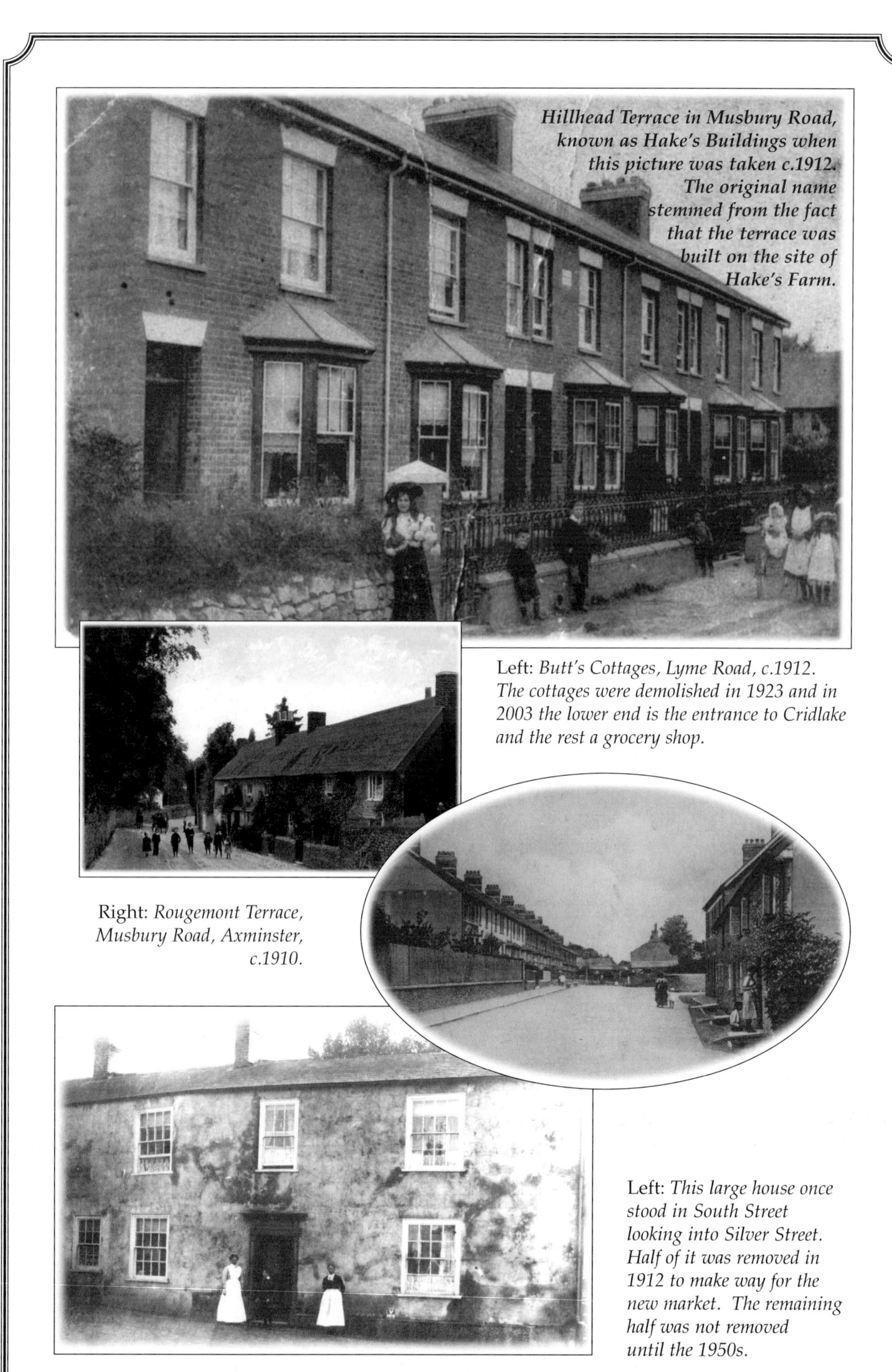

Hillhead Terrace in Musbury Road, known as Hake's Buildings when this picture was taken c.1912. The original name stemmed from the fact that the terrace was built on the site of Hake's Farm.

Left: *Butt's Cottages, Lyme Road, c.1912. The cottages were demolished in 1923 and in 2003 the lower end is the entrance to Cridlake and the rest a grocery shop.*

Right: *Rougemont Terrace, Musbury Road, Axminster, c.1910.*

Left: *This large house once stood in South Street looking into Silver Street. Half of it was removed in 1912 to make way for the new market. The remaining half was not removed until the 1950s.*

Left: *West Street, Axminster. The picture must predate 1883 because Thomas Kibby Cawley, the name on the wagon, was the landlord of the New Commercial Inn in Trinity Square from around 1870–83. He was also a delivery agent for the London & South Western Railway.*

Above: *Looking into Victoria Place from the top of Castle Hill around 1890. Most of the balustrade on the right has vanished. The nameplate above the shop on the left bears the name E. Dawkins.*

Above left: *Charlie Down, manager of Eastmans Ltd's butcher's shop at the bottom of Lyme Street, c.1918. The business became a branch of Dewhurst and closed in 1992. In 2003 the Busy Bee flower shop occupies the premises and a branch of Nat West Bank plc is on the right.*

Left: *West Street, Axminster, c.1948. Gray's Motor Cycle and Bicycle Shop is on the left with its petrol pumps on arms that were swung out over the pavement. Anyone leaving a car parked by the church wall in 2003 would soon find a ticket stuck to his or her car door. The church wall was taken back to make room for street widening and the provision of a pavement. It was at that time that the small building on the right was demolished. Its purpose has been lost in the mist of time.*

Right: *Trinity Square, c.1958.*

Axe Vale Devon Dairy Supplies.

Axe Vale Devon Dairy Supplies, Gammons Hill, Kilmington, c.1907. Vic Hurford is in the doorway of the milk department with Edward Cuming, the proprietor, in the milk vat (top of picture). *The steam engine that drove the dairy machinery and a grinding mill can be seen in the bottom picture. They were later removed to the company's shop in West Street, where they were used for many years. Mr Cuming is on the left* (below) *helping Jack Sanders and his wife to pack butter.*

the guard's compartment.

An extensive set of sidings bore evidence of the considerable amount of freight that the railways then carried, but these vanished in less than 20 years because it was possible to receive a more efficient service by road. Goods arrived from all over the country and, if you were desperately awaiting a certain item, Dick Underhill or Frank Matthews, with a glance at their waybills, would be able to tell you if it had arrived.

Next door to the Plaza cinema, where Jack Newbery would later run a motor business, was the first home of Webster's Garage. Moving from the cinema towards Trinity Square one would pass Charles Walker's ironmongery shop, Groves the greengrocers, Moon's Stores, a small family grocer's shop, Bristol House, opposite the Western Hotel (now Goldini's) and a drapery run by a Mr Packer. He had display cabinets fixed to the wall of W.G. Potter & Son that faced down Anchor Hill. Potter, of course, came next. W.G.'s widow served in her late husband's shop, and her son, Jack, took over the family business, which included an undertaking department. One of the side-lines was hiring out folding chairs and tables for shows, whist drives and other occasions. They were carried to the various events by horse and flat-bottom wagon by Mr Maeer who was one of the last persons in Axminster to regularly wear a stiff-winged collar.

Another of Axminster's characters was Mrs Parsons who ran a sweet shop between the archway to Potter's yard and what became Tesco's Walk. She was often seen, summer and winter, walking to and from the shop with several layers of clothing, generally of a waterproof nature. Indeed, she even wore a pair of men's spats.

Harold Gray ran the motorcycle shop next door. We then arrive at the Church Rooms (the old school), the venue for whist drives, concerts, auction sales and dances. One of the town's favourite bands was the Harmony Aces Dance Band with Charlie Turner playing the fiddle, Bob Newbery and Dolly Dare, as she then was, as accordionists, Tom Vowden on the drums and little Miss Owen on the piano.

Collard's jewellery store was run by the two Miss Collards, before Bert Leslie and Bill Bulled, together with their wives, ran a drapery shop there that catered largely for the older generation; it stocked items such as winceyette nightdresses and antimacassars.

On the corner of West Street and Castle Street (then known as Phoenix Lane, an allusion to the Phoenix Inn part way down on the left) was the Axe Vale Devon Dairy Supplies run by Mr Cuming. In the front shop the butter was patted into oblongs or rolls by the use of a pair of wooden strips (sometimes known as Scotch hands). Cut to size, the final process was the stamping of the firm's logo on the top before it was enclosed in a paper wrapping. The creamery also collected eggs from the surrounding farms and cottages. They were brought to the rear of the premises for grading, sorting and packing before dispatch to all parts of the country.

On the opposite corner to the creamery was W.J. Harris' grocery shop, certainly among the finest in East Devon and where such delicacies as quails in aspic, pheasants, jugged hares and other exotic foods were all delivered as a matter of course. Harris' bakery department included a café that was next door. This was also the agency for sending and receiving parcels on the Devon General buses to Exeter and beyond. Harris' was founded by Joe Harris and succeeded by his son Ted. It passed into other hands and, finally, became one of the early victims of Tesco's arrival in the town.

The dominating feature of Trinity Square's business life was Frederick Baker's dress shop. Formerly Overmass, it held the agency for K shoes, at that time reckoned to be the shoe equivalent of the Rolls Royce. At the end of the premises was a tiny watch repair shop where a Mr Gosling was more often seen in the doorway smoking his pipe than inside mending clocks and watches. Next, in the former Post Office, was the wartime Ministry of Food (now Boots). The local Midland Bank, the now-closed Old Bell Hotel, Chick's butcher's shop and Dawkins' furniture department completes our 1940s view of the north side of Trinity Square and Victoria Place.

On the corner of Market Square was another butcher's shop, Wally Hoy's. Market Square itself was the scene of two horse fairs a year when the animals on offer were run down Castle Hill and back up again; no mean feat – for the horse as much as the vendor who was hoping to prove the fitness of his animal. Apparently a considerable amount of whisky was available for the man who 'galloped'. No mention was made as to what prize the horse received.

In the far corner of Market Square were the steps that led through an archway to Phoenix Lane. Near to these was an old Nonconformist chapel, which, at the end of the war, was being used as a furniture store. It was known as the Lace Room (where lace was repaired), below which a temporary wartime mortuary had been prepared in case of heavy casualties. On the other side of the steps was Seager's stores, well known for home-made ice-cream; during the war it was used by the American Army hospital until it was taken over by Dawkins as a workshop where Fred Hallett renovated furniture.

The Regent cinema, which fronted Market Square, is dealt with elsewhere, as are the two brush factories at the bottom of Castle Hill. However, going down Castle Hill, there was a Co-op store on the bottom corner of Phoenix Lane. This became a bookmaker's shop and then a private house. Lower down was Eveleigh's the bakery and, near the bottom of the hill, was the grocer's shop run by Mr and Mrs Len Duke. Right at the bottom was Norrington & Sons' foundry and, along Valley Path, the town's gasworks.

Returning to the town, there was a cycle repair shop run by a Mr Rice, as well as Mr Carter's shoe-repair shop on Castle Hill. On the corner of Castle

James Seager,
Grocer, Confectioner,
TEA and TOBACCO DEALER,
MARKET PLACE,
AXMINSTER.
Sole Maker and Proprietor of the most Wonderful Remedy
Seager's Pills
(LATE JOSHUA HOARE'S).
WARRANTED FREE FROM POISONOUS DRUGS.
For NEURALGIA, TOOTHACHE HEADACHE, EARACHE, DEAFNESS, SCIATICA, LUMBAGO, INDIGESTION, RHEUMATISM, INFLAMMATION, SWOLLEN FACE, GIDDINESS, COLDS, SORE THROATS, LOSS OF VOICE AND APPETITE, NERVOUSNESS, &c., &c.,
Price 7½d. and 1s. 1½d. per Box. Post 1d. extra
Cough & Asthma Mixture 1/1½ & 2/3 per Bottle.
POST 2d EXTRA.
MAKERS OF THE FINEST ICE CREAM.

Above: *James Seager's grocery shop in Market Square, c.1910. As well as a grocer, Seager was a tobacco dealer and the sole maker and proprietor of that wonderful remedy Seager's Pills.*

Right: *Chick's butcher's shop on the edge of Trinity Square next to the Old Bell Hotel, 1905.*

Hill and the now-blocked-off original entrance to North Street was Castle Hill House, the home of the Rural District Council before it moved to Oak House in Chard Street in 1945. On the higher side of that North Street entrance was Carr & Quick's, the Castle Inn in 2003. Next came Manchester House, the nerve centre of the Dawkins' empire.

Turning into Chard Street, and after passing Oak House and the Cottage Hospital on the left, we turn opposite the entrance to the school and, passing the site of Dawkins' boot factory that was destroyed by the Luftwaffe during the Second World War, we come back towards the town passing the Legion (now Axe Vale) Club and the Town Club (long-since closed). Then came one of Axminster's longest-standing businesses, Mr Imber Parsons' chemist and photographer's shop. Bateman's, the opticians, are found on this site in 2003.

Edwin Dawkins & Son Ltd's boot factory in Chard Street. Luftwaffe incendiary bombs destroyed it during the Second World War.

George Street, one of the shortest streets in Axminster, was home to the drapery business run by the two McNeil brothers. On the corner with Lyme Street, Graham Newbery established a wireless shop after moving from King Edward Road in 1945.

In Lyme Street there were two pubs, the now-closed White Hart, almost next door to Graham Newbery, and the Red Lion, on the other side of the road. Apart from these two establishments, Lyme Street was mostly residential.

Looking into South Street from Musbury Road, c.1905. The shop on the left became Stuart's butcher's. Of interest is the fact that the private house in the centre became, in turn, the café for the market (and thus English food), a Chinese take-away and restaurant and, in 2003, an Indian take-away and restaurant.

South Street, which, perversely, runs almost parallel with West Street (as does North Street) begins on its corner with Lyme Street with Matthews the ironmongers – in 2003 a Chinese take-away and restaurant – owned and run by Charles Pengelly, a deacon at the Congregational church in Chard Street. Further along the street, at Buckland House (once a girls' school) was Axminster's third ironmonger's business, known as 'middle Matthews' to avoid confusion with the other Matthews ironmongers, which, for obvious reasons, was known as 'corner Matthews'.

LYME, SOUTH AND CHARD STREETS.
AXMINSTER, 19/12
Mrs J. Parsons
Dr. to MATTHEWS BROTHERS,
FURNISHING & GENERAL IRONMONGERS, CUTLERS,
Oil and Colourmen, Plumbers, Whitesmiths and Gas Fitters.
COPPER AND TIN PLATE WORKERS.
Head Establishment: HONITON.

Jany 31	Cutting 2 Firebricks to pattern	2	0
Feby 16	1 qrt Benzoline		4½
		2	4½

South Street, Axminster, looking towards Lyme Street, c.1905. The shop on the immediate right became Jack Sansom's wet-fish and fish-and-chip shop in the 1920s.

Looking up Lyme Street with South Street on the right, c.1904. Smythe's on the right was a general grocer. The sign over the pavement on the left was that of the White Hart Inn that closed during the 1960s.

S. Sheppard & Co.'s grocery in Lyme Street. In 2003 it is the South Street car park. This photograph was taken around 1910 when a case of good German wine would cost you less than £1.

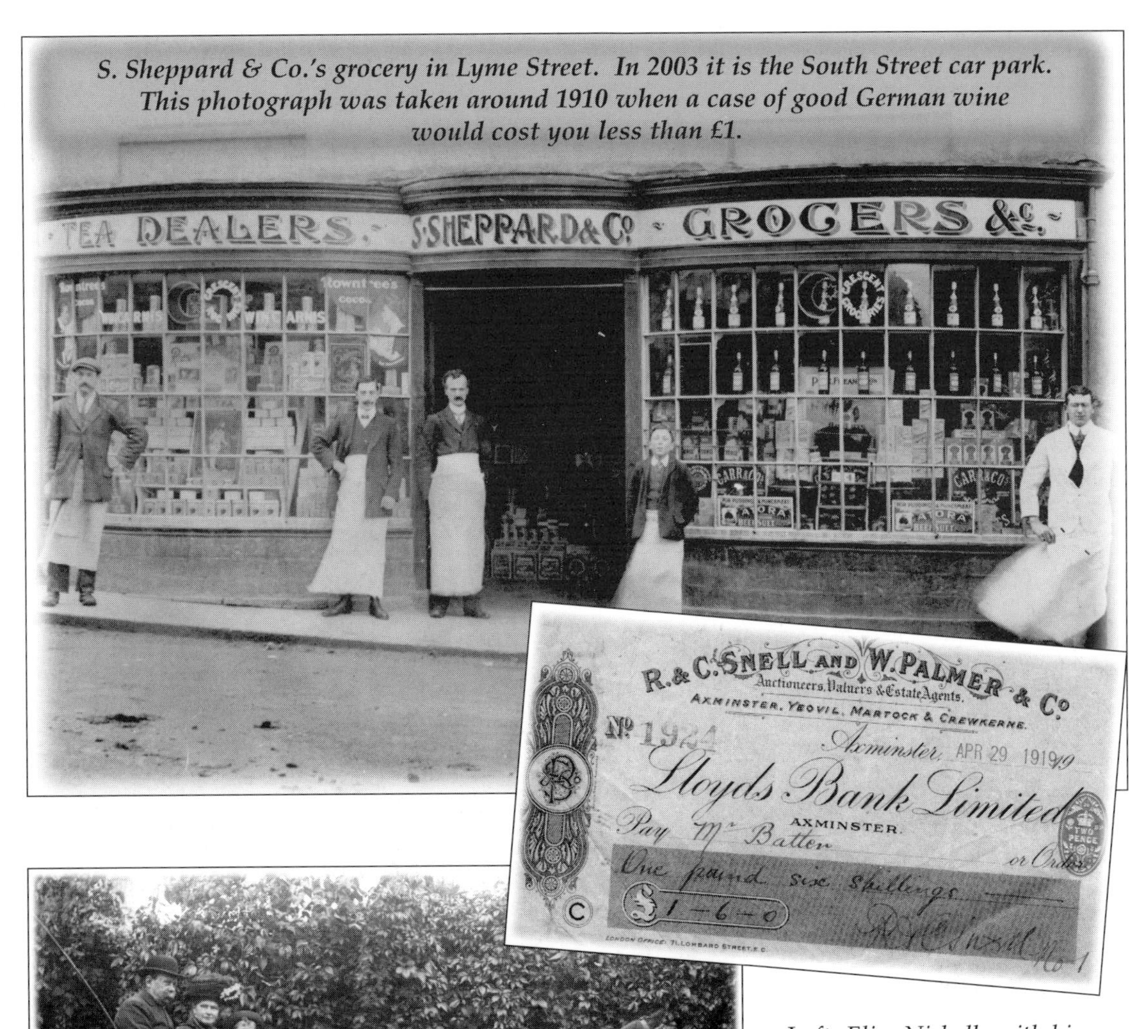

R.& C. SNELL AND W. PALMER & Co
Auctioneers, Valuers & Estate Agents.
AXMINSTER, YEOVIL, MARTOCK & CREWKERNE.
No 1924
Axminster, APR 29 1919
Lloyds Bank Limited
AXMINSTER.
Pay Mr Batter or Order
One pound six shillings
£1-6-0

Left: *Elias Nicholls with his second wife and their grandson Gilbert Love (born August 1910) in the cobbled courtyard of their Tudor Cottage home in South Street, c.1913. In 2003 Gilbert is 93 years of age.*

Tudor Cottage, probably one of the oldest buildings in South Street in 2003. The land is recorded as far back as the late-twelfth century. The cottage was burnt down in 1644 during the reign of Charles II and rebuilt almost a century later in 1733 during the reign of George II. Inside, much of the 1733 building remains including a bread oven, a large inglenook fireplace and beams.

Right: *Fred Ball outside his saddler's shop in Trinity Square, c.1925.*

Below: *A Love family wedding outside Axminster's Congregational church in Chard Street, 1935. The arched doorway, in the ivy-covered wall* (left) *can still be seen in 2003. Three Axminster families can be seen here: the Nicholls and Loves* (left), *and the Seagers* (right).

Left: *During the 1978 blizzard a queue formed outside King's bakery at the top of Castle Hill.*

Inset: *The scene in Lyme Street on the same day.*

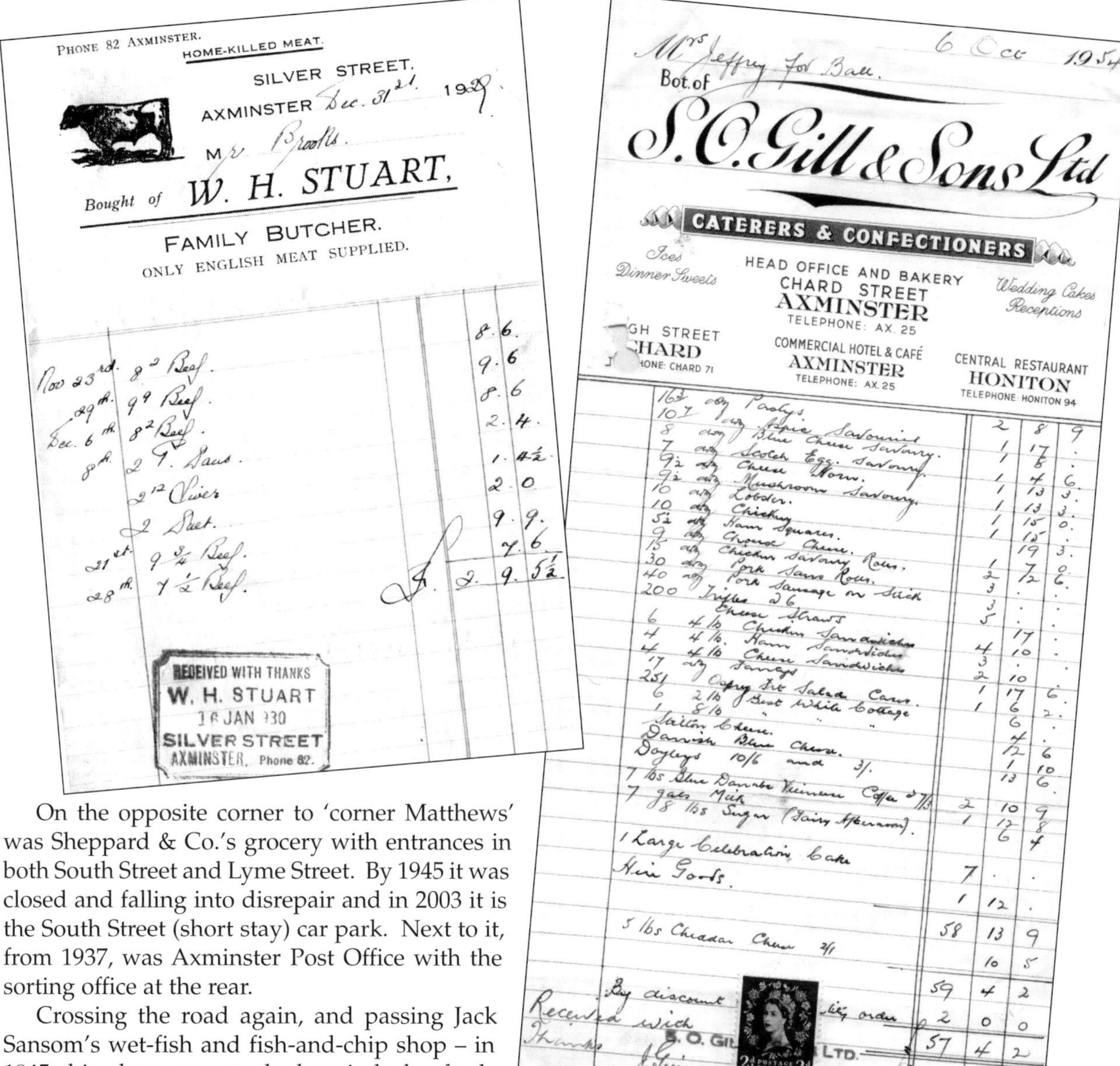

PHONE 82 AXMINSTER.
HOME-KILLED MEAT.
SILVER STREET,
AXMINSTER Dec. 31st 1929
Mr Brooks.
Bought of W. H. STUART,
FAMILY BUTCHER.
ONLY ENGLISH MEAT SUPPLIED.

Nov 23rd	8 2 Beef	8. 6.
29th	9 9 Beef	9. 6
Dec. 6th	8 2 Beef	8. 6
8th	2 9. Saus	2. 4.
	2 12 Liver	1. 4½
	2 Suet.	2. 0
21st	9 ¾ Beef	9. 9.
28th	7 ½ Beef	7. 6
		2. 9. 5½

RECEIVED WITH THANKS
W. H. STUART
16 JAN 1930
SILVER STREET
AXMINSTER. Phone 82.

Mrs Jeffry for Ball. 6 Oct 1954
Bot. of
S. O. Gill & Sons Ltd
CATERERS & CONFECTIONERS
Ices
Dinner Sweets
HEAD OFFICE AND BAKERY
CHARD STREET
AXMINSTER
TELEPHONE: AX. 25
Wedding Cakes
Receptions
GH STREET
CHARD
HONE: CHARD 71
COMMERCIAL HOTEL & CAFÉ
AXMINSTER
TELEPHONE: AX. 25
CENTRAL RESTAURANT
HONITON
TELEPHONE: HONITON 94

	£	s.	d.
16½ doz Pastys.			
10 ½ doz Aspic Savouries	2	8	9
8 doz Blue Cheese Savoury.	1	17	.
7 doz Scotch Egg. Savoury.	1	8	.
9½ doz Cheese Horns.	1	4	6.
9½ doz Mushroom Savoury.	1	13	3.
10 doz Lobster.	1	13	3.
10 doz Chicken	1	15	0.
5½ doz Ham Squares.	1	15	.
9 doz Grouse Cheese.		19	3.
15 doz Chicken Savoury Rolls.	1	7	0.
30 doz Pork Saus Rolls.	2	12	6.
40 doz Pork Sausage on Stick	3	.	.
200 Trifles 26	3	.	.
Cheese Straws	5	.	.
6 4 lb Chicken Sandwiches		17	.
4 4 lb. Ham Sandwiches	4	10	.
4 4 lb Cheese Sandwiches	3	.	.
17 doz Savarys	2	10	
251 Cups Ice Salad Cases.	1	17	6.
6 2 lb Best White Cottage	1	6	2.
1 8 lb " " "		6	.
Stilton Cheese.		4	.
Danish Blue Cheese.		12	6
Doyleys 10/6 and 3/.		1	10
7 lbs Blue Danube Viennese Coffee @ 7/3		13	6.
7 gals Milk	2	10	9
8 lbs Sugar (Fairy Afternoon).	1	12	8
		6	4
1 Large Celebration Cake			
Hire Goods.	7	.	.
	1	12	.
5 lbs Cheddar Cheese 2/1	58	13	9
		10	5
	59	4	2
By discount	2	0	0
	57	4	2

Received with Thanks J. Gill
S. O. GILL ... LTD.
27 Oct 54.

On the opposite corner to 'corner Matthews' was Sheppard & Co.'s grocery with entrances in both South Street and Lyme Street. By 1945 it was closed and falling into disrepair and in 2003 it is the South Street (short stay) car park. Next to it, from 1937, was Axminster Post Office with the sorting office at the rear.

Crossing the road again, and passing Jack Sansom's wet-fish and fish-and-chip shop – in 1945 this shop was stocked entirely by fresh fish from the fishermen at Seaton and Beer. There were two greengrocers almost next door to one another: Brian Vicker, and Mr and Mrs Enticott. The site of the latter's business is the home of *Pulman's Weekly News* in 2003. Opposite, Mayo's bakery, one of Axminster's long-established businesses, was famed for its produce.

The last business in South Street (going roughly south) was Lionel Stuart's butcher's shop, which looked out at a market from which much of his meat came. His slaughterhouse was a few yards away at Purzebrook in Musbury Road.

Returning to Lyme Street and turning towards Trinity Square, Mrs Hawkins' fish shop (later the Co-op) was followed by Webster's Garage, which is closed in 2003, but likely to be developed. Then came Eastmans' butcher's shop, the Nat West Bank and Nicholl's Bazaar (Victoria Place). Inside the latter, the ceiling was covered with hooks from which hung an amazing collection of teapots and crockery.

Fred Ball was a fortunate man. He ran his saddler's shop in the corner of Trinity Square. When business was slow he had but to cross the road to meet his customers at the bar of the Old Bell Hotel. In 1945, he did not need to press the button and WAIT as today's pedestrians are ordered to do by the light-controlled crossing.

Wedged between Llewelyn's chemist shop and Gill's café and bakery was Mrs Hooper's tiny sweet shop, which, in 2003, is still there, albeit in different hands, of course. For a spell, Gill's opened a branch in Chard. Like Mayo's in South Street, it enjoyed a reputation for good-quality baking.

From Gill's onwards into Silver Street was, for want of a better term, Axminster's commercial centre, with Lloyd's Bank, auctioneers and estate agents R. & C. Snell, various solicitors' offices, plus the registry office, presided over in 1945 by Miss Gage.

Odd man out was the old Axminster Carpet factory that, in turn, has served as the Cottage Hospital, the Drill Hall and, in 2003 is again in the carpet factory's hands. Part of the building, however, is used by the Conservative Club.

Committee members and helpers pose after watching Mrs Audrey Banner cut the first sod at the Flamingo Pool site in September 1997. Left to right: *Sir Peter Emery, MP for East Devon, Diana Church, Michael Hodges, Joan Swarbrick, Colin Chesterton, Don Self, Deputy Mayor, Gay Boalch, Sarah Bevis* (in front), *Jane Broom, Hilary Sutton, Wendy Bevis, Shirley Parris, Audrey Banner, Tony Drake, county councillor. The young boy in the front is Brandon Turner.*

Axminster Rotarians

The Rotary of Axminster received its Charter on 3 November 1959 and became active shortly afterwards. The 29 founder members were: John Banner, Bruce Beckingsale, Bill Beavis, Bill Beviss, Harold Bolton, Noel Carey-Potter, Norman Cawley, Peter Coleman, John Cotter, Wally Fellender, Bruce Gould, Ted Harris, Alec Hayter, Wally Henning, Eric Hicks, Wally Hoare, Cliff Hodson, Fred Kett, Alan Lodge, Jeffrey Lovatt, Jim Matthews, Jim Medley, Harold Pratt, Frank Rowe, Roy Shand, Les Spoor, Charles Tissington, Jack Webster and Alan Wood. The group has been active in its support of other local organisations. Those that have benefited from the Rotarians' community spirit include: Axminster Gateway Club, the town's Abbeyfield retirement home, Axminster Probus Club, an annual hanging-basket competition and local senior citizens' events.

The Flamingo Pool

A long-felt need in Axminster had been for a heated, indoor swimming-pool. This need was finally realised on 12 September 1998 when the Flamingo Pool was opened next to the Axe Valley School and Community College. A steering committee was formed in 1991 with the idea of building a 25-metre indoor pool in the Axe valley as a community project. Its first chairman was the Revd Barrie Swift. He suggested £100,000 was enough for success and, with hindsight, he was not far out; the total cash raised was £159,792. That sum gave rise, in turn, with a lot of hard work from councillors, to a grant of £500,000 from the East Devon District Council. Once the pool was started it became possible to apply for a grant from the Sports Council Lottery. The total grant was £1,440,240, without which it is highly unlikely that Axminster would have had its swimming-pool. The total grant from the East Devon District Council was £556,191 and, in all, the pool cost £2,156,233.

The architect, Mr Michael Hodges, and committee member John Banner, travelled the length and breadth of England to look at other pools, which guided them towards the final design for Axminster's, which included a hydrotherapy pool.

The pool was scheduled to be opened at 3p.m. on Tuesday 16 September by Sports Minister Tony Banks, but he was conspicuous by his absence. It seems he had been held up at a prior engagement in Bath. Consequently, the opening was delayed but the minister returned to London so the Revd Barrie Swift performed the opening ceremony instead.

Hannah Thomas and Sarah Bevis brought the first car that travelled on Axminster's bypass, 10 November 1991. They took part in the sponsored walk to raise funds for the Flamingo Pool.

Aged 92, Mrs W. Kirby was the oldest person who participated in the sponsored walk on Axminster bypass in November 1991. She is pictured here with the youngest participant, Angela Hill, who was aged just 14 months at the time.

A New Court-house

Around the time Axminster was gaining an indoor pool, it was losing its court-house. Formerly in Church Street above the old police station (now Axminster Museum), Axminster's court moved to a new home in Lea Combe where it was handily placed adjacent to the new police station. After much speculation and official denials 600 years of legal history were swept away on 3 May 2001 when the court sat for the last time. The magistrates present were: Richard Birnie, Colonel Ronnie Dowden, Patricia Swinburne-Johnson and Michael Stacey. A teenage car-tax dodger was the last 'customer', but he failed to put in an appearance.

Mayors of Axminster

In 1978 Axminster Town Council decided to have a mayor. The first to be elected was Bob Newbery, a member of a popular Axminster farming family. Elected in 2003 for the second time, Douglas Hull joins Michael Steer as the only mayors to have served two separate terms of office.

Above: *Bob Newbery, who farmed at Hunthay Farm, was Axminster's first mayor.*

Axminster's Mayors

R.E. Newbery, 1978–79
M.P.J. Steer, 1980–82
Mrs D.J. Hull, 1983
K.A. Smith, 1984–85
M.P.J. Steer, 1986–88
D.R.H. Hull, 1989–90
B.A. Draper, 1991–93
H.J.A. Jeffery, 1994–96
D. Hallett, 1997–98
D. Self, 1999
Mrs S. Spiller, 2000–01
M. Symes, 2002–03
D.R.H. Hull, elected 2003.

Above: *Local militiamen, saying their goodbyes as they wait to entrain for service in August 1914. The water tower and the passenger bridge have long-since been removed.*

Below: *An armoured-car convoy taking a breather in Trinity Square and West Street during the First World War whilst en route to Exeter. The car on the right is flying the White Ensign that suggests a Naval connection. Imagine the same scene with the level of traffic that we often see in the early-twenty-first century.*

9

Axminster At War

The outbreak of the First World War on 4 August 1914 found Axminster well prepared as far as Axminster Territorials, H (Axminster) Company, 4th Battalion Devon Regiment, were concerned. They had moved into their new headquarters on 29 January 1913. It is not known where they had previously met but the new base consisted of a spacious Drill Hall, an armoury, an orderly room and office on the ground floor; a sergeants' room, a refreshment bar, a recreation room, bath and lavatory accommodation on the first floor, and dwelling apartments for the sergeant instructor on the second floor. The brand-new Drill Hall was to the rear of the building that had once been Thomas Whitty's carpet factory.

Despite rain falling throughout much of the day there was a large attendance at the opening ceremony, which was performed by Major-General Donald, who was commanding the Western Division of the Territorial Forces. He arrived by train and was taken by motor car to Trinity Square where he inspected a guard of honour under the command of Captain W.H. Percy-Hardman (a good name for a British soldier). The guard consisted of members of H Company.

Major-General Donald was received by Colonel Marwood-Tucker (commanding 4th Battalion Devon Regiment), Major Duncan DSO (Chief Staff Officer, Wessex Division), Captain Graham W. Forward, and other officers. By this time the Drill Hall was full, those present being entertained by the company's band under Bandmaster Wench. The large gathering included a good sprinkling of local National Reservists with Lyme Regis being well represented, Axminster's Boy Scouts under Mr McLennan, and the Axminster's Church Lads' Brigade under the command of the captain, the Revd Nicholas.

During his opening speech Major-General Donald made a special mention of Mr Bowden, the architect responsible for the building, as well as Messrs J. Clarke & Son, the Axminster-based building contractors. He also mentioned that the Territorial Association was in the course of spending around £60,000 in the erection of similar buildings in various parts of Devon.

During his annual report Captain Graham Forward said that the strength of H Company at the end of the previous year had been 78 and was distributed as follows: Axminster (47), Lyme Regis (19) and Chardstock (12). Since then, a couple more recruits had joined at Lyme Regis and a further 16 at Axminster, which made the total 96. He added that all of the 60 trained men that fired the musketry course had passed with an average of 62 points per man. All but five of the 21 recruits taking the recruits' musketry course passed, evidence of the general improvement in shooting on the rifle range, an impetus to which had been the introduction of the Commanding Officer's Cup. During the year there had been 21 drills with each man averaging around 16 attendances.

In closing, thanks were given to Mr R. Cornish of Axminster, the former owner of the building, and to the members of Axminster's Conservative Club who sold the building to the Territorials. The annual dinner, attended by 200 people, was held in the new Drill Hall that evening. Mr S.O. Gill, a sergeant in H Company and one of Axminster's leading bakers and caterers, provided an excellent meal. Needless to say there were many long speeches.

The training of all Territorial companies, including Axminster's, was to stand Britain in good stead in 1914 when their discipline played a large part in the orderly retreat from Mons.

WELCOME HOME DINNER.

To all service and ex-service men who served in the Great War.

AXMINSTER.
JANUARY 14TH. 1920

MENU.

ROAST LEG PORK.
Apple Sauce.
BOILED BEEF. ROAST BEEF.
BOILED LEG MUTTON.

POTATOES.
(Boiled and Baked)
PARSNIPS. TURNIPS. CABBAGE.

PLUM PUDDING.
APPLE TART. MINCE PIE.
CHEESE SALAD.

The town's way of saying 'thank you' to all its men who had served in the First World War.

To The Glory of God And In Grateful Memory Of These Men Of Axminster Who Died For Their Country In The First World War, 1914–18

Bertram P. Bowles
Henry A. Bruce
John S. Channing
Charles F. Chant
Francis F. Chick
William C. Chick
Edward C. Claybyn
Thomas P. Claybyn
William A. Claybyn
Alfred A. Coote
Frederick W. Coote
William Dimon
Gerald C. Elson
Arthur Enticott
Charles Enticott
Samuel B. Enticott
Joseph Farmer
Alfred W. Fish
John Froom
Percy H. Gribble
Archibald J. Harris
John Harris
William Haysom
Ben Hoskins
Reginald Hoskins
Leonard W. Lethaby
Thomas Loud
Archibald N. Luff
Francis C. Lumbard
Albert C. Maidment
Frederick D. Maidment
William C. Mence
Ernest J. Moulding
Ralph Pace
Albert H. Parker
Thomas F. Pavey
Ernest W. Peach
William Percy-Hardman
Frederick C. Perham
John Perham
Frank Perryman
Thomas L. Phippen
James Pomeroy
Ralph Pomeroy
John H. Richards
Colin T. Rough
William J. Russell
William R. Silk
Albert J. Sloman
Edwin A.W. Snell
Tom S. Snell
John Spiller
William J. Spiller
Charles F. Sprague
Leslie W. Sprague
Reginald C. Sprague
Frederick J. Stentiford
Harry Strawbridge
Charles E. Sweetland
Sidney J. Tucker
Frederick C. White
Frederick C. Willey
William H. Woodland
Charles Young
Philip Young

Right: ***The memorial plaque at St Mary's Church dedicated to the men of Axminster who died for their country in the First World War, 1914–18.***

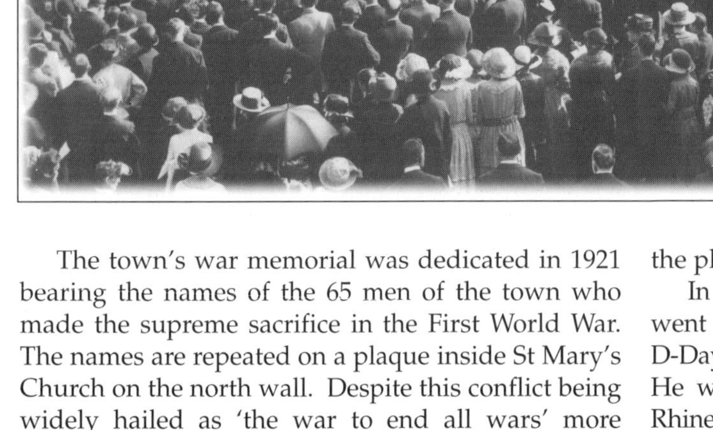

This picture: ***The dedication of Axminster's war memorial in 1921.***

The town's war memorial was dedicated in 1921 bearing the names of the 65 men of the town who made the supreme sacrifice in the First World War. The names are repeated on a plaque inside St Mary's Church on the north wall. Despite this conflict being widely hailed as 'the war to end all wars' more names were added to both the war memorial and the plaque after the end of the Second World War.

In this later conflict Axminster man Dick Sweetland went to Normandy as a parachutist, as part of the D-Day invasion, although he arrived by landing-craft. He was among the first British troops to cross the Rhine, doing so by boat. During the early days of the Normandy campaign Dick was largely responsible

Armoured vehicles passing through Axminster during the First World War. The tall ladder beside the drinking fountain belonged to the local fire brigade and was permanently parked in Trinity Square during this period.

Bottom left and below: *Second World War anti-tank defences outside the old Trout Inn on Chard Road. The theory was that if an enemy tank was seen approaching, two girders were fitted into the slots in the concrete blocks on each side of the road. The houses opposite the Trout Inn were demolished during the 1970s.*

Above: *Willhayes Cottage, North Street, Axminster, which was hit by incendiary bombs during the Second World War.*

The 315th Station Hospital built in 1943 just off Chard Road on what is now part of the Millwey Rise housing estate. Built by local labour for the US Forces in readiness for the D-Day landings, many of these buildings were taken over by squatters after the war and later converted by the Rural District Council into accommodation for local residents.

for the production of the first edition of what became *The Swedebasher*, a front-line newspaper for troops. It was continued after the war as the mouthpiece for former members of the 12th Devons who kept in touch through the many reunions that it inspired. Dick was its editor for 42 years, work that led to him receiving the BEM in the New Year's Honours List on 1 January 1987. His work with the Rural District Council led to his moving to Sidmouth in 1974 when the newly formed East Devon District Council gobbled up that admirable body.

Another Axminster man, Cecil Sansom of South Street, a member of D Company, 8th Devon Territorial Army who was called up at the outbreak of war, had two humorous experiences, although they may not have seemed such at the time. Almost immediately he was posted to Axminster in what had once been Fred Ball's saddlery in Trinity Square, about 100 yards from his home. When his particularly sadistic sergeant (Topper Brown) discovered this fact he took great delight in marching Cecil, and the rest of the squad, into South Street for a lengthy arms drill outside Cecil's father's fish-and-chip shop.

Later in the war Cecil volunteered to join the newly formed SBS (Special Boat Service, the forerunners of the SAS). This led to his being parachuted behind enemy lines in Greece and Yugoslavia. On one such occasion, he was dropped in the dead of night and his 'chute became entangled in a tree in the darkness – and he had no idea how far off the ground he was. Unable to drop free for fear of breaking a leg, he hung in the dark for some hours before spotting approaching lights. It was the partisans who were looking for him – and he was only four feet off the ground!

Axminster Home Guard held its stand-down parade at the end of 1944 when the threat of a German invasion had long-since vanished.

Above: *Officers and non-commissioned officers of No. 4 Platoon (Axminster) 'B' Coy. 19th N. Batt. Devon Home Guard on parade in Queen Alexandra Road.* Left to right, back row: *Cpl W. Dimon, L/Cpl T. March, L/Cpl J. Hayball, Sgt O. Chapple, Cpl J. Menniss, L/Cpl F. Manley, Cpl S. Wench, Cpl E. Parker;* middle: *L/Cpl I.D. Venn, L/Cpl W. Manley, L/Cpl J. Board, Sgt A. Henley, L/Cpl R. Bird, L/Cpl C. Gapper, Cpl A. Perham, Sgt T. Wilson;* front: *2nd Lieut A. Hayter, 2nd Lieut J. Potter, 2nd Lieut C. Cross, Lieut J. Wraight, Lieut. D. Snell, CMS T. Young, 2nd Lieut A. Hill, 2nd Lieut E. Bridle.*

In the years when our Country
was in mortal danger

MARTIN JOHN HENRY BRIGHT

who served 28 Aug 1942 to 31 Dec 1944
gave generously of his time and
powers to make himself ready
for her defence by force of arms
and with his life if need be.

George R.I.

THE HOME GUARD

Stan Davis, another Axminster man, ended his war on Luneberg Heath on 4 May 1945 as a member of Field Marshall Montgomery's staff and, as such, was a spectator when General Jodl arrived to surrender all enemy forces in north-western Europe.

Apart from a few pillboxes in surrounding fields that have escaped demolition, Axminster's most enduring reminder of the Second World War is the Millwey Rise housing estate that was constructed on the site of the American Army hospital (built in 1943) on

WE REMEMBER ALSO THOSE MEN OF THE PARISH WHO GAVE THEIR LIVES IN THE SECOND WORLD WAR, 1939–45

Jeffrie R.D. Bartlett
Cyril H. Carter
Wilfred C. Coleman
Sidney R. Foster
John J. Fry
Frederick W. Goddard
Percy Lambert
Gilbert J. Long
James R. McNeil
Frederick W. Moulding
William W. Nicholls
Cecil Percy-Hardman
Brian Pinter
Keith H. Rosewell
Harold G. Spurway
Robert Strawbridge
Charles F.J. Willey
Vincent C. Pascoe

The standard party marches through Church Street on its way to the service, as part of the 1977 Remembrance Sunday parade.

land to the east of Chard Road. Its purpose was to accommodate the wounded that were expected after the invasion of Normandy in 1944. However, there were less wounded men than the authorities expected and the hospital was seldom more than half full. After the war squatters moved in, most of whom stayed until the new council-houses began to replace the army buildings from around the mid-1950s. The first houses to be built were those facing Chard Road and around the Post Office and shops.

Axminster Town Council named the first two roads in the estate First Avenue and Second Avenue as a reminder of the American connection. This link is also mentioned on the plaque that was placed at the entrance to First Avenue to mark the 50th anniversary of the estate's construction.

News that the war in Europe had officially ended reached Axminster late in the evening of 7 May 1945. The following day was declared a holiday, which gave local schoolchildren a double reason for celebrations (and most took two days off in any case). Although Axminster's celebrations were said to be of a quiet and thankful nature it was not long before the flags and bunting began to cover the town. The flag of St George fluttered bravely from the tower of St Mary's Church, the Union Jack being hoisted on the flagpole that had been recently erected by the Urban Council in Trinity Square. (For more details of how Axminster celebrated the conclusion of the Second World War, see Chapter 16.)

It was not all celebrations, however, as the local Royal Observer Corp kept their last watch at their post on Trinity Hill. According to the local press, the only thing they heard was a nightingale singing in the nearby woods.

If the good people of Axminster were getting fed up with all the flags and bunting and the ringing of bells after the Japanese surrendered in August 1945 they could always spend an evening in one of the local cinemas.

Film buffs at Axminster's Plaza (later the Guildhall) were able to enjoy the film *The Port of Forty Thieves* with Richard Powers. That was on Monday, Tuesday and Wednesday – the rest of the week they could regale themselves with *Can't Help Singing* (Robert Paige and Deanna Durbin).

At the end of the war a garden party was held at Raymonds Hill at Windyridge, the home of the pastor, Revd W.J. Bavis, in aid of funds to build a new Congregational church on the opposite side of the road from Master's Garage (demolished in 2002). The original church had been constructed in timber and galvanised, iron sheets and was on a site near where the Post Office is located in 2003. The new building was built a few yards further up the road. It is no longer there, having been replaced by a bungalow.

10

CHURCHES AND CHAPELS

St Mary's Church at Axminster is among the oldest of East Devon's many lovely churches; its foundations are said to date back to AD786 when Cyneheard founded the site as a place of worship shortly before his death.

He was King of Wessex, descended from Cerdic, the first of the Wessex kings, and a man from whom almost all our subsequent monarchs can claim descent, including Queen Elizabeth II. There is an unconfirmed claim that it was Cyneheard's bones that were unearthed at St Mary's in 1782 (see page 10).

St Mary's dominates the centre of the town, standing on the same site that its predecessors occupied for 12 centuries. None of the first building remains, although the oldest feature still to be found is the exceptionally fine Norman door at the east end of the aisle. Davidson claimed that it was moved from its original position in the nave when the south aisle was added in 1800. This is highly unlikely. Gervase de Prestaller's church was shorter than the modern building; the hagioscopes in the piers of the tower prove this. In addition there were originally two transepts, but the south one (the Drake aisle) was pulled down in 1800.

The tower, of which the lower part dates from the thirteenth century, is the church's finest feature. It once contained nine bells, but one was removed from the peal after John Brocas was accidentally hanged on its rope; it was only used for tolling afterwards. Not surprisingly it became known as the Brocas Bell.

Two interesting effigies in the chancel, once thought to be two of the Saxon earls killed in the Battle of Beandun, are now said to be Alicia de Mohun and Gervase de Prestaller. Gervase was the first known vicar of Axminster; he was certainly ministering in the town from around 1200. Alicia

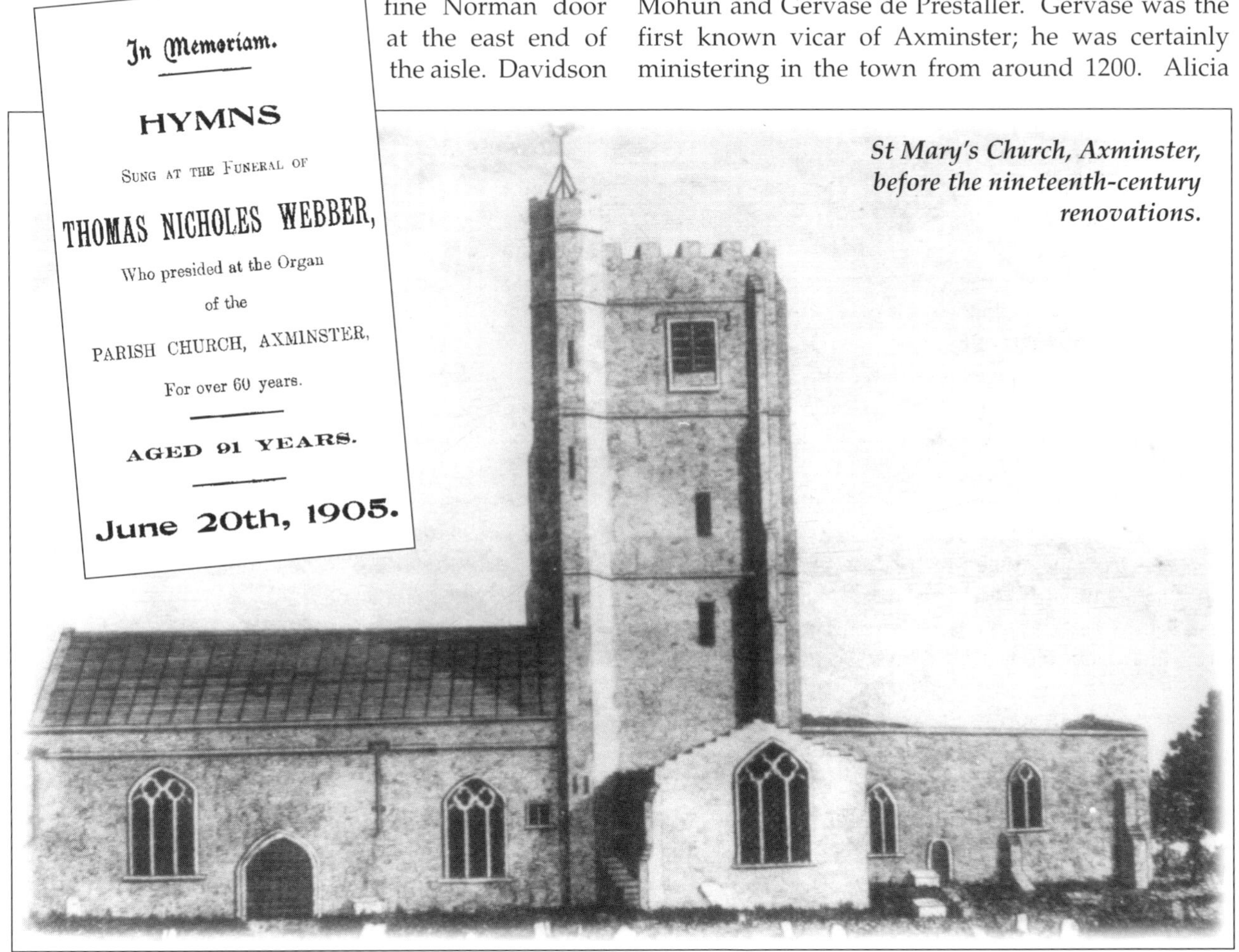

In Memoriam.

HYMNS

Sung at the Funeral of

THOMAS NICHOLES WEBBER,

Who presided at the Organ

of the

PARISH CHURCH, AXMINSTER,

For over 60 years.

AGED 91 YEARS.

June 20th, 1905.

St Mary's Church, Axminster, before the nineteenth-century renovations.

VICARS OF AXMINSTER

Date	Vicar	Date	Vicar
Late 1100s	Gervase de Prestaller	12 Jul. 1520	Cuthbert Marshall
c.1215	Matthew de Apulia	30 Apr. 1534	John Underhill
c.1244	John Maunsel	31 Oct. 1537	Emery Tuckfield
c.1258	Walter de Awlescombe	30 Apr. 1554	Robert Hicks
c.1265	John Pyte de Bridport	1559	Emery Tuckfieldc
5 Feb. 1292	John de Ilminster	30 May 1577	John Creech
1293	Not known	21 Mar. 1601	William Knowles
1310	John ?	Not known	Richard Cresson
Before 1316	William Sarestrepe	13 Feb. 1660	Bartholomew Ashwood
24 Sep. 1328	Roger Pedefer	Not known	Thomas Ayshford
1330	John de Clyve	21 Nov. 1662	Joseph Crabbe
4 Feb. 1331	John de Wilton	19 Nov. 1699	William Langford
18 Jul. 1332	William Russell	21 Oct. 1741	John Pester
13 Jan. 1349	Roger de Hackels	15 Jul. 1765	Philodeth Dommett
Mar. 1352	Thomas Welsh	20 Mar. 1780	Benjamin Symes
19 Mar. 1361	Thomas Sage	8 Jun. 1782	Charles Steer
20 Nov. 1361	John Attchurve	22 Apr. 1836	William Daniel Conybeare
Not known	John Langley	4 Aug. 1838	William John Conybeare
Aug. 1374	John Gray	13 Jan. 1855	Francis Tate
23 Aug. 1392	William Rothewell	7 Sep. 1867	William Bulmer Bailey
Sep. 1393	John Wattecombe	21 Mar. 1885	Arthur Newman
20 May 1401	Henry Peck	25 Oct. 1911	Edward Adams
Not known	John Matthue	19 Jul. 1915	Ernest Bramwell
Nov. 1420	John Hille	24 Dec. 1919	Frederick Hayne Sanders
Aug. 1427	John Matthue	17 Mar. 1953	Noel Carey Potter
Apr. 1437	John Clerc	19 Sep. 1971	John Wilkes Graves Molland
Before 1450	John Hembury	21 Jul. 1977	Frederick Harold Lockyer
6 Mar. 1491	John Waty	30 Jun. 1987*	Richard Barry Swift
26 Apr. 1519	Thomas Scanescy	7 Mar. 1995	John Hobart Good

*In 1983 Axminster became part of the team ministry with Chardstock, All Saints and Combpyne.

was the sister and heiress of William Brewer, and had carried the manor of Axminster with her, by marriage, into the Mohun family. For 12 years she paid for all the stone used in the building of Salisbury Cathedral.

The royal coat of arms at St Mary's Church date from 1767 (the reign of George III). They cost £9.14s.0d. (£9.70 in modern money). Also in the church are a curious bust of woman with a seventeenth-century hairstyle thought to be Ann Bazly who died in 1643; the painting of the Last Supper; a piscina and sedilia, all of which are well worth a look.

Around 1200 the prebendaries appointed Gervase de Prestaller as the first (known) vicar of Axminster. He was the chaplain to Lord Brewer as well as his steward of the manor of Axminster, which King John had just granted Lord Brewer. During the thirteenth century the Bishop of Exeter, the King, and the Abbot of Newenham all presented vicars at different times when vacancies arose. However, in 1293, the prebendaries clawed back the right, although, when they were dilatory, the bishop presented his choice 'by lapse'.

John Knight bought Hilary House in 1763 and fitted up a room as a Catholic chapel to serve the needs of the growing Roman Catholic community. In 1831 Mr Henry Knight, of Terrace Lodge in Lyme Road, built St Mary's as a Roman Catholic church on the opposite side of the road to his home. The original building was taken down and a new church was erected, together with a school and priest's residence, in 1862 at a cost of nearly £3,000, chiefly contributed by the Knight family. It was built in stone and in the Gothic style.

Axminster's Wesleyan community was born when the town was visited by the movement's founder, the Revd John Wesley (1703–91). The first chapel was situated at the corner of South Street and Combe Lane (often known as Back Lane). Wesley himself contributed to the building fund, and, on a couple of occasions, he visited the town and preached in the market-place. For a while, after the destruction of the derelict chapel in South Street, services were held in the Congregational chapel.

A new chapel was opened in 1796 adjoining the market-place in a building that was later used for repairing lace. The building in Lyme Street, which

Left: *St Mary's Church, Axminster, after 1887 when the new clock was erected to commemorate the golden jubilee of Queen Victoria. The iron railings and ornate gate were taken down during a Second World War salvage drive.*

Right: *The belfry, in St Mary's, 1877.*

Left: *Tom Vowden winding the church clock for the last time, c.1967. The mechanism was electrically operated after this date, the cost of it being met by Miss Jess Whitwell of Horselears in memory of her brother Jack.*

The interior of St Mary's Church in 1877. It looked like this between 1870 and 1925 after which the church was completely rearranged and the pews removed.

in 2003 is the home of Axminster's Wesleyan congregation, was opened in 1894 to seat about 300 persons. The register of births and baptisms dates from 1809.

The Congregational chapel was founded in 1662. The building that is still used in 2003 was erected in 1828 in plain stone with seating arrangements for 400 persons. The registers belonging to the chapel date from 1786. Part of the modern Axe Valley School and Community College stands on the site of the original building. Among the better-known graves in its graveyard is that of Thomas Whitty, the founder of the town's carpet industry.

Lady Tullock, who also endowed Woodbury School, which had to be conducted on strict Church of England principles, contributed to the building of Woodbury Holy Cross Mission Church in 1875.

The Methodist church in Lyme Street, c.1914. The wall in front of Lion (now Lyme) House was moved back when the road was widened. The trees on the left were also removed and a pavement put in their place.

Wally Fellender was the district reporter for the Axminster and Lyme Regis area for Pulman's Weekly News *for over three decades. The dedicating and placing of a seat in his memory at St Mary's Church reveals the immense respect that was felt for him by the people of the town.*

11

NEWENHAM ABBEY

The positioning of Newenham Abbey a mile to the west of Axminster obviously depended on the lush water-meadows that surrounded it and the plentiful supply of water from the River Axe on its doorstep.

The notion that Newenham has been occupied since Roman times and was, indeed, the site of the lost town of Moridunum, is fanciful. During the building of the Axminster bypass in the early 1990s excavations brought to light some Roman remains but this was of the Roman road that followed the pre-Roman track, the Icknield Way, into the West Country. The track crossed the Axe to the south of Axminster (although the *Daily Telegraph* at the time wrongly called this route the Fosse Way). To place the site of the abbey anywhere simply because a Roman road exists nearby is utterly flawed.

Newenham was the third Cistercian abbey to be founded in East Devon or south-west Somerset. The first had been at Forde, near Winsham, also on the River Axe, which was founded in 1140 from Waverley in Surrey, the base of the order in England. William, Lord Brewer, who served three successive English Kings (Richard I, John and Henry III), founded the second at Dunkeswell. The manor of Axminster belonged to the Brewer family, King John having granted the manor the right to a weekly Sunday market in 1210 at an annual rent of £24 in 1204. In 1215 the King also granted an eight-day fair commencing on St John's Day.

The manor of Axminster passed through marriage to Reginald de Mohun and, in due course to his eldest son, another Reginald. The second son, William, received permission from his brother to found an abbey 'for the greater glory of God'. He had the choice of three sites: Minehead, Fleming's Ottery or Axminster. He passed the choice of a site to the Cistercians who chose Axminster, almost certainly for the reasons given above. However, they may have also been infuenced by the tradition that claimed Joseph of Arimathea landed at Axmouth or Seaton with the holy grail on his way to build the first church at Glastonbury.

The first community at Newenham consisted of an abbot, 12 choir monks, and four lay brothers. All were selected from the existing abbey at Beaulieu and walked to Axminster; they arrived on the Feast of Epiphany (6 January) and were greeted by the de Mohun brothers and a large crowd. Work started immediately on a chapel and simple living accommodation for the monks, Reginald de Mohun having promised a substantial annual sum of 100 marks for his lifetime towards the building work.

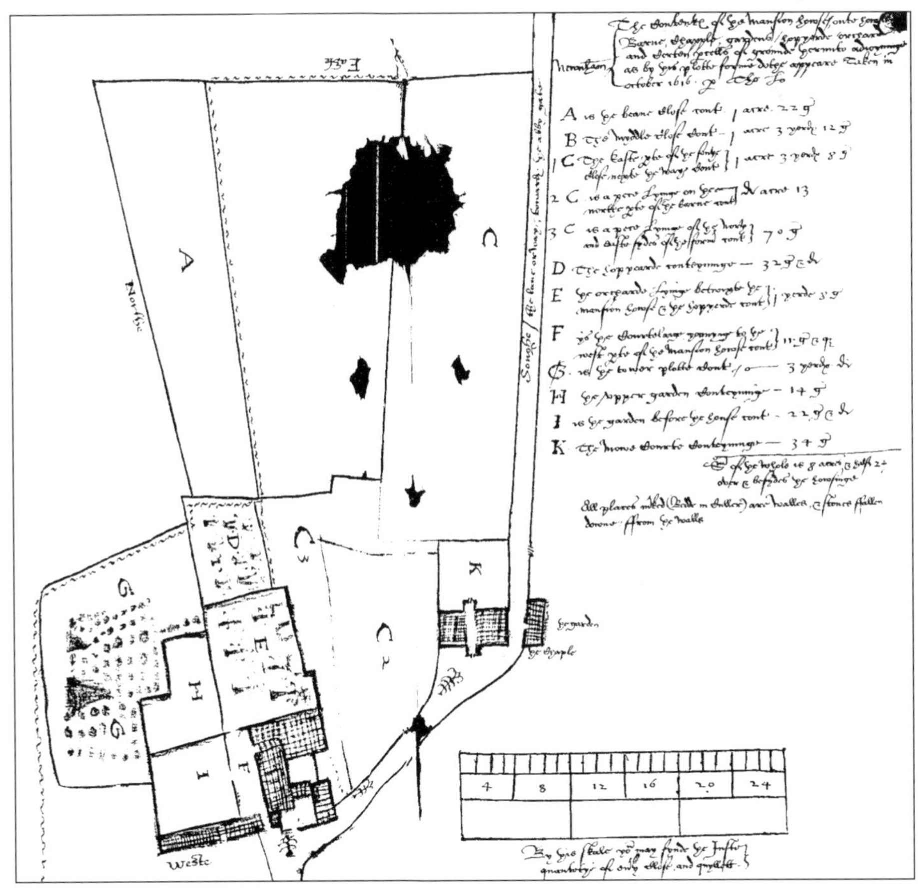

Newenham Abbey, c.1500.

The first abbot was John Godard and the prior was Walter of Huntspill. The Cistercian life was harsh. Poverty, chastity and obedience were the ideals of the order, and they were strictly enforced. The monks worked in the fields and had to sing the services at the prescribed hours, which included matins at 2a.m., lauds 70 minutes later, and prime at 4a.m. The chapter, the business meeting, dealt with confessions of faults and assignment of both punishment and works, the latter starting at 5a.m. Four times a year the monks had to submit to bloodletting for the sake of their health. They wore white habits that were thick and woolly in winter, but made of thin linen in summer. The lay brothers wore brown.

Newenham Abbey was constructed to strict Cistercian rules. The church had to be cruciform, with presbytery, transepts and a nave, but no apse. Only a small bell turret was allowed with one bell. The chapter house was next to the church in the angle of the south transept. The eastern range included the monks' dormitory; the southern included the washrooms, the calefactorium, the only room that was heated, the infirmary and the refectory. The western range consisted of the kitchen, cellarium, from where the cellarer carried on the business of the abbey, and the abbot's parlour and lodging.

The abbot ruled Newenham with the prior as his deputy. The monasteries of the Cistercian order were exempt from episcopal visitations and appointments, tithes and excommunication, and had a great deal of power. Newenham was permitted to celebrate Divine Services in the granges (farms).

On 6 July 1250, Richard Blond, Bishop of Exeter, dedicated the abbey to the Holy Trinity, Our Blessed Lady and All Saints. Reginald de Mohun laid the foundation-stone in 1254 but it took three years before enough of the work had been done for the church to be used. Even then it was almost 30 years before the work was completed.

In 1257 Walter de Bronescombe was appointed Bishop of Exeter. For some reason the new bishop, who was born at nearby Branscombe, did not meet with the approval of Newenham and its sister abbeys at Forde and Dunkeswell. From this stemmed the refusal of Bishop Bronescombe in 1262 to accept Hugh de Cokeswell as the new abbot at Newenham. He was the choice of the Cistercians and had previously been the porter at Beaulieu. Bishop Bronescombe witheld the customary Bishop's Benediction from the new abbot and presented his own rector, Nicholas Corbyn de Honiton, to the living of Axminster. Meanwhile de Cokeswell, claiming the advowson, presented John Pyte de Bridport, which, in 1265, meant that Axminster had two rectors at the same time.

Events took a mysterious turn. Hugh de Cokeswell went to Beaulieu to see the abbot and offered his resignation. However, he returned to Newenham and pretended that he was still the abbot and sent the monks into the countryside on various pretexts.

Meanwhile, a new abbot (John de Northampton) and 12 monks were sent by sea from Beaulieu to Charmouth and, singing the *Te Deum*, marched via Trinity Hill and Wyke to the empty abbey and took possession of it.

By 1277 the choir was completed and the bishop then dedicated the high altar to the Holy Trinity and St Mary, and the three south transept altars to St John and All Apostles and Prophets, St Anne, Mother of Mary and All Widows, and St Nicholas and All Saints and Confessors. In 1279 the church was finally completed in what, for the standards of the time, was good going: Forde having taken almost a century and the rebuilding of Exeter Cathedral almost as long.

Not all the abbots incumbent at Newenham could claim to be godly in their ways. Richard of Chichester, elected abbot in 1288, was said to be a 'sensual and irreligious man' and was deposed, leaving the abbey in debt. Richard of Petherton, who cleared the debt before resigning in 1297, followed him. At the turn of the century the dovecotes were built at Bewshayes and Furseleigh to ensure a supply of fresh meat for the abbey during the winter months.

Probably the best-remembered abbot was Walter de la Houe. Elected in 1338 after being the porter there, he completed the refectory, built the bakehouse and enclosed the grange (farm) at Shapwick. He also erected a cross at Abbey Gate and provided a bell called Grandisson after John de Grandisson, Bronescombe's successor as Bishop of Exeter.

It was during de la Houe's time at Newenham that the Black Death struck Axminster (1348–49), soon after it first arrived in the country through Melcombe Regis, now part of Weymouth. A total of 20 monks, three lay brethren and 88 others were killed by the disease. Only the abbot himself and two monks survived. The Black Death marked the end of Newenham's heyday; the names of half a dozen more abbots are recorded, but after that the register gives little information. It is known that Henry VII (1485–1509) was present at the abbey in November 1497 on his way to Exeter at the time of the Perkin Warbeck rebellion.

The last three abbots were John Ellis, John Ilminster and Richard Gyll. It was Gyll who surrendered Newenham to the King's commissioners on 8 March 1559, when its annual value was given as £227.7s.8d. and the tithe £22.14.9d. The monks were paid pensions. After the Dissolution of the Monasteries, Katherine Parr, Henry VIII's third wife, had a life interest in the abbey, after which the building and its lands passed to the Howards of Arundel, the family of the Dukes of Norfolk. Lord Petre owned the estate in the eighteenth century, and it was subsequently divided into smaller holdings.

One of the auditors after its suppression was John Drake, a member of a family that had held the Ashe estate since 1415. His great-grandson, another John, had a daughter, Elizabeth, who married a Dorset knight called Winston Churchill. Their daughter, Arabella, was the favourite mistress of James II

(1685–88) and one of their sons, John, became the great Duke of Marlborough.

All that remains of Newenham in 2003 are a few mouldering stones. As far back as 1796 the Revd John Swete, in his *Tour of Devon*, said that 'little remained of the abbey... little is there to justify antiquarian research... [it is a] mere jumble of ruins.'

Peter Orlando Hutchinson, the celebrated antiquarian from Sidmouth, made a drawing of the corbel on the east wall of Lower Abbey Farm. In 2003 three depressed arches can be seen inside a barn that were part of the wall between the church and the cloister. Walls of the farmhouse probably form part of the western range, which might make this the oldest house in Axminster. There are also steps leading underground, probably to a water-supply and drainage channels.

The Archway Bookshop in Church Street with its doorway arch that was taken from Newenham Abbey.

Some of Newenham's fragments can be seen around the town of Axminster. Probably the most well known is a window that now forms the doorway of the Archway Bookshop in Church Street. Similarly, some of the cloister windows can be found in a house in Lyme Road. Some floor tiles from the abbey are on display in Axminster Museum and it is thought that some of the stones were used to build (or rebuild) the mansion at Ashe.

The notion that some dressed-stone walls at Sisterhood Farm in Axminster came from Newenham is supported by the fact that in the guidebook for the Cistercian Tintern Abbey in south-east Wales, founded in 1131, the Welsh word for Cistercian is given as Sistersiadd.

George Pulman, the celebrated Victorian historian, in *The Book of the Axe* covers the history of Newenham at some length, while James Davidson's *History of Newenham Abbey* goes into even more detail. Both are recommended reading for anyone interested in the subject.

The house in Lyme Road that has the windows taken from Newenham Abbey. Since this photograph was taken (1990s) a conservatory has been built which incorporates the end window.

Left: *Thomas Whitty junr, the son of the founder of Axminster's carpet industry.*

SAM^{L}. R. WHITTY,
Carpet Manufacturer;
AXMINSTER.

Turkey Patterns 22
India & Persia 26
Superfine Axminster 42

per Sq.

NB. Brufsells & Kidderminfter Carpeting.

Below: *The Law Chambers, Silver Street, in 1995, formerly the home of Thomas Whitty and his family.*

Axminster Carpets Ltd have run a skittle team in the Axminster Skittle League since its formation in 1968–69 when it won the first ever title. It also won in 1970–71. Known as the Carpetbaggers, the team seen here played during the 1970s. Posing, with one of the firm's products are, left to right: *Arnold Sparks, Ray Fowler, Graham Turner, Stan Manley, John Knight, Bill Stuckey, Merv Knight, Reg Davis, Vic Ford, Chris Neale, Percy Downton, Sid Pascoe.*

12

Trade and Industry

Axminster Carpets

Thomas Whitty, the undoubted father of Axminster's carpets, came from middle-class Devonian stock and a family that had settled in and around the town of Axminster in the middle of the sixteenth century when John Whitty (Thomas' great, great, great-grandfather) moved from Wells to Kilmington where his son, another John, was born in 1555.

The second John's great-grandson, the second Thomas Whitty (1694–1756) married Sarah Braddick, a mercer's daughter from nearby Lyme Regis. Together they had nine children, our Thomas Whitty and eight daughters, none of the latter seeming to have children.

All the Whittys from John (1581–1634) down to Thomas Rampson Whitty (1846–1912) had a son called Thomas, the last being killed on the Somme in 1916. It tends to make the family history rather hard to follow. Therefore, for the purposes of clarity within this publication, and starting with the founder of the carpet industry in Axminster, we will name the four Thomases who ran the family business as Thomas I, Thomas II, Thomas III and Thomas IV.

In the sixteenth century the most dangerous period of life was early childhood. Thomas I had a dozen children (six sons and six daughters), of whom only two sons, Thomas II and Samuel, survived infancy. Samuel's family died out by 1820. Indeed in the Whitty family tree provided by Bertram Jacobs in his *Axminster Carpets (Hand Made) 1755–1957*, Thomas I is shown as having 12 children. However, elsewhere in the book Jacobs states that 'he married Sarah Rampson at Axminster... and raised a family of five daughters and two sons...' Thomas IV, the son of Samuel Rampson Whitty and a nephew of Thomas III, who died without issue at the age of 35 in 1810, was one of 14 children and the only one of the 14 to continue that particular line of the family.

Above: *An original Thomas Whitty carpet dating from the late-eighteenth century.*

Thomas I was born into a family of tanners and mercers, his father one of the former, his father-in-law the latter and, as far as is known, he joined his father's business. However, when aged 24, he left to start his own weaving firm in 1737. For 13 years he went quietly about his life, doing well enough to have to employ several weavers. Unfortunately for him, or so it seemed at the time, the competition supplied by the new textures of the Huguenot weavers, who were fleeing religious persecution on the Continent, was playing havoc with the traditional English styles. Consequently, some of the Wilton weavers adapted their horizontal looms to make carpets and, by the mid-eighteenth century, they were successfully producing loop-pile Brussels and velvet-pile Wiltons.

As we would say today, Thomas I was forced to diversify and tried his hand with some large seamless carpets of a type that he spotted in a friend's house in London, where a large bale of imported Turkish carpets included some as big as 36 feet by 24 feet. Pierre Norbet also made such carpets in London. Rather out of character for a staunch son of Axminster's Congregational church, Thomas I took advantage of Norbet's absence and, posing as a relative, was taken on a guided tour of the factory. A shrewd businessman, he soon spotted that Norbet's methods were too slow and that he was employing too many people to produce any real profit. He was also well versed in his trade and quickly realised that Norbet's horizontal looms were far too narrow.

Returning to Axminster he designed and built a

new loom with a perpendicular frame on which he quietly trained his five daughters and Elizabeth, a sister, to work. On midsummer's day 1755, when the factory was empty, Whitty and his family workforce produced the very first Axminster (knotted) carpet. This carpet was obtained by a Mr Cook of Slape Manor, Netherbury, on behalf of Mr Twynihowe, steward to the Earl of Shaftesbury, who was so impressed that he promised to give Whitty all the support that he could. The first service, and the best as it happened, was that he mentioned the carpet to Lady Shaftesbury who promptly obtained the carpet from Mr Cook because 'she wanted to have the first carpet of that manufactory.' It was, of course, for Thomas I, a foot in the door of the best market in England. After all, the gentry, landed or otherwise, were the people with the money. The Shaftesburys would become regular patrons of Axminster Carpets.

Whitty's factory was in Silver Street on the site of what later became Axminster's first hospital and, fittingly, in 2003, it is again in the hands of Axminster Carpets Ltd. The family dwelling, the town's chambers in 2003, was next door to the factory and both, seemingly, were cramped enough to force Thomas I to look elsewhere for a showroom when his business flourished enough to make one necessary. For this purpose he rented a site in South Street from his father-in-law, Samuel Rampson.

In 1828, when the Silver Street factory was destroyed by fire (being run at the time by Samuel Rampson Whitty), it was rebuilt on the same site, although not necessarily along the same lines. It is of more than passing interest that *Pigot & Co.'s Devonshire Directory* for 1824 lists Samuel Rampson Whitty as the local agent for the Globe Insurance firm.

Mrs Mary Anne Hoare, who lived at the top of Castle Hill, said in 1890, aged 90, that she could recall a lively interest throughout the town when a carpet was finished. She said:

> *It was counted* [as] *a grand event, bells were rung, carriages came from a distance, on this gay day. All the work was done by means of needles and the hand, and the whole work, as well as the dyeing of the materials, was done in the town. At one time it was the custom for a very large number of people to assemble in the Congregational church, where thanks were given for the completion of a fine carpet to be sent abroad.*

The Whitty family worshipped at the Congregational church in Chard Street (the United Reform church in 2003).

Both James Bradford and John Welch had told Davidson that they could well remember such occasions. They recalled a particular carpet being sold to the Sultan of Turkey – it required between 20 and 30 men to carry it from the factory to the church! It incorporated a pattern that represented the sun, the moon and the stars, and was such a great size that it covered almost the entire area of the chapel, only one aisle being left free to allow visitors to view 'this remarkable piece of work'.

Another large and valuable carpet, which was made for Goldsmiths' Hall in London, was seen when in the making, and on the works, by a Thomas Webber. Mr Webber, as well as James Bradford

Just how much modern machinery has made a workman's life easier can be seen by the size of these trees which then had to be manhandled or moved by horses. The employees of G. Heal & Son, seen here at Sector Lane are, **left to right, in front of the tree:** *Jack Selway, Fred Selway and Jack Gapper.*

Below: *Staff of G. Heal & Son at their Axminster factory at the bottom of Castle Hill, c.1890. The business was taken over by the Exeter-based firm, Norrington & Sons.*

Opposite: *G. Heal & Son displays some agricultural machines in Trinity Square. The date is unknown but it has to be pre-1912, the year the market was moved to South Street.*

and John Welch, knew Mr Samuel Rampson Whitty and his son Thomas personally. The latter was the last of the family to make carpets in the town. He was the great-grandson of the Thomas Whitty who founded the business. The works closed in 1835.

Harry Dutfield brought the carpet industry back to Axminster in 1937, where it still flourishes in 2003. In 1997 Axminster Carpets Ltd bought the garage premises formerly occupied by Moto of Axminster and which had become an eyesore at the western entrance to the town. The whole site was tided up and became the firm's shop.

Cloth Manufacture

Davidson claims that there was a cloth factory in Axminster before the carpet factory was opened and that, after it closed in 1835, several other industries sprang up in its place. These included, in Willhayes Lane (North Street), a small tape business that existed there for around 70 years. At the bottom of Castle Hill there was, for a while, a manufacturer of tow and flax for cordage, until the building was burnt down and the industry was moved elsewhere. George Pulman, writing in 1875, claimed:

> *The manufacture of tape was carried on in Axminster in the early part of the nineteenth century, and there is still a factory for the preparation of flax for cordage and sacking, but not worked to the same extent as formerly.*

For a spell a Mr Boon owned a wool storage store at the foot of Castle Hill, which, in turn was taken over by the brush factories of Coate & Co., and Bidwell, Bidwell & Co. At that time (1890) there were also Castle Hill Iron Foundry (later Norrington & Sons), Millbrook Saw Mills & Box Making Works, Weycroft Roller Flour Mills, Tolcis Lime & Stone Works, a cabinet manufacturer and a carriage works.

Cider

Axminster would not be a Devonshire agricultural town if it did not have some connection with cider. There was a time when almost every farmer made his own 'scrumpy' and it was made under conditions that would horrify the gauleiters of the common market. Even as late as the 1960s it was not uncommon to see a rat's head or its tail sticking out of cider cheese on a floor covered with cobwebs and other interesting bits of flotsam or jetsam. 'It do give it a bit of bite', one grizzled old Axminster cider-making expert solemnly affirmed when an over-fastidious visitor pointed out the dead rat.

However, one place that had to comply with the regulations was Fordwater Farm, located at the foot of Tytherleigh Hill, where Messrs H.R.D. Coles made:

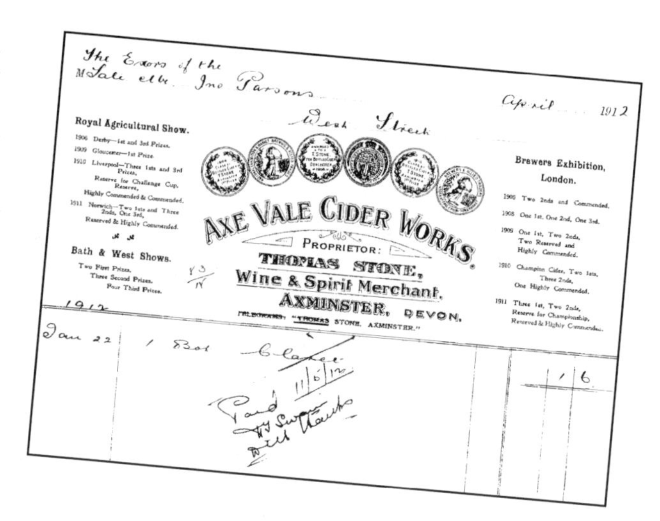

The Exors of the Late Jno Parsons

West Street

April 1912

Royal Agricultural Show.
1906 Derby—1st and 3rd Prizes.
1909 Gloucester—1st Prize.
1910 Liverpool—Three 1sts and 3rd Prizes, Reserve for Challenge Cup, Reserve, Highly Commended & Commended.
1911 Norwich—Two 1sts and Three 2nds, One 3rd, Reserved & Highly Commended.

Bath & West Shows.
Two First Prizes, Three Second Prizes, Four Third Prizes.

AXE VALE CIDER WORKS.
PROPRIETOR:
THOMAS STONE,
Wine & Spirit Merchant,
AXMINSTER, DEVON.
TELEGRAMS: "THOMAS STONE, AXMINSTER."

Brewers Exhibition, London.
1906 Two 2nds and Commended.
1908 One 1st, One 2nd, One 3rd.
1909 One 1st, Two 2nds, Two Reserved and Highly Commended.
1910 Champion Cider, Two 1sts, Three 2nds, One Highly Commended.
1911 Three 1st, Two 2nds, Reserve for Championship, Reserved & Highly Commended.

1912 Jan 22 | 1 Box | 1/6

Paid 11/6/12

> *Pure Devonshire Cider under ideal conditions unrivalled as a delicious health-giving and appetising wine – and as a specific* [treatment] *for Rheumatism, Gout, etc. and an aid to digestion.*

Although Mr Coles' best years (his family had been in the cider-making industry for centuries) were before the Second World War, cider was nevertheless still made at Fordwater until the 1950s.

At the risk of bringing tears to our readers' eyes, we should mention that in 1925 Mr Coles' cider cost 2s. a gallon delivered in the Axminster district. Just imagine it! Real Devonshire cider delivered to your door for a shade over an old penny a pint. And you could have it in 4½, 12½, 30 and 60-gallon casks. The 60-gallon cask cost just £6. For the man with a smaller capacity, champagne cider quarts were available at 12s. (60p in modern money) a dozen.

Axminster's Brush Industry

Messrs Bidwell, Bidwell & Co. Ltd's Castle Mills Brush Factory most likely stood on the site of the two town mills recorded in the Domesday Book (1086). Formerly a rope factory, according to their price list, Bidwell's was established in 1839 and arrived in Axminster in 1881, staying there until 1955 when the firm went into liquidation.

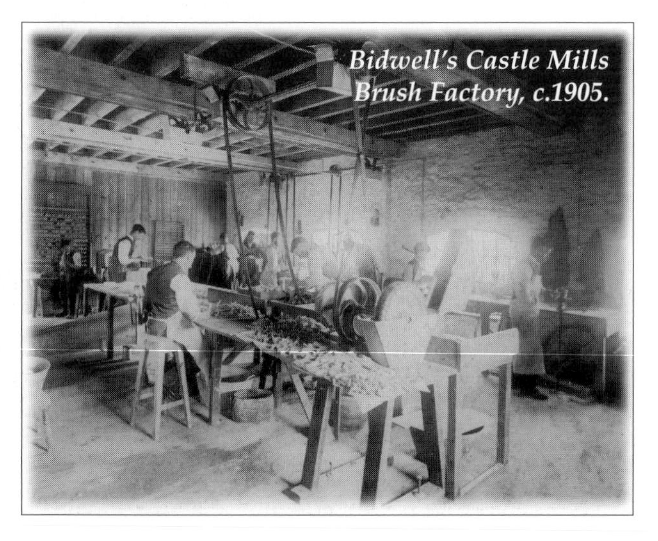
Bidwell's Castle Mills Brush Factory, c.1905.

The shaping room at Bidwell's Castle Mills Brush Factory at the foot of Castle Hill around 1910.

Left: *James Coate, proprietor of Coate & Co.*

This picture and left: *Coate & Co.'s brush factory at the foot of Castle Hill, c.1905. Of interest are the hand-operated level-crossing gates on the left that were later replaced by a single gate. Bidwell's Brush Factory can also be seen on the left of the inset picture.*

The satin wood or rose wood used in the brushes came from either the East or West Indies. It was brought in logs to London and, after being sold at auction to timber dealers, it was cut up and distributed to the various brush manufacturers.

The bristles came from the backs of semi-wild hogs in Siberia that were driven into enclosed yards where men went in among them to pull the bristles off their backs. Bristles were also collected from the trunks of trees which the hogs used as 'scratching posts'. The bristles were sorted into lengths and exported in casks in which a quantity of camphor was placed to kill off vermin or maggots. On arrival at Bidwell's factory the bristles were sorted into the various colours (white, black or yellow) and then machine-washed, bleached and cut into the various required lengths.

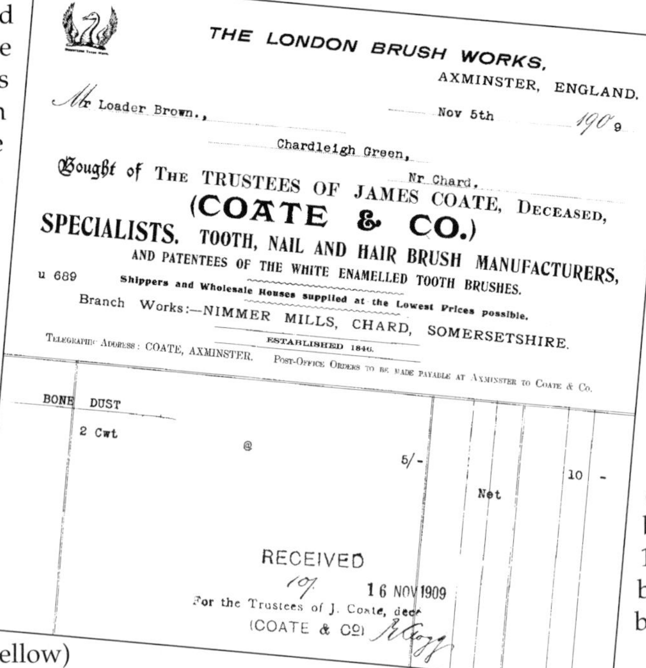

THE LONDON BRUSH WORKS,
AXMINSTER, ENGLAND.

Mr Loader Brown., Nov 5th 1909
Chardleigh Green,
Nr Chard.

Bought of THE TRUSTEES OF JAMES COATE, DECEASED,
(COATE & CO.)
SPECIALISTS. TOOTH, NAIL AND HAIR BRUSH MANUFACTURERS,
AND PATENTEES OF THE WHITE ENAMELLED TOOTH BRUSHES.
u 689
Shippers and Wholesale Houses supplied at the Lowest Prices possible.
Branch Works:—NIMMER MILLS, CHARD, SOMERSETSHIRE.
ESTABLISHED 1840.
TELEGRAPHIC ADDRESS: COATE, AXMINSTER. POST-OFFICE ORDERS TO BE MADE PAYABLE AT AXMINSTER TO COATE & CO.

BONE DUST			
2 Cwt	@ 5/-	Nett	10 -

RECEIVED
19/
16 NOV 1909
For the Trustees of J. Coate, decd
(COATE & CO)

Tooth and nail-brush handles were made out of bone that had been collected from butchers' shops by bone boilers. The only part of the bullock's skeleton used in brush manufacturing was the middle bone of the leg. It was sawn into the size required and shaped by machinery before being finished by hand. After going through about ten different processes, polishing, drilling, bleaching, etc., the 'stock' (toothbrushes) or 'block' (nail-brushes) were ready for the bristles.

GOLD MEDAL. CASTLE MILLS
TRADE MARK
BIDWELL BIDWELL & CO. LIMITED.
ESTABLISHED 1839. AXMINSTER.

"Desideratum" In Transparent Tubes. White or Yellow Bristle. Medium or Hard. 4-row, 14/-; 3-row, 12/- dozen.

"Defiance" In Transparent Tubes. White or Yellow Bristle. Medium or Hard. 4-row, 14/-; 3-row, 12/- dozen.

"Defiance de Luxe" 4-row, 16/-; 3-row, 14/- dozen. As above but in "Gloria" Silverdrawn quality.

"Gloria" No. 1 Short hard knots prevent bristles crushing. Hard or Medium, 17/- dozen. In Transparent Tubes. REGD. 090700.

"Gloria" No. 2 Strong in centre where strength is required. Hard or Medium, 17/- dozen. In Transparent Tubes. REGD. 314272.

Double Tooth Brush 20/- per dozen in cartons. Highly recommended by Dental Profession. D. 21.

IMPORTANT.—Tooth Brushes should be rinsed free from dentifrice, water tapped out and Brush hung up. Bristles will then keep stiff and sweet.

These stocks or blocks were given to cottagers (outworkers) who put the bristles into the handles. In all, and including the outworkers, Bidwell's employed around 300 people. On return to the factory the backs of the brushes were cemented, washed, polished, graded, stamped and packed for delivery to the retail trade, but only after having been through, from start to finish, some 70 different processes.

Bidwell's manufactured a total of 72 types of toothbrushes at Axminster. Each type came in a dozen different qualities and four degrees of stiffness. There were also 200 different patterns of hairbrushes made at the factory. Bidwell's shipped their brushes all over the world on a weekly basis (shipments often amounted to 100 grosses at a time).

Next door to Bidwell's factory was the Coate & Co. Brush Factory that manufactured brushes along the same lines as its neighbour. During the First World War it supplied over 15,000 brushes to the Armed Forces. The firm also produced brushes at Nimmer Mills near Chard. The Axminster factory closed in 1936 but Nimmer Mills continued to produce brushes until at least the 1950s. The buildings became derelict but are being renovated in 2003.

The products of both firms may be seen in Axminster Museum. Work at Chard was regularly taken to Axminster for finishing – and vice-versa. This work was carried by donkey cart, the two carts meeting at Tytherleigh to exchange their loads.

Edwin Dawkins & Son

Edwin Dawkins & Son was, without question, Axminster's leading shop and played a prominent part in the town's commercial life for over a century. It was founded around 1874 and traded until its closure in 1978.

During its heyday, the 1920s and 1930s, a feature of the year was the July sale when a four-piece circular printed in red contained details of the special offers to be found in each of the stores' 13 departments. The circulars were distributed in Axminster, Honiton, Seaton, Lyme Regis and Chard. Train or bus fares were refunded for purchases of £1.10s.0d. (£1.50p) or over. On the first day of the sale

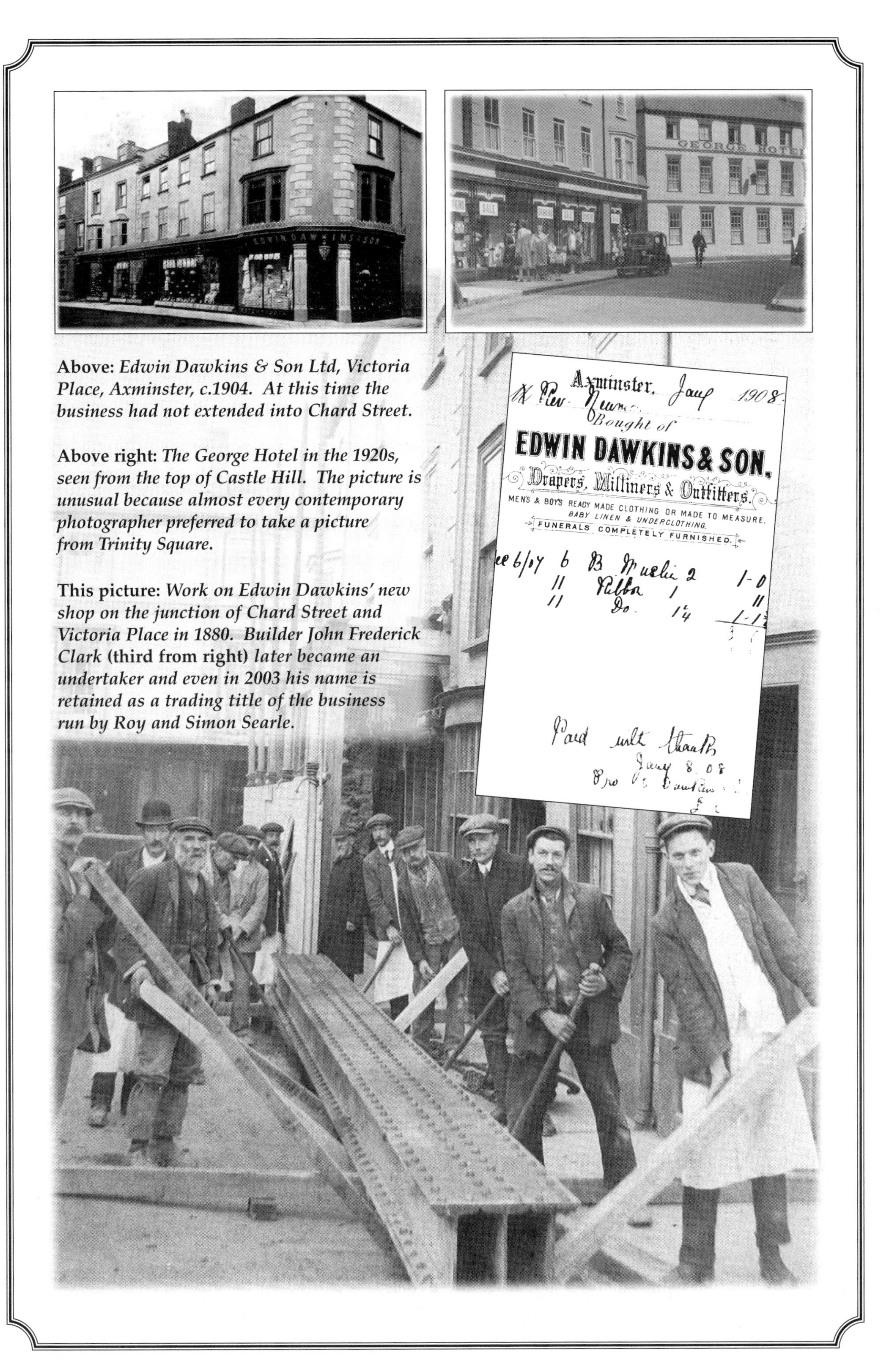

Axminster, Jany 1908
Rev. Newman
Bought of
EDWIN DAWKINS & SON,
Drapers, Milliners & Outfitters.
MEN'S & BOYS READY MADE CLOTHING OR MADE TO MEASURE.
BABY LINEN & UNDERCLOTHING.
FUNERALS COMPLETELY FURNISHED.

Paid with thanks
Jany 8. 08

Above: *Edwin Dawkins & Son Ltd, Victoria Place, Axminster, c.1904. At this time the business had not extended into Chard Street.*

Above right: *The George Hotel in the 1920s, seen from the top of Castle Hill. The picture is unusual because almost every contemporary photographer preferred to take a picture from Trinity Square.*

This picture: *Work on Edwin Dawkins' new shop on the junction of Chard Street and Victoria Place in 1880. Builder John Frederick Clark* **(third from right)** *later became an undertaker and even in 2003 his name is retained as a trading title of the business run by Roy and Simon Searle.*

outside staff were not allowed to go home for dinner but went to Oak House for a meal of cooked ham and tea as and when they could be spared. (Oak House in Chard Street, formerly a private school, had been purchased in 1920–21 by Mr Harold Dawkins, son of Edwin, the company's founder, and used as a live-in hostel for members of staff.) They were allowed just 30 minutes away from the shop.

Customers began queuing as early as 8a.m. for the sales and police were stationed at all the doors to control the queues. The doors opened at 9a.m. Employees were allowed to have a cup of tea in the workroom above the shop and the male outside staff helped to pack the customers' purchases. Rather unkindly, the staff lost their Wednesday half-day the week before the sale in order to help with the preparations. On the other side of the coin they received commission of 3d. in the pound ($1\frac{1}{4}$p), which was paid at the end of the month and in some instances was a considerable sum.

A man's navy-blue, all-wool serge, two-piece suit was sold for 4s.11d. (a fraction under 25p in modern money). Other bargains were work shirts, also 4s.11d., socks at a 1s. a pair (5p), underwear from 1.11d. ($9\frac{3}{4}$p) and made-to-measure suits from £2.15s.0d. (£2.75p), a skilled carpenter's weekly wage at the time. Better quality suits cost £3.15s.0d.

When the company went public the heads of each department were each asked to buy £100 worth of shares. Mr Dawkins acted as guarantor for those who had to borrow money from the bank. He guaranteed $7\frac{1}{2}$ per cent but paid 10 per cent at a time when the bank rate was $3\frac{1}{2}$ per cent, which undoubtedly made him a pioneer in workers' participation schemes.

When Mr Harold Dawkins had a mild stroke in 1924 the Staff Ball was cancelled but, as a sop, all members were allowed in turn to go and visit him at his home at Brookland in Musbury Road. While he was away Mr Rose, from Green's of Exeter, became a director and when Mr Dawkins died shortly afterwards he took charge. Harold Dawkins' two sons were pupils at Rugby School and they did not come into the business when they grew up; one became a missionary, the other an accountant in Cheltenham.

Mr Rose did not want to own the company and a Mr Burroughs, who owned a Bournemouth company at the time, purchased the Dawkins' empire. He ran down some of the stock lines and all non-essential and out-of-date goods were cleared in the 1930 July sale. Mr Burroughs also introduced three representatives to cover the immediate area in a successful effort to both boost sales and collect outstanding debts. Each was provided with a good, second-hand car and received commission on their sales. One covered the Chard area, another Lyme Regis and Charmouth, the third Seaton, Honiton and the villages in between.

At the time the firm had a boot factory in Chard Street next to the entrance of what is now the Axe Valley School and Community College. It was destroyed during the Second World War and never rebuilt (see page 70).

Miss Emmy Sheppard was the company secretary, but she purchased the major shares in 1943 when Mr Burroughs had become disenchanted with a businessman's life when seemingly endless regulations were thought up by the Board of Trade, a situation made worse by wartime shortages of goods and staff.

The business continued until May 1973 when the advancing years of the directors led to the decision to sell both it and the premises. Frederick Baker, the

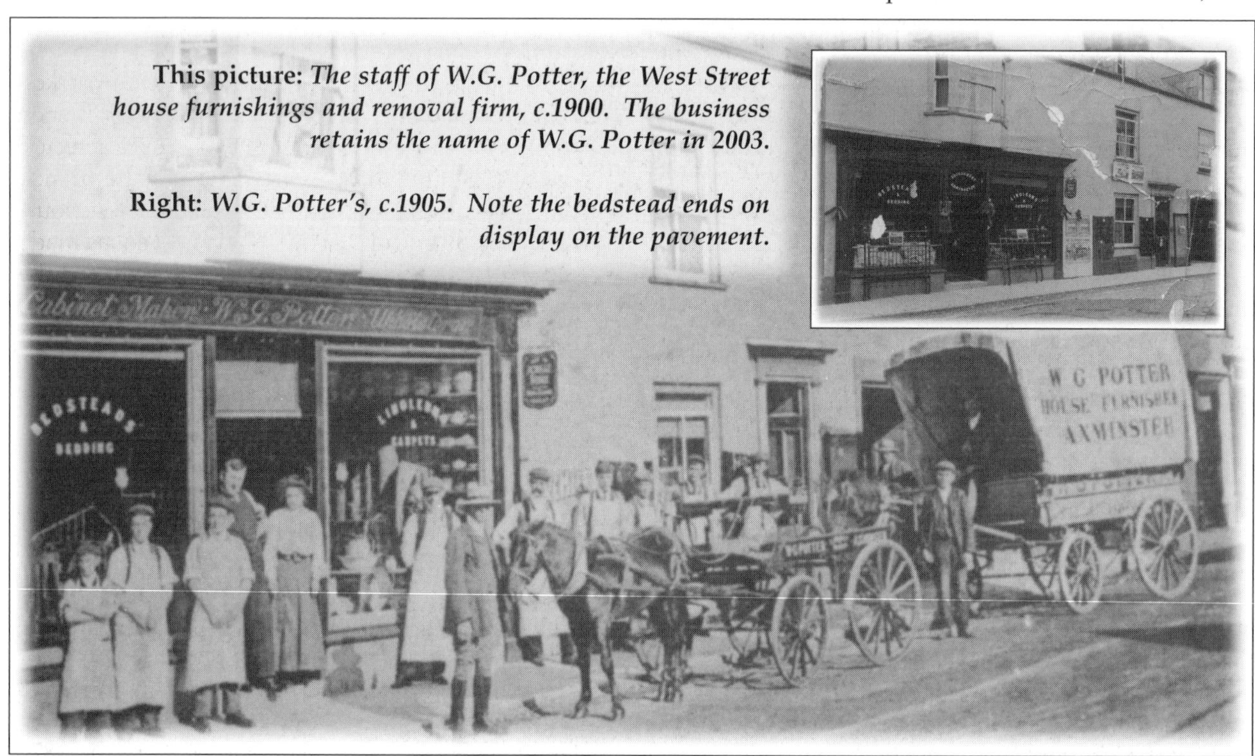

This picture: *The staff of W.G. Potter, the West Street house furnishings and removal firm, c.1900. The business retains the name of W.G. Potter in 2003.*

Right: *W.G. Potter's, c.1905. Note the bedstead ends on display on the pavement.*

Trinity Square drapers, snapped up the business and its stock for £135,000. Four years later Baker's went into voluntary liquidation and the business closed, the Dawkins' premises being sold to a developer for a rumoured £350,000. That part of the Dawkins' empire on the junction of Victoria Place and Chard Street was converted into several smaller shops on the ground floor with flats above. W.G. Potter's, a furniture business (part of Fords in 2003, the well-known Sidmouth firm), purchased the premises opposite and have their kitchenware department there.

Axminster Power Tool Centre

Axminster Power Tool Centre started life in the late 1960s as a light engineering production and electrical assembly workshop. The company was founded by Mr Ron Styles and the late Mr Graham Brown, and was first known as Styles & Brown. The difficulties they encountered in obtaining the necessary tools and materials for their line of business prompted them to open a small shop in the early 1970s when Ron's eldest son Bernard joined him. Eventually the production was overtaken by the demands of the tool shop, which grew rapidly into a private business. Ron's youngest son, Ian, set up the mail-order side of the company in 1982 and this has flourished ever since; Marjorie (Bernard's wife) and Katina (Ian's wife) also worked within the company.

One of the most significant developments in the history of the firm was the introduction of their *Tool and Machinery Catalogue*. From single bargain sheets in the 1970s, this free publication has grown in both size and stature over the years and the 2003 edition boasts over 600 colour pages and supports a world-wide mail-order business offering a friendly and personal service to many thousands of customers, both professional and amateur. To supplement the catalogue, and to keep the customers up-to-date with what is happening on the tool front, an in-house quarterly magazine *Review* was launched, offering an informative and light-hearted read.

The 11th Axminster Tool and Machinery Exhibition ('Tools 2002') was staged in the October of that year at The Bath and West Showground before the exhibition was held at West Point, Exeter, in 2003. Back to its roots in Devon!

Ever-changing developments in the retail side of the business have followed with a tool-hire shop opening in Chard Street in the 1980s. In addition, a CNC (Computer Numerical Control) machine shop was set up and produces chucks and other machine items, plus a new Wood Turning and Craft Centre where courses in wood turning, routing and wood-carving have taken place since its creation. Such innovations have ensured the growth and success of the company, which, in 2003, employs over 150 staff.

To service the retail side, a new warehouse, together with office accommodation, was built in 1995 on the Millwey Rise industrial estate. Since then a further warehouse and a relocation of the machine shop has taken place.

The company opened a branch shop in Faversham, Kent, after premises were acquired in 1999. This side of the business is continuing to grow steadily. Two new moves in the twenty-first century have seen the setting up of a new company, Jet Tools & Machinery Ltd, and the purchase of the former Axe Vale Engineering premises in the town. As a result of the latter, it is envisaged that, by 2004, all of the firm's retail shops in Axminster will be under one roof.

Despite the continuous expansion and diversification, Axminster Power Tool Centre still remains a family concern with three generations of the Styles family actively involved at every level of the business. Several members of staff have also been with the company for many years; Andrew Parkhouse, who joined as school-leaver in 1983, is now a director of the company, as is Ian Huntley who joined in 1986. There are also husbands and wives and almost complete families who work within the various departments of the company, adding towards the feeling of a family firm.

R.J. Luff Ltd

R.J. Luff Ltd, a family coal and builders' merchants flourished for many years in Woodmead Road. The firm had the first lorry in the town around 1912 – it was solid-tyred and served the business for many years. Luff's was still in existence after the Second World War but was finally bought out by rivals Bradford & Sons, who moved to Yeovil for some years before returning to occupy Luff's premises in Woodmead Road.

Mole Avon Trading Ltd

Mole Avon Trading Ltd, the farmers' 'supermarket' that was founded in Crediton in 1968, opened a branch in Station Approach in 1976. Mr Ted Cross, a director, played a large part in the establishing of the branch whose first manager was Robin Mallet. Business flourished to such an extent that, in 1990, a move was made from the old railway carriages, which first housed the firm, into a modern shop and office complex. Five years later the neighbouring Jewson business was acquired and a warehouse built on the site.

In 2003 there is 10,500 square feet of retail area, the staff has risen from 5 to 18 and the annual turnover is over £4,000,000.

Weycroft Mill

Weycroft Hall stands on a bluff overlooking the old Fosse Way where it forded the Axe just outside Axminster on its way to the coast near Seaton. For centuries a mill on this site has utilised the water of the river to power its grinding machinery.

Henry Morrish bought Weycroft Mill around 1870

In 2002 Mr and Mrs Rowe of Newton Poppleford presented a model of Weycroft Mill to Axminster Museum, where it has since been displayed. The left-hand picture shows the 60hp Blackstone diesel engine that replaced the old gas engine in 1941. Its flywheel weighed 3½ tons. The picture on the right is of special interest to author Gerald Gosling; in 1955 he started work as a clerk in the bottom left-hand room, which, by that time, was serving as the main office. This view of the mill is of that part which faces the main road.

and, in 1885, he engaged the Ringwood firm of Armfield & Co. to replace the old water-wheel with two water turbines. Most likely this was done to provide the extra power needed to run the roller mills, which had been supplied by Robinson's to replace the old flat, circular grindstones. At the same time a four-storeyed, brick extension was built to house more milling machinery and the large chimney built into a corner of this extension was used for making gas to fuel the engine, which is believed to have been installed at the time.

A 1909 photograph shows the mill bearing the sign 'W. Morrish & Sons – Roller Mills'. So the old millstones had clearly been supplanted by that date, if not in 1885. In 1911 Armfield & Co. was again employed, this time to install wheat-cleaning machinery and storage silos.

By 1920 there were 20 employees at the mill and five cart-horses were kept busy making deliveries within a 10-mile radius. A farm was also run and two of the employees, Bill Gigg and Tom Hallett, were kept as 'floaters' who could be employed either in the mill or on the farm.

The former was worked 24 hours a day, six days a week, and even Sundays were productive in another way, for on Saturday nights an eel trap was placed in

The Cotley Harriers at Weycroft Mill in 1908.

the sluice which bypassed the turbines. This often yielded a fine catch and this practice was still taking place in the 1960s.

Much of the mill's supplies, such as oil-cake slabs, were brought by cart from the Southern Railway's sidings at Coaxden where they served a small lime and cement works. The oil-cake slabs were taken to the mill for 'kibbling' (breaking into small cubes) and then used in the making of cattle food cubes.

In 1925, after George Morrish had inherited the business, a Sentinel steam lorry was purchased and it considerably extended the trading area that had been covered by horse and cart. Mr Barnes, a Yarcombe farmer, recalled that the steam lorry came to his farm in 1934 to collect the 11 tons of wheat that he produced from a 10-acre field, for which he was paid £54.

George Morrish's employees knew him as a 'character', although his family referred to him as a 'Tartar'. Indeed, his language, away from the church and his family, was strong. Unknown to him, one day his grandchildren were in the mill and heard him using strange words. The most repeated word they heard they referred to as the 'buggy' word and, from that day forth, both family and employees knew him as Buggy.

Charlie Matthews, the cowman on the farm, was usually sacked at least once a week but always turned up the following morning. 'I thought I'd sacked you yesterday', George would say. 'Aarh youm did, but I knowed you dunnun mean it', he would reply. This performance was repeated week after week, year after year. Finally, Charlie failed to turn up the next morning; he had found a quieter job. Buggy was devastated and for days mooched disconsolately around the mill.

The arrival of a three-ton petrol lorry in the 1930s signalled the end of the horse and cart era and the horses were gradually sold off. In 1941 the old gas engine inside the mill was replaced by a large, single-cylinder, 60hp Blackstone diesel engine. It took a week to install and then all and sundry (a euphemism for the important people) were invited to the mill to view the largest engine that Axminster had ever seen. It had been purchased second-hand from an airfield in the Bristol area. Although there was a dynamo for lighting the mill and the house, it could not be used for cooking or heating. The installation of mains electricity in the 1940s meant the end of cooking on a paraffin stove but the dynamo was still used for lighting the mill.

The employees at the mill were exempt from military service during the First World War and the official notice to this effect was still in place in 1992. During the Second World War there were 15 employees and two horses, the latter having been brought out of retirement for deliveries during the wartime fuel rationing.

Buggy died in 1951 and the business was sold to Bakers of Colyton the following year, although his son, Leslie, remained as managing director. During the war bakers were restricted in their choice of flour suppliers; much of Weycroft's trade was lost and was never recovered. Flour was still ground there, however, until the early 1960s.

In 1970 the diesel engine was taken out of service and replaced by a new three-cylinder Lister engine that was very troublesome and noisy by comparison. Production ceased altogether in 1977 and the old Blackstone engine was sold to a local farmer in 1978, although it has since changed hands again.

Sadly perhaps, the mill has been converted into dwelling-places and a modern generation will never know what it was like to wander around inside the working mill. Happily Mr and Mrs D. Rowe of Newton Poppleford have painstakingly constructed a six-foot long model, which they have presented to Axminster Museum. It is on display in a special cabinet that was made in the workshops of Axminster Carpets Ltd and funded by a grant from the East Devon District Council.

Plans by Mrs Lillie Pettitt of Bridport to restore the mill and turbines, along with plans to create a shop, craft and antique centre, museum, restaurant and living accommodation for her family, were passed by the local authority but a further application for a 169-vehicle car park and staff accommodation was rejected in 1997 by both Axminster Parish Council and the East Devon District Council.

Mill Brook

Barely a mile towards Axminster the Mill Brook passes under the A358 on its way from its source at Furzeleigh Farm to its junction with the River Axe below Cloakham Bridge. The brook once drove the mill at Prestaller Manor. Part of the stream was sold to the town of Axminster and diverted to become the watercourse that fed the leat in Lyme Road. At one time the owner of the mansion at Weycroft had the right of grinding corn at this mill free of charge.

Trivett's Toys

The firm of A. Trivett & Son was in Axminster for almost the entire twentieth century and was the last of the old Axminster family-name businesses to stop trading. The first of the family was Albert Henry Trivett who, after beginning work as a newspaper delivery boy around the 1890s, was sacked for refusing to work on a Good Friday. He then completed an apprenticeship with George Pile, a saddler and harness maker, before starting his own saddler's business in a wooden building on Anchor Hill. He then moved to West Street after buying a bakery and a photographer's shop around the end of the First World War. He converted the two shops into one saddlers' shop where, at one time, he employed as many as 13 men. In time his son, also an Albert, took over the business and, with the advent of the radio, and later TV, and the decline in the call for leatherwork, the business made an abrupt turn towards being a radio shop. It took another turn when it became a toy shop and finally closed in 1999 through Mr Trivett's failing health.

Tesco Comes to Axminster

Tesco arrived in Axminster at the old Shand's factory site on Monday, 3 August 1998 in a blaze of publicity. The opening ceremony was performed by local teenager Kathryn Every, nominated for the job by her grandmother, Mrs Winnie Every of Millwey Rise, who won a competition run by *Pulman's Weekly News*. Kathryn was taken to the new store in a chauffeur-driven Rolls Royce and walked down a red carpet to open the new store. The first two customers, David Thomas and Hilda Fowler, were presented with bottles of champagne.

There were many opponents to the new shop; most of them arguing that its presence would lead to the death of many small local businesses. It did. Tesco manager Trevor Shimell claimed 750,000 customers had visited the store in its first year and spent over £15 million there. Of course not all that £15 million would have been spent elsewhere in Axminster if Tesco was not there, but much of it would have made many a small shopkeeper feel that the Tesco claim that 'Every Little Helps' meant that his or her own 'little' was getting even littler.

Other Small Businesses of Axminster

Not all of Axminster's businesses or industries have been large employers. Many one and two-men concerns have thrived down the years, and they were usually owned or run by craftsmen who took a pride in their work. One such one-man business was that of Charles William Feesey, who had his workshop at Symondsdown, near Old Park Buildings and roughly opposite where the old A35 out of Axminster joins the new A35 bypass just below the Hunters Lodge. Charles, who was an antique restorer and cabinet-maker of some repute, came to the Axminster area in 1925 from his home at Henley-on-Thames to do some restoration work for a Mr Gibb of Old Park House. He eventually settled in Raymonds Hill and lived at The Beeches, a bungalow at the rear of the teashop and Post Office owned by his sister-in-law, Miss Annie Wright. In 1931 he built a new workshop at The Beeches and carried on the business with his son Jack, working mainly for the big houses around Axminster and Lyme Regis.

While operating at the Symondsdown workshop he was very proud of three large oak tables that he made for Harcombe House near Uplyme, in 1927, using only his skill and hand tools (there was no electricity in the workshop at the time). Over half a century later Charles Feesey's grandson John wondered what ever happened to those tables. The authors of this book, through the offices of *Pulman's Weekly News*, were able to trace them from Harcombe House, which had become a boarding-house, to the Woodroffe School at Lyme Regis, where they were still being used and can be seen just inside the front door.

David Badman, a member of staff at the school in 2003, said:

> *The tables would have been made to the order of Mrs Francillon, who ran Harcombe House as a Domestic Science College. During the early 1950s this moved to Rhode Hill and Harcombe became the girls' boarding-house for Lyme Regis Grammar School (now Woodroffe School). The tables were used for meals and homework. In 1969 the girls moved into Rhode Hill and the tables were moved to the main school.*

A few paragraphs back we mentioned Annie Wright's shop on the opposite side of the A35 trunk road to the Hunters Lodge. It was there, in 1925, that Annie purchased some property with a large piece of land adjoining where she opened a shop in a tiny, galvanised hut, a remnant of the First World War. There she sold groceries, sweets mineral waters and tobacco, and then opened a teashop and a small library and, later, a Post Office.

She also bought a tramcar that was brought from London for extra accommodation; one of her sheds contained a Petters generator that provided electricity for the shop. It was a monster, but Annie handled it with ease. Around 1934 she handed the running of the shop over to her niece, Ethel Bridel, but she retained the Post Office side of the business. Fred Bridel started a delivery service and covered a large area around Raymonds Hill.

In 1939, a few weeks before the outbreak of war, a brand-new Post Office and stores was opened. A conventional building, it was erected by neighbour Mr John Hoole. The business still flourishes in 2003. The original buildings have long-since vanished but, for a while, they were used as a meeting-place for Raymonds Hill WI, for social events such as whist drives, and as a place of worship, a Sunday school and a well-used youth club. Annie Wright died in 1962 at the age of 90.

The Lodge, Cloakham House, Chard Road, before its demolition in the 1980s.

Real horse power at Mill Brook, c.1910.

Above: *The bridge over the Axe near Cloakham House, c.1905. Although the majority of the ornamentation has gone, most of the bridge is still standing in 2003.*

Left: *Charles Neale's blacksmith's shop in Lyme Street (opposite the Red Lion) in 1921.*
Left to right: *E. Anning, ? Fritzby, Charles Neale.*

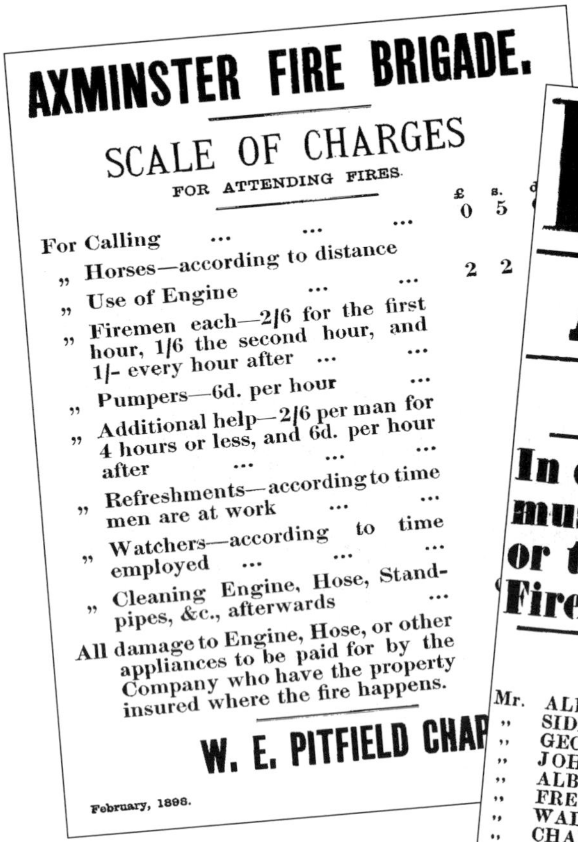

AXMINSTER FIRE BRIGADE.

SCALE OF CHARGES

FOR ATTENDING FIRES.

	£	s.
For Calling	0	5
" Horses—according to distance		
" Use of Engine	2	2
" Firemen each—2/6 for the first hour, 1/6 the second hour, and 1/- every hour after		
" Pumpers—6d. per hour ...		
" Additional help—2/6 per man for 4 hours or less, and 6d. per hour after		
" Refreshments—according to time men are at work		
" Watchers—according to time employed		
" Cleaning Engine, Hose, Stand-pipes, &c., afterwards ...		

All damage to Engine, Hose, or other appliances to be paid for by the Company who have the property insured where the fire happens.

W. E. PITFIELD CHAP

February, 1898.

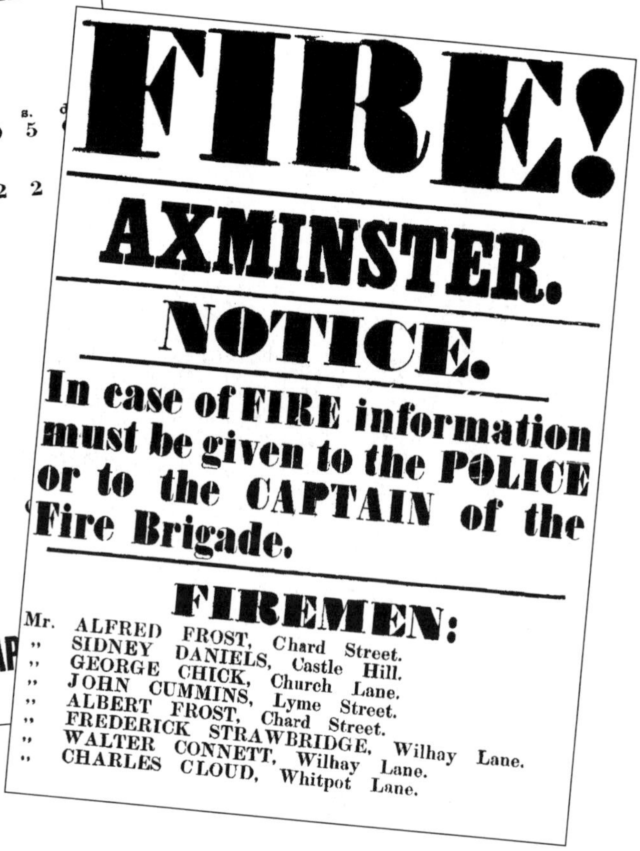

FIRE!

AXMINSTER.

NOTICE.

In case of FIRE information must be given to the POLICE or to the CAPTAIN of the Fire Brigade.

FIREMEN:

Mr. ALFRED FROST, Chard Street.
" SIDNEY DANIELS, Castle Hill.
" GEORGE CHICK, Church Lane.
" JOHN CUMMINS, Lyme Street.
" ALBERT FROST, Chard Street.
" FREDERICK STRAWBRIDGE, Wilhay Lane.
" WALTER CONNETT, Wilhay Lane.
" CHARLES CLOUD, Whitpot Lane.

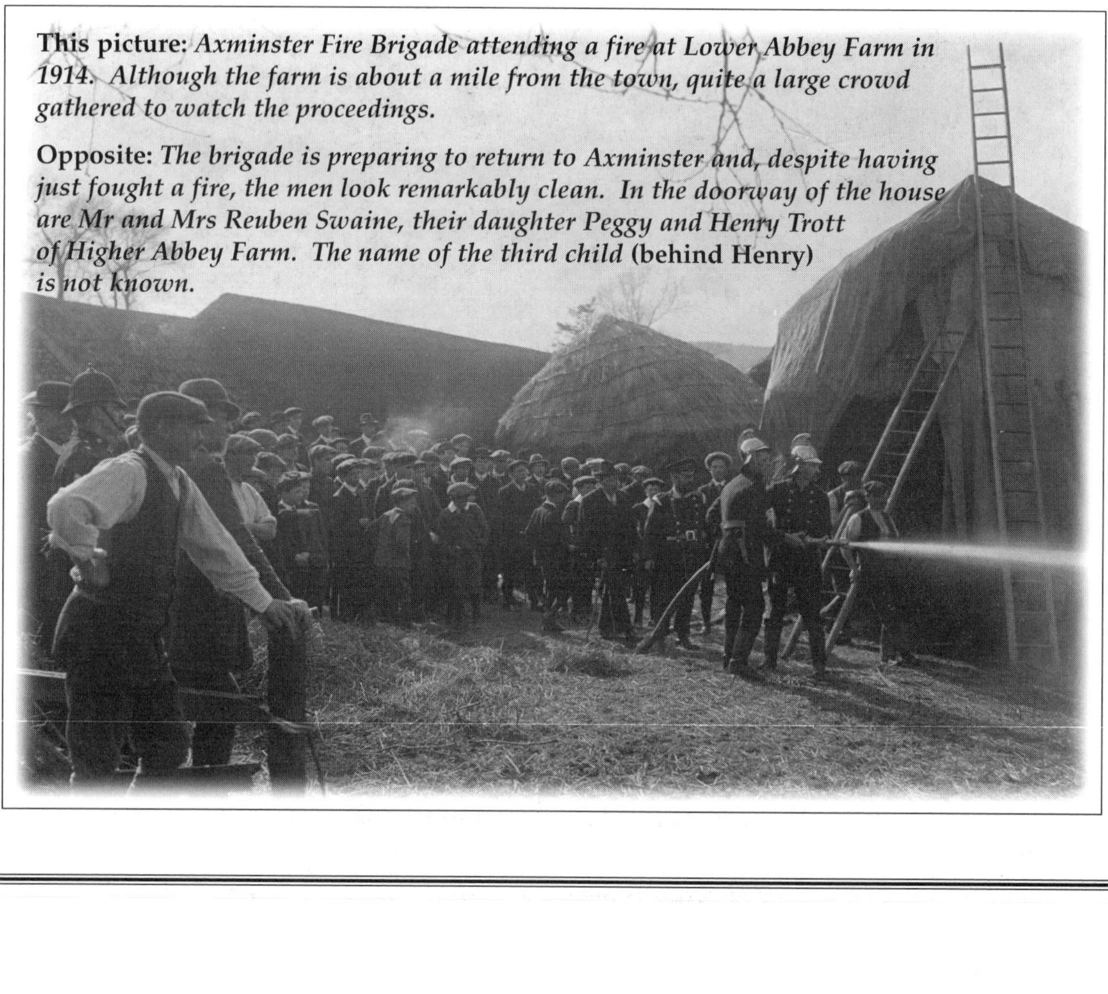

This picture: *Axminster Fire Brigade attending a fire at Lower Abbey Farm in 1914. Although the farm is about a mile from the town, quite a large crowd gathered to watch the proceedings.*

Opposite: *The brigade is preparing to return to Axminster and, despite having just fought a fire, the men look remarkably clean. In the doorway of the house are Mr and Mrs Reuben Swaine, their daughter Peggy and Henry Trott of Higher Abbey Farm. The name of the third child* (behind Henry) *is not known.*

13

THE FIRE BRIGADE

Axminster's first fire-engine was manually operated and did service for many years before wearing out in 1898 when the town was without any appliance for some months. Public concern was such that a meeting was held to discuss the obtaining of a new fire-engine. At the meeting the fire brigade's Chief Officer, W.E. Pitfield Chapple, suggested that a steam engine should be obtained. Those present at the meeting felt that the cost should be defrayed out of the rates, supplemented by voluntary subscriptions. The approval of the Parish Council, the Rural District Council, and the Board of Guardians had to be sought; they all gave their blessing. On 22 December 1898 the new machine went on public view outside the fire station in West Street before it was drawn to Trinity Square to be officially christened 'The Duke of Marlborough'. That noble lord's permission had been sought by Mr Pitfield Chapple, who spoke to the Duke in person on the telephone. The Duke's interest stemmed from the fact that he was the president of the National Fire Brigade's Union, and his celebrated ancestor, Jack Churchill, First Duke of Marlborough, is thought to have been born at Ashe, a couple of miles south of Axminster, and christened in St Mary's Church.

Included in the large crowd that had gathered were the Chief Fire Officers R. World of Seaton, L. Whetham of Bridport, Mr Pett of Exeter and Mr Gillingham of Chard. The vice-chairman of the Parish Council, Mr S.J. Bucknole, asked Miss Chapple to perform the ceremony, which she did to the sound of hearty cheering.

The horses were positioned and the engine driven to the mill leat, at the bottom of Castle Hill, where Miss Chapple set light to the engine's fire and 'full steam' was soon up. The pumping power of the engine was first tested with a long hose and a jet was thrown about 100 feet high. After that a trial was made with two short lengths, which also proved satisfactory. Exeter's Chief Fire Officer Pett conducted the test.

Left: *Axminster's fire station, West Street, decorated for what would appear to be a royal event, possibly King Edward VII's coronation in August 1902. The building on the left was the old National School (now the Post Office). The fire station was moved first to North Street, then to Lyme Street and finally to its home in Lyme Close.*

The engine, being of Merryweather's patent Gem pattern, was similar to those already in use in several West Country towns and able to pump at the rate of 300 gallons per minute. Many householders were insured against fire, which probably meant that charges for the brigade attending a fire were covered. Anyone who was not insured had to pay 5s. (25p) for a call-out, £2.2.0d (£2.10p) for the use of the engine, and a mileage rate for the horses. Afterwards there was a 10s.6d. (52½p) charge for cleaning the engine, hoses, etc.

Not everyone was happy with the new fire-engine. At the Annual Parish Meeting four months later a Mr Barnes wanted to know how the town stood with regard to the new engine and claimed that it was quite unnecessary for Axminster because they had hydrants about the town. He also pointed out that if 300 gallons a minute were pumped out of a well or small stream it would become dry in a short time. A further point was that neighbouring villages got the use of the appliance if they contributed £5 but the town of Axminster was saddled with a 6d. (2½p) rate. Mr Pitfield Chapple vigorously defended his pride and joy. The rate was much lower and would last for only two years, he claimed.

In 1910 Axminster found itself without a fire brigade, a situation that came about because the Chief Fire Officer and the chairman of Axminster Parish Council was one and the same person – Mr W.E. Pitfield Chapple, a local solicitor and a colourful character of late-Victorian Axminster. He resigned from the brigade in a fit of pique in April 1909 after failing to be re-elected to the Parish Council of which he had been chairman for 16 years. There were 23 candidates for the 15 seats and Pitfield Chapple came 18th with only 99 votes, 14 short of the 15th successful candidate, Mr W.J. Harris.

When he went, he took all the fire brigade's uniforms and most of the hose with him. It turned out that he had paid for them himself. Consequently all they were left with was an engine and the fire escape.

The fire brigade figured large in the discussions of the Parish Council during the next few years, *Pulman's Weekly News* telling us some time after Mr Pitfield Chapple's departure that there had been wanton damage at the fire station (at that time located in the next-but-one building to the right of the walkway down to the Tesco store).

The Parish Council sub-committee appointed to consider the fire brigade question reported that in spite of the instructions given to the caretaker of the fire station (Mr F. Silk), brackets and foundations had been pulled down from the walls of the station and taken away. As the inventory of the council's property at the fire station was not taken on the previous Friday evening, when the newly elected council first met, the committee had no idea of other articles that might have been removed. Mr Silk informed the committee that his son had removed the fittings from the walls of the station and, as he had been given express instructions not to allow anyone in the station except the members of the council, he had breached his instructions and the committee suspended him pending advice from the council. The sub-committee also reported that they had made an inventory of the appliances at the fire station.

Mr Hearn of the Parish Council stated that he intended to move at the next meeting the rescinding of the resolution that Mr Silk was caretaker of the council chamber as well as the fire station.

A further attempt by Mr Stocker, also of the Parish Council, to discuss the matter of the caretaker was blocked by the chairman because it was due to be considered at the next meeting. The council appointed Mr W.J. Enticott as captain of the fire station and he was instructed to test the fire escape and the hose at the station as soon as possible.

Mr Pitfield Chapple was a prime suspect as the man behind the removal of the fittings at the station, at least in the eyes of the council. Clerk John Gage was instructed by the council to seek him out and enquire whether he had given instructions for the brackets to be torn off the walls of the fire station. No trace of the outcome of those enquiries survive.

At a meeting on 12 September 1911 Mr Enticott,

Axminster Fire Brigade, c.1910, in Trinity Square.

A fire brigade practice night, c.1905. Although the bridge is almost certainly one over either the River Yarty or the River Axe, the precise locality is unknown.

the captain of the fire brigade, presented his annual report on the work of the brigade for the year ending 30 April. After the report he asked that the council consider supplying his force with 200–300 yards of new hose, plus a canvas dam. In the discussion that followed it was pointed out that according to the rules the captain's report should have been presented at the end of March, while the charges made by the captain for the engine attending fires and its not being used as often as possible were much criticised.

At that time the Parochial Sanitary Committee put forward the notion that the fire brigade should use the steamer (the engine) for pumping water from the river to flush the town sewers that it could reach, while the sewers on the higher levels could be flushed with water from the water cart. The Parish Clerk told the meeting that the fire brigade had been asked to flush the sewers on previous occasions, but had done so (as many as ten times a day) with the water cart. It seems that the fire brigade (or Mr Enticott at least) argued that the steamer should not be used for the purpose of flushing. It was a subject that was dragged out over many Axminster Parish Council meetings.

The cost of new uniforms was estimated to be around £120 and *Pulman's Weekly News* suggested that the people of Axminster had only themselves to blame – if they had voted for Mr Pitfield Chapple he would not have taken the equipment with him when he left!

Fire at Uphay Cottage on Sunday 20 June 1971.

14

AXMINSTER'S HOTELS AND PUBLIC HOUSES

Few would argue with the statement that the George Hotel was, and is, Axminster's premier hotel. It can certainly claim to be the town's oldest remaining watering-hole, occupying as it does, the same spot that it has filled for some five or six centuries. Along with its adjoining brew house (brewery) it was the property of Newenham Abbey, a connection that led to its earlier name of Cross Keys, which stemmed from the fact that part of the Papal coat of arms contained crossed keys.

Its fate after the Dissolution of the Monasteries, when Henry VIII left its parent abbey in ruins, is rather sketchy, but it did become the property of the lord of the manor of Axminster who, probably in the 1880s, sold the hotel to the Chard-based brewers Mitchell & Toms (later Mitchell, Bruton & Toms). The Cross Keys was destroyed by fire in 1759 but the following year arose phoenix-like from the ashes as the George Hotel. It may never be known for certain whether the hotel was named after George II (1727–60), his grandson George III (1760–1820) or indeed, England's patron saint. George II did not die until 25 October 1860, which leaves little time for his grandson to be the George in question.

George III visited the George Hotel on 13 August 1813, along with his Queen Sophia Charlotte of Mecklenburg-Strelitz, when he came to the town to visit Thomas Whitty's carpet factory. First he alighted 'at the turnpike gate' (Eastgate) from where he was borne by the gentlemen of Axminster into the town.

It was the height of the coaching era and the 16 coaches that passed through Axminster daily all arrived at and left from the George. One London coach bound for Exeter, via Salisbury, Dorchester, Bridport and Honiton, even advertised that passengers (on arrival in the early hours of the morning), could be 'shaved

GEORGE HOTEL, AXMINSTER.
FIRST CLASS FAMILY COMMERCIAL AND POSTING HOUSE
BILLIARDS
'BUS MEETS ALL TRAINS.
JAS NEWBERY.
JAS NEWBERY, PROPRIETOR.

M The Axminster Fat Stock Show — Jany 6 1912

1911			£	s	d
Nov 30	To 26 Cold Luncheons	@ 2/.	2	12	0
	" 5 Judges Dinners			12	6
	" 2 Reporters			5	0
	Drinks & Cet for Judges			7	6
			3	16	0

Settled By Cheque Jany 6th 1912 J Newbery

Right: *The bill for the Axminster Fat Stock Show committee's dinner held 30 November 1911 but not presented until 6 January the following year. If the George Hotel of the time produced fair up to the high standards of 2003, and we are sure James Newbery did, the diners had a treat for just 10s. (50p in modern money).*

Left: *The George Hotel, c.1946. Axminster's coaching inn can be seen here behind the now-demolished wall that once surrounded the car park.*

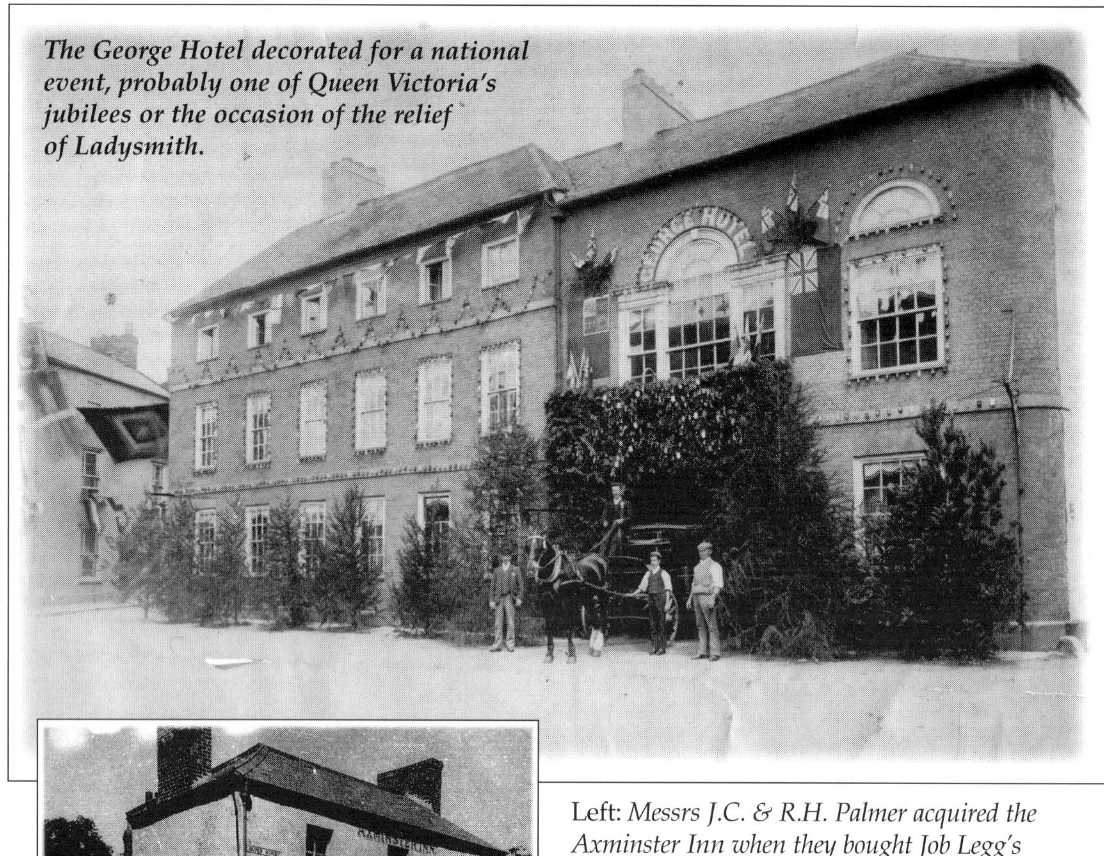

The George Hotel decorated for a national event, probably one of Queen Victoria's jubilees or the occasion of the relief of Ladysmith.

Left: *Messrs J.C. & R.H. Palmer acquired the Axminster Inn when they bought Job Legg's brewery in Bridport in 1892 and renamed it the Old Brewery. This picture was taken after 1892.*

Below: *After the Second World War, the narrowness of Lyme Street between the George Hotel and Webster's Garage was proving to be a traffic hazard. Its widening meant that part of the hotel, as seen here, was demolished around 1960.*

at Axminster by a lady barber'. One visitor who found the cuisine on offer at the George to his liking was Denison who called in on Axminster after the closure of the carpet factory. He records in his *Chronicles of the Coach*, that the only business of Axminster was that of 'the manufacture of tooth-brushes'. He did get a good lunch at the George, however.

In time the railway sealed the doom of the coaching era, and the motor car almost did the same to the railway. As both of these forms of transport became outmoded, so went some of the George Hotel's prosperity. It met the challenge of the railways head on by its acquisition of a horse-drawn bus that 'met all trains'. It did not say so, but one suspects that passengers only got a ride into the town if they were booked into the George. It remained as a posting inn until the 1920s and was popular with commercial travellers who could hire a pony and trap in order to make deliveries into the surrounding villages.

OLD BELL HOTEL,
AXMINSTER.
First-Class
Family and Commercial.
FREE HOTEL.
Posting in all its Branches.
BILLIARDS.
PROPRIETOR: W. J. DICKS.

By the 1940s the part of the George Hotel that looked up into Lyme Street had become an eyesore. It was only improved when that side of the hotel was removed in order that the road might be widened – it had become almost impossible for two vehicles to pass each other outside what was then Webster's Garage. Happily, the Adam fireplace in the Adam Lounge was just that little bit too far away from that part of the hotel to be in danger.

The principal hotel in Axminster before the George was the Dolphin, which was on the east side of Market Square. It closed in 1804 and the building was destroyed by fire in 1881 and rebuilt as a private dwelling.

The George Inn, as opposed to the George Hotel, was situated in the old Purzebrook House, reputed to have been built in the fifteenth century and an inn since the seventeenth. It was certainly an inn in 1830 when Axminster's Victorian historian, James Davidson, wrote about it. He had some strange ideas about Axminster streets, claiming that the George Inn was on Musbury Road 'in the time that it was the high road from London to Exeter that passed through White Pot (now Wide Post) Lane.' This has to be open to question – West Street and Anchor Hill were there at the time.

The motorists hurrying down what became the busy A35 trunk road in search of the West Country's sun and sand would have been horrified had they been confronted by the Cotley Harriers seen here outside the Hunters Lodge in 1911.

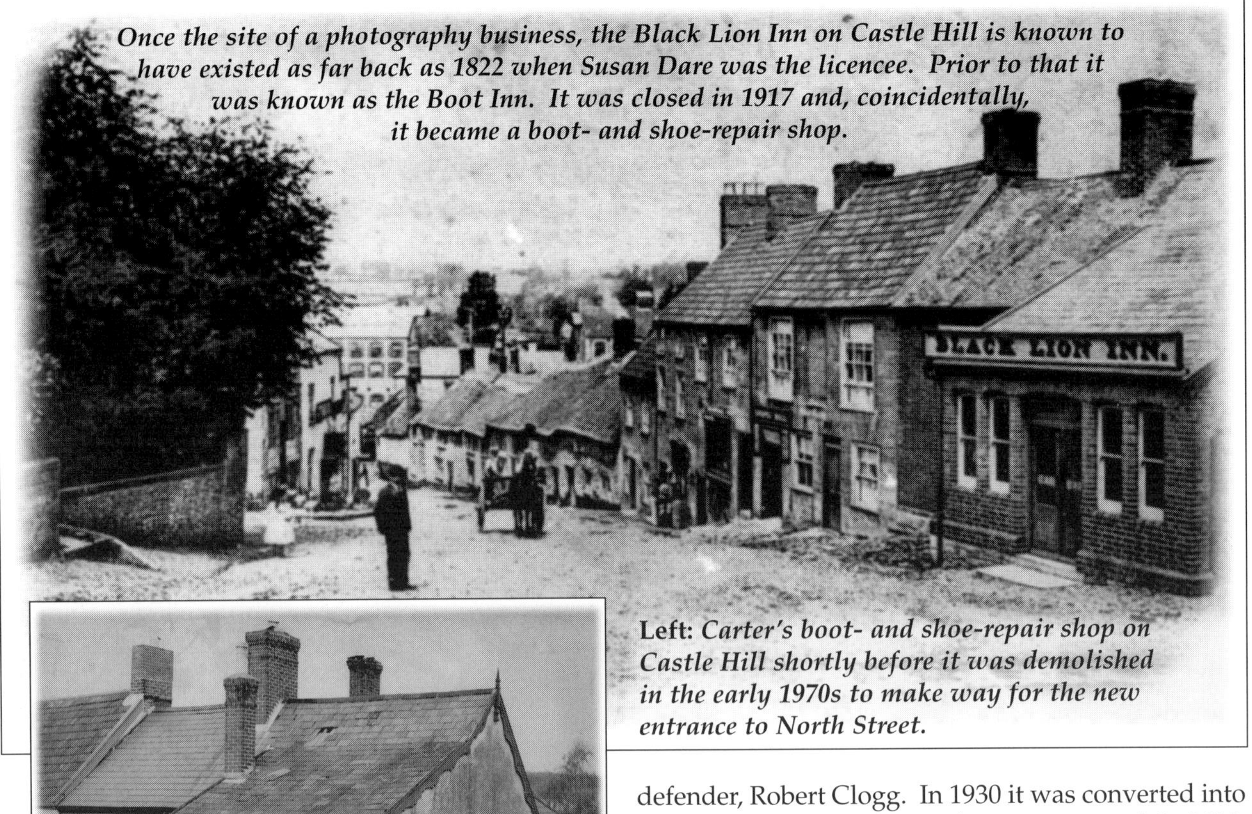

Once the site of a photography business, the Black Lion Inn on Castle Hill is known to have existed as far back as 1822 when Susan Dare was the licencee. Prior to that it was known as the Boot Inn. It was closed in 1917 and, coincidentally, it became a boot- and shoe-repair shop.

Left: *Carter's boot- and shoe-repair shop on Castle Hill shortly before it was demolished in the early 1970s to make way for the new entrance to North Street.*

In 1830 Matthew Drake was the innkeeper and held the property on lease from the manor of Axminster. There had been an earlier George Inn, said to have been where the South Street car park is located in 2003, and when it closed the sign of the George was taken up by the inn in Musbury Road. A Charles Henry Ewens took over the property in 1882. It seems to have ceased being an inn by 1891 when it was converted into two parts, one of which was occupied by Charles Gage, the Axminster auctioneer, the other by a well-known Axminster Town Football Club defender, Robert Clogg. In 1930 it was converted into three separate dwellings and remains as such in 2003.

The Old Bell Hotel formed an important part of Axminster's accommodation for visitors. Its proprietor between the 1940s and 1960s was Bill Hart. Probably apocryphal, it was said that it was dangerous to stay too long in the spacious entrance hall; lorries trying to negotiate the bend in the road on their way into Trinity Square had, on more than one occasion, crashed into the porch. Although the bypass, which was being discussed in 1945 and was finally opened in 1991, was said to be designed to put an end to this problem, in 2003 even bigger lorries still bring all other traffic to a standstill as they try to negotiate that bend. The problem is also exacerbated at the other end of the square where 'road narrowing' causes even more jams.

One of the more historic inns in the area is the Hunters Lodge at the junction of the B3165 and A35. Despite its claims to the contrary, it was not a

Two pictures of the lounge bar of the Old Bell Hotel in Trinity Square, c.1946. The Bell closed in 1971, the site being converted into a small shopping arcade.

coaching inn (there would have been no need to change horses just over a mile away from the George Hotel, which definitely was a coaching inn, and any casual coach passengers for Lyme Regis would have alighted at Red Lane, the main road to Lyme Regis).

The Lyme Road that in 2003 runs outside the inn was cut around 1850, which disproves the old fable that a highwayman was hanged at the crossroads outside the inn. Indeed there were no crossroads at this point, nor is there any proof that a highwayman was hanged there. It is far more likely that any such highwayman would have met his grisly end at the crossroads that did exist – half a mile up the road at the junction of Green Lane and Red Lane with the main coaching road.

Hunters Lodge was a small sixteenth-century inn that has been considerably altered down the years. It has become long and two storeyed, made from stone and cobb and with a bow porch. Over the years it had served as a farm and a blacksmith's shop and, between the two world wars, it even sold petrol from two pumps that stood in the corner nearest the end of what later became the car park.

During the nineteenth century the inn had an estate of 100 acres that included closes of orchards, meadows and pasture, plus arable land including the long-since demolished Borough Shot Farm. A private householder conjured up a roadside sign giving the area the name of Burrowshot, but this is in fact inaccurate.

The inn has never been short of personalities among its customers. His grandmother took Albert Manley, a local historian, to the inn in 1921 for his first drink – lemonade. That was during the tenancy of Mr Willmington. In 1991 the then landlord, the Australian opera singer Craig Sullivan, threw a party to mark Albert's 70 years as a customer. The first drink was on the house – but it was not lemonade!

It was Craig Sullivan who discovered the inglenook fireplace in the lounge bar behind a rather mundane and modern open fireplace. It has since been restored to its former glory. It is now one of the outstanding features of the place.

The Swan was near the junction of Musbury Road and White Pot (now Wide Post) Lane and was closed by 1817.

The Green Dragon has had two homes in the town. According to the Tithe Map of 1754 the first was on the opposite side of the road to what is now Goldini's Wine Bar (originally the Western Hotel and later the Cavalier). It closed in 1785 and moved to the foot of Castle Hill where it looked into Vale Lane. At one time it opened at 6p.m. for the convenience of the workers at the brush factories that were next door. It closed around 1988.

George Pulman is on record as saying that there was an inn at Weycroft called the 'Sine of the Sammon' (Sign of the Salmon). It had been closed for some time when Pulman produced his first edition of *The Book of the Axe*. Pulman also mentions a Red Lion on the road to Membury near Uphay, a small and virtually separate hamlet at the time.

Other long-since vanished or closed inns known to have existed include the Old Angel in Chard Street, the Anchor at the top of Anchor Hill and the Boot Inn at the top of Castle Hill (it changed its name to the Black Lion in 1822). There was also a Bear in Silver Street and the Railway Hotel at the foot of Anchor Hill. In addition, Trinity Square was home to the Golden Lion.

There have been a number of casualties among Axminster's inns and pubs since the 1960s – including the Phoenix, Trout, Green Dragon, White Hart, Old Bell, New Commercial and the Millwey. The latter opened in 1970 but in 2002 it was demolished, the site being scheduled for housing development.

Axminster 100% Charity Carnival, 1926.

A Prize of Half-a-guinea is yours if you can guess the combined weight of

Dr. W. LANGRAN	Our President,
Mr. H. JACKSON	Our Treasurer,
Mr. ARTHUR GAGE	Our Secretary
and	
Mr. JAMES CHADWICK	Winner of the Great Popular Election of 1925.

WHOSE AGES TOTAL $202\frac{3}{4}$ YEARS and HEIGHT 21ft. $10\frac{1}{2}$ins.

Fill in and sign your estimate on the Coupon below and sent it to the General Secretary not later than Saturday, October 23rd, when the correct weight will be ascertained by Dr. A. L. Crockford and published in *Pulman's Weekly News* of October 26th.

COUPON, PRICE 2D.

I estimate the total weight of the four Gentlemen named above to be ....

Name ....

Address ....

Alterations will cancel the entry. **(Please write clearly).**

You may send as Coupons as you wish.

Above: *Bill Stuart, landlord of the Axminster Inn, seen here receiving the carnival perambulator derby trophy won by his team in 1954. Making the presentation is Jim Medley.*

Below: *Irene Newbery, Axminster's carnival queen in 1953. Her attendants are,* left to right (wearing gowns): *Joy Male, Mary Huntley, June Boyland, Ethel Norman and Margaret Board.*

15

AXMINSTER CARNIVAL (THE BEST IN THE WEST)

The date of the first carnival in Axminster is thought to be 1891, when a local press report stated, '... a carnival was celebrated at Axminster last evening. It was by far the largest demonstration held in Axminster in the memory of the oldest inhabitants.'

During the evening, hundreds of people flocked into the town by rail and road and at 7.30p.m. the masqueraders met at the railway station and, headed by an escort of police, marched in procession to the town. Two steeds drew the Mayor, accompanied by his son and private secretary, in an elegant chariot. The Band of the Axminster Zouaves followed, playing an inspiring air. Axminster's fire brigade, with its engine fully horsed, showed that it was ready for any emergency. The fire brigades from Honiton and Chard were also present.

Among the tableaux were the Eddystone Lighthouse, with a revolving light, members of the past and present Axminster Fife and Drum Band, the Beer Smugglers and Guy Fawkes.

During the evening collections were made and the sum of £4.11s.8d. (£4.58 in modern money) was raised and, to accommodate visitors, late trains had been laid on to neighbouring towns.

At the start of the twenty-first century the East Devon carnival season starts in September (the 1900 carnival in Axminster was held on 24 May but, within a few years, switched to a November date). Early carnivals were one-day affairs and held on a Wednesday because that was Axminster's early-closing day and Thursday was market day, into which the jollities often overflowed. The 1900 festivities centred on a 'Grand Torch Light Procession'. As the Boer War was still raging there was an air of jingoism about the floats, which included The Relievers of Mafeking, Britannia's Daughters and the Capture of Kruger. As on any other important occasion, the Pride of the Axe Band was present.

By 1905 the programme had doubled from two to four pages and advertisements had made an appearance. That year the carnival was changed to a November date and was styled as the Nelson Centenary Carnival with the proceeds going to Axminster's Cottage Hospital. At the time the president was Dr William Langran, the chairman was Revd Newman and the secretary was Mr J.J. Payne. Among the advertisements was one from Messrs Southwoods, the Victoria Place wine merchants, offering ALS whiskey at 42s. (£2.20p) a dozen – 3s.6d. (17½p) a bottle! The Old Quay whiskey was even cheaper.

Samuel Enticott offered fish, fruit, game and rabbits from his South Street shop, while Sid Gill drew attention to his wedding cake speciality, his celebrated St Ivel sausages (fresh daily) plus refreshments in his café. The names of Enticott and Gill would persist on Axminster shop fronts until almost the end of the twentieth century.

The early carnivals gathered at the railway station and paraded through a town gay with flags and bunting and past a grand array of sideshows that offered prizes.

One of the entrants was Sambo the White Elephant, captured in Combpyne Alps, trained by Professor Barnham and giving penny rides. It is purely coincidental that Axminster Town Football Club's entry was next to 'a troupe of lively clowns'.

By 1925 the Southern Railway was offering cheap day tickets to Axminster from places such as Yeovil and Exeter as well as the intermediate branches for trains that arrived in Axminster between 2.00p.m. and 8.00p.m. The long-since forgotten Grey Bird Bus Company ran a late service to Lyme Regis and Bridport and the Devon General Company offered buses from Ottery St Mary at 2.45p.m. and 4.15p.m. via Honiton (3.20p.m. and 4.45p.m.). Ottregians missed the later fun – their last bus left for home at 9.00p.m.

The 1925 carnival programme included 'A Gorgeous Eastern Bazaar' in Trinity Square, which was said to come from 'the Sands of the Desert and would be attended with all the mysteries of the Orient.' The programme also told us that:

An Axminster Inn tableau for the 1907 carnival.

Below: *This picture is believed to have been taken in the grounds of the Shrubbery (now the West Street car park) in 1905. Although it is not certain that these characters were dressed up for the carnival, the people in the picture are,* left to right: *W.E. Pitfield Chapple, Jimmy Payne, W.G. Potter, 'Barney' Heal* (in the stocks), *Albert Silk, 'Titch' Plaster, Howard Sutton, Edwin Snell.*

HMS Victory, *a float entered in the 1905 carnival.*

Goods and chattels of every kind may be bought at the stalls and among them you'll find, the Refreshment Buffet very clean and so nice, where you'll get a sound meal at a moderate price.

If sweets and some 'baccy should next be your choice, push on through the crowd and lift up your voice.

Fitting gifts for your friends will be easily found, at the Chowringhee stall, so all gather round,

As the fun of the fair will there be conspicuous, but if you buy 'teazers' we pray you won't tickle us!

Confetti gives fun so please scatter a lot, and chance if the wife will be angry or not,

Our boatload of gas balloons sent in mid-ocean, so get one of air with no fear of explosion,

And if your pocket runs low and you wish to refill it, have a few shots at hoop-la – run by Ali Mehelit,

But don't rush at it madly, or you'll come down a cropper, as your pence you will need for the hundred-weight copper.

Then old Salad Ud Din and El Asis Es Saud have more things to show you, than Madam Tussaud.

We could write a lot more of our wonderful show, but time and the printer won't let us, and so, to enjoy the delights that await you today, be sure that you get here and don't stay away.

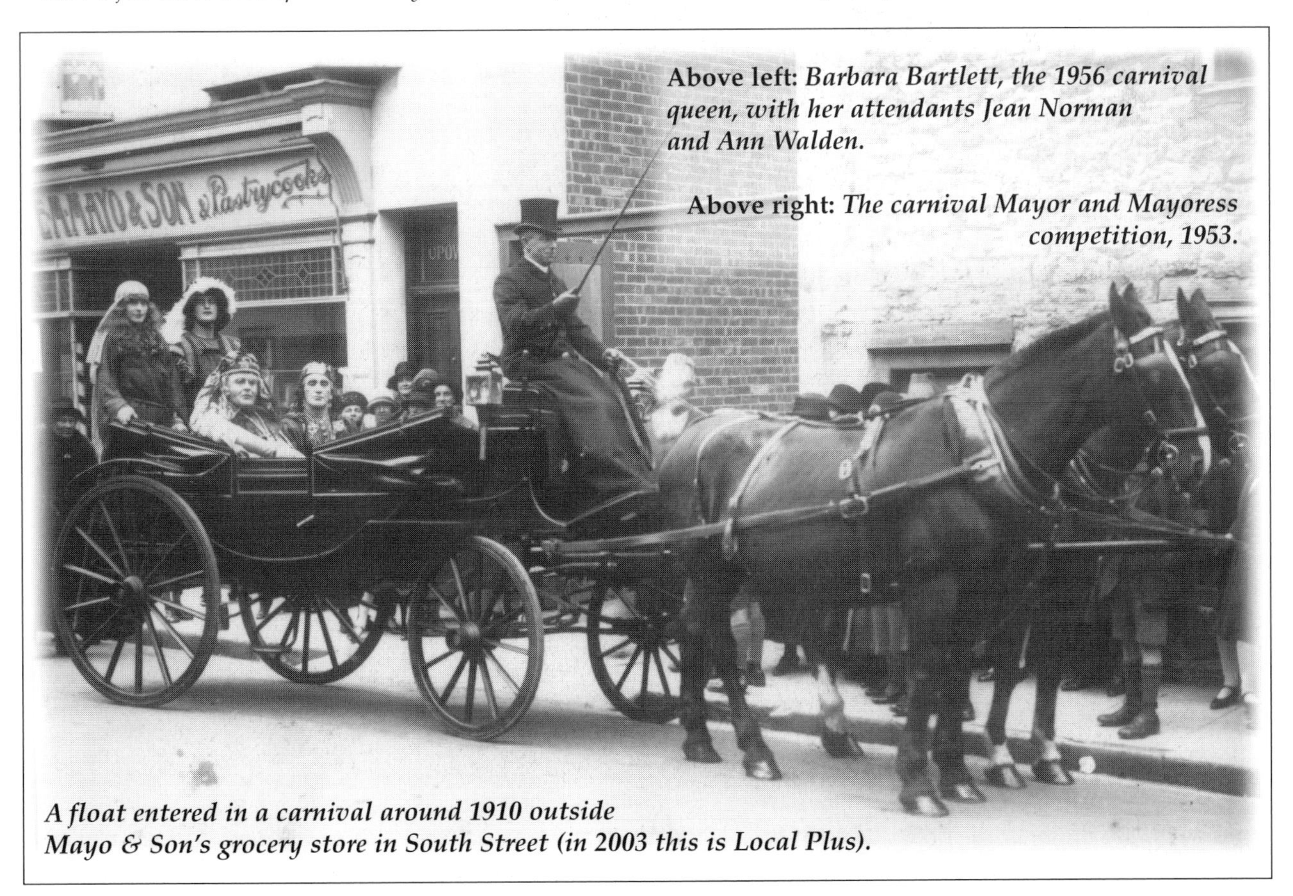

Above left: ***Barbara Bartlett, the 1956 carnival queen, with her attendants Jean Norman and Ann Walden.***

Above right: ***The carnival Mayor and Mayoress competition, 1953.***

A float entered in a carnival around 1910 outside Mayo & Son's grocery store in South Street (in 2003 this is Local Plus).

Right: *The 1957 carnival queen with her attendants.* Left to right, back row: *Frank Rowe, Tom Mayo, Emmy Sheppard, W.G. Paynter;* front: *Eunice Broom, James Rowe* (in front), *Prudence Hiscox (queen) Cicely Brown, Wendy Crockett.*

Below: *Elaine Huxford, carnival queen in 1992* (left). *In the centre is Mrs Barry Draper with Tracey Knight, the princess, on the right.*

Unlike modern carnivals, where the emphasis is on bigger and better floats aimed at bigger and better prize money, Axminster's early carnivals were almost entirely aimed at fun and laughter and one went to them prepared to get the occasional soaking!

Indeed, from time to time the carnival has been postponed because of wet weather. This was the case in 1999, but, a year later in 2000, it was postponed because of the fuel crisis that had resulted from protesters picketing major oil depots.

There have been many stalwart workers on behalf of the carnival. Emmy Sheppard and Frank Rowe are mentioned elsewhere in this book. The carnival's secretary in 2003 is Geoff Enticott whose first official post was that of vice-chairman in 1978. He has served in many ways ever since. Nellie Weller is another who will be remembered for her work, especially behind the scenes with the fancy-dress competition.

After seven years' break because of the Second World War, the carnival restarted in 1947, when its first officers were: chairman, Ernie Gill; secretaries, Arthur Gage and Val Enticott; treasurer, Stuart Yeo. Mr Yeo, who lives in Seaton in 2003 at the grand of age of 99, held the treasurer's post until 1963. From 1971 until 1987, Mr Gordon Dendle handled the financial affairs. Among many secretaries were Frank Rowe, Mrs A. Jeffery and Jackie Lack. Peter Perryman, the chairman in 2003, took office in 1986.

There are no records of pre-war carnival queens, and the only two postwar queens to have served for successive years are Tracey Graham (1987 and 1988) and Elaine Huxford (1991 and 1992). Since 1994 the reluctance of girls to come forward has meant that there were no carnival queens in 1994, 1995, 1996, 1998, 1999, 2001 or 2003.

Looking back on four years as either princess, attendant or queen, Elaine Voysey (née Huxford) remembers:

The first year I entered (1987) I was made the princess' attendant only I really wanted to be the princess as I wanted to wear the tiara. But we had a great time, I think I was about 12 and I remember getting home from school and having tea before getting dressed in my lovely pink dress. I think it was my Mum who had the most fun, as she would spend ages styling my hair. We both walked miles selling tickets that year. The following year I made princess' attendant again. This time we went to the Guildhall and were judged on personality and looks and suitability, as it was deemed dangerous to send children off selling tickets alone.

In 1991 I again entered the competition where you had to face a panel of judges. This time I got to wear the crown – third time lucky as they say. Although I was now older and could cope with the late nights, there were not as many functions to attend.

My final year as part of the royal party was 1992 (although who knows what might happen now that I have two girls of my own). That year I was allowed to pick the material for my own dress – I chose a white flower material. I was almost 18 and had a wardrobe full of long dresses that no longer fitted me. But I did have four years of great fun!

The royal party after the crowning of the queen in Trinity Square in 1991. **Left to right:** *Debbie Thompson (princess), Joanne Lack (princess), Debbie Stewart (attendant), Elaine Huxford (queen).*

Postwar Axminster Carnival Queens

1947 Eileen Harrison/ Doreen Evans
1948 Audrey Sparks
1949 Peggy Denslow
1950 Nancy Bishop
1951 Peggy Davey
1952 Margaret Duke
1953 Irene Newbery
1954 Rosemary Hooper
1955 Marina Bowditch
1956 Barbara Bartlett
1957 Prudence Hiscox
1958 Christina Welch
1959 Shelia Taylor
1960 June Loftus
1961 Maureen Key
1962 June Williamson
1963 Not known
1964 Not known
1965 Linda Matherick
1966 Jennifer Brooks
1967 Valerie Soaper
1968 Lynne Jaquet
1969 Jenny Parsons
1970 Sharon Neill
1971 Pamela Bowditch
1972 Heather Aplin
1973 Pat Clark
1974 Sandy Sharland
1975 Anita Edgerton
1976 Caroline Davis
1977 Yvonne Chick
1978 Susan Thompson
1979 Carol Pridden
1980 Penny Babbs/Sharon Taylor
1981 Marie Lacey
1982 Joanne Ambrose
1983 Rebecca Shephard
1984 Not known
1985 Michelle Demkiw
1986 Julia Horn
1987 Tracey Graham
1988 Tracey Graham
1989 Claire Enticott/Sheila Perham
1990 Michele Cloud
1991 Elaine Huxford
1992 Elaine Huxford
1993 Lisa Cowling
1994 No queen
1995 No queen
*1996**
1997 Kerry Chamney
1998 No queen
1999 No queen
2000 Claire Kelland
2001 No queen
2002 Jessica Chapple
2003 No queen

** In 1996, in the absence of a queen, nine-year-old Jenna Wellman, the carnival princess, led the procession in the queen's float.*

Axminster en fête for Queen Victoria's diamond jubilee in 1897. Most of Axminster's other great occasions began either in the church or Trinity Square. Here the town, in procession, marched to The Latches on Chard Street for sports followed by tea and buns.

16

OTHER HIGH DAYS

Axminster's townspeople have always shown great enthusiasm when celebrating a great occasion. The diamond jubilee of Queen Victoria on 20 June 1897 was one such occasion and, according to *Pulman's Weekly News*, was 'right loyally celebrated'.

A committee had been formed under the chairmanship of Mr W.E. Pitfield Chapple, who seemed to have had a hand in almost every Axminster pie of the time. Its secretary was Mr G.R. Stevens. The inhabitants of the town had been asked to do all they could to decorate their premises and they responded magnificently. From every house bunting was hung and each shop displayed emblems of loyalty in doors and windows. Where possible, lines of flags crisscrossed the streets, each bearing suitable mottoes. At the residences of Messrs Pitfield Chapple, A. Paul, W.J. Enticott, Nicholls, W. Gapper and Harris among others, as well as in front of the George Hotel, some ornamental trees were planted.

The most conspicuous decorations were in front of the George Hotel, where fairy lamps and greenery had been installed. Others of note included those at Hilary House and the town's inns and pubs. Ornamental arches had been erected at suitable vantage points, such as the entrance to Trinity Square, the top of Anchor Hill and the end of South Street. The Royal Standard (wrongly) was flown from the church tower and the Union Flag from the Constitutional Club and Council Room.

Celebrations for Queen Victoria's diamond jubilee in 1897 in Trinity Square. The seemingly disused building on the right became the Midland Bank. The scaffolding around the church tower was for the benefit of the workmen who were replacing the outer stonework that was crumbling away. Some cannon balls and musket shots, which had been embedded there during the Civil War, were found at the time and in 2003 can be seen in Axminster Museum.

Queen Victoria's diamond jubilee, 1897. After the ceremony in Trinity Square the children paraded through Victoria Place towards the sports field at The Latches in Chard Street.

That morning the good people of Axminster would have breakfasted early after being woken up by the noise of cannon fire. The band of the H Company of the 3rd VBDR (Volunteer Battalion Devonshire Regiment) assembled in Trinity Square and played the National Anthem. At midday the members of the entire company assembled in the churchyard under the command of Sergeant Instructor Hastings, and a *feu de joie* was fired. The National Anthem was again played and a large crowd joined in by singing.

A procession was then formed and, headed by the band, it marched through the town. After the band came the Volunteers, followed by the schoolchildren, ladies of the town, tradesmen and members of the various friendly societies. Also present were the Axminster Church Lads' Brigade, with their band, the Wesleyan Fife and Drum Band and several

Men at work erecting the floral arch at the entrance to Trinity Square to mark the Queen Victoria's golden jubilee (1887). The George (in the background), *is the sole survivor of Axminster's three town-centre inns that can be seen here. The other two, the Old Bell on the left and the New Commercial on the right, were both closed towards the end of the twentieth century.*

V. R.

"FOR HEARTHS AND HOMES."
"DEFENCE NOT DEFIANCE."

H Company (Axminster) 3rd Volunteer Battalion Devon Regiment.

PROGRAMME

OF TWO

EVENING CONCERTS

To be held at the

BOARD SCHOOLS, AXMINSTER,

ON

Friday & Saturday, April 29th & 30th, 1898.

Proceeds in aid of the erection of the New Range and Targets at Marsh Farm, Dalwood.

PRICES OF ADMISSION

FRIDAY—Reserved Seats, 3s.; Second Seats, 2s.; Third Seats, 1s.

SATURDAY—Reserved Seats, 3s. (limited); Front Seats, 2s.; Second Seats, 1s.; Back Seats, 6d. (limited).

Plan of Room at Mr. E. Snell's, Stationer, &c., Axminster.

Doors open each evening 7.30 p.m. Commence at 8 p.m. Carriages 10-15 p.m.

GOD SAVE THE QUEEN.

Like the rest of the town, South Street was decorated for Queen Victoria's golden jubilee. At its junction with Silver Street a decorated archway nears completion.

Above:
Axminster Militia Band forcing its way into a crowded Trinity Square during the diamond jubilee celebrations.

Axminster Wesleyan Sunday-school outing, c.1900.

mounted youths in fancy dress.

On arrival at Cloakham Lawn in Chard Road, cheers for the Queen were given before Mr Real of the Green Dragon provided an excellent hot dinner in a very large marquee. From the list of names given in *Pulman's Weekly News* it seems that only the great and the good of the town actually had dinner.

Sports followed and the jollities, including alfresco dancing in Trinity Square, went on until the early hours and, because there were no licensing hours at the time, the pubs did a roaring trade.

Like Axminster, Kilmington woke to find itself bathed in glorious June sunshine. The bells of St Giles' Church that began pealing at 6a.m. probably helped the waking process! At noon there was a full choral service that was conducted by the Revd Owen with Miss Scott at the organ. On leaving the church the congregation joined the procession that was forming outside and, headed by the band of H Company (Axminster), 3rd VBDR, everyone made for Coryton Park where a free dinner was provided for the men beneath the trees. *Pulman's Weekly News* ended its report of the day with 'a free tea was also provided for the women and children.' Between the two meals there were many speeches, mostly based on the theme of 'God Save the Queen', but 'the Bishop and clergy of all denominations' were not forgotten. Nor were Messrs R. & C. Snell for placing the grounds (of Coryton Park) at the village's disposal. Sports were 'indulged in', as was dancing, and there were a large number of visitors present (from where they came is not clear as Shute and Whitford held their own jollifications).

Although the coronation of Edward VII was delayed for a couple of months because of the King's ill health, when it did take place in August 1902, Axminster again celebrated the occasion in style.

The day began when Mr Pitfield Chapple, chairman of the Axminster Parish Council, fired a one-gun royal salute from a new 7lb cannon that he had acquired. On a more peaceful note the bells of St Mary's pealed out across the roofs of the old Minster town calling the people to a Holy Communion Service held at 8a.m. The bells rang intermittently throughout the day and Axminster groaned under the weight of the flags and bunting that hung from every building.

Decorated arches, made with tree branches and flags, were again placed at strategic points throughout the town. Mr Pitfield Chapple had erected a particularly large one outside his Shrubbery home on Anchor Hill where the West Street car park and Co-op superstore are located in 2003.

It was a matter of honour for the tradesmen of the town to come up with the best decorated premises. A leading contender in 1902 was the Western Hotel, later the Cavalier (in 2003, Goldini's Wine Bar). It was just along the road from Mr Pitfield Chapple's arch, which it rather put in the shade, no doubt much to the annoyance of that august leader of Axminster society!

Other premises that were worthy of mention included that of Mr Parsons, the West Street coach builder and, in Trinity Square, W.G. Harris' grocery

The registry office in Silver Street at the turn of the last century. The railings were utilised as part of the war effort during the Second World War.

shop, Mr Boas' New Commercial Hotel, and Mr E. Snell's auction house.

The best, however, had to be the George Hotel – among the flags that covered the front of the building was a gas jet marked with the initials ER. The Post Office, in Chard Street at the time, also attracted much admiration, even if the stamps inside still bore the head of Queen Victoria. The new postboxes marked ER rather than VR had probably not yet made their appearance (one of the latter can still be seen at Weycroft Mill).

There was a mid-morning service at St Mary's Church, where the entire handsome iron railings (later requisitioned during the Second World War's salvage drive) were almost hidden under a myriad of fairy lamps. Afterwards a procession formed outside and, with the band of H Company at its head, marched to Cloakham Lawn where Mr George Heal of the Green Dragon Hotel provided a hot dinner for around 500 people. In the afternoon a free tea was also given. Sports and maypole dancing followed before the evening fireworks display and more dancing in Trinity Square.

Even the inmates at the workhouse were remembered with presents and extra rations, but not, it would seem, to the extent of being allowed to mingle with the diners at the free meals in town.

News that a peace treaty to end the Boer War (1899–1902) had been signed reached Axminster on the first up train on the morning of 4 June 1902. Immediately the old Minster town vanished under a sea of flags and bunting and Axminster made merry while cannons and detonators were discharged. Although *Pulman's Weekly News* of the time doesn't say so, it is safe to assume that every pub in town did a roaring trade as toast after toast was made to England, its monarch and the men responsible for bringing the Boers to the peace table.

The Union Flag fluttered proudly in the early summer breeze, peal after peal of bells drifted over the roof tops and the band of H Company under Bugle-Major Frank Fry, and Axminster's Town Band, The Pride of the Axe, under Bandmaster George Fry, played in different parts of the town. All the schools, shops and businesses were closed.

St Mary's was crowded at noon for the Thanksgiving Service at which the Volunteers were in attendance. The Revd Slipper (Kilmington) conducted the service supported by the vicar of Axminster, the Revd A. Newman, who 'preached an excellent sermon'.

A quickly arranged married v singles match took place at the old cricket field in North Street that afternoon; the married men lost. In the evening, the cricket field was packed with dancers enjoying the music of the Volunteers. We trust the groundsman kept them off the square!

The towns of Seaton and Lyme Regis wired Axminster asking for aid with bands to help with their own jollifications. Seaton had a Fife and Drum Band at the time, but obviously wanted reinforcements, and it is unthinkable that a seaside resort such as Lyme Regis would not have had a band. Lyme's SOS was answered when the Pride of the Axe Band went there that evening to play.

Unlike the coronation of his father (Edward VII), that of George V took place on time in the age-old fashion of English monarchs in Westminster Abbey on 22 June 1911.

It was celebrated in style throughout his kingdom as well, especially in the West Country, which, apart from aberrations in the shape of the Duke of Monmouth in 1685 and, three years later, the arrival of Dutch Billy (William of Orange, later to become King William III), has been steadfast and true in its support of the monarchy.

Axminster was again awash with flags and bunting and the standard of decorations were said to have been the best for many years. It was, after all, an age in which little excuse was needed to get the flags out, as is evidenced by the fact

Left: *An outing to the caves at Cheddar for the staff of W.G. Potter & Son's furniture business around 1925. Mr W.G. Potter is standing; Mr 'Jack' Potter is in the seat behind the driver (Wally Newbery).*

that even the local cricket club's annual track and sports meeting found the town en fête.

There was a temporary, rustic bandstand in Trinity Square, which was decorated with red, white and blue bunting and was illuminated at night by 'fairy lamps and other devices'. The decorations and lighting of the bandstand had been undertaken by Edwin Dawkins & Son Ltd, whose business premises in Victoria Place, 'decorated in an artistic and pretty style', had been declared the best in town by the judges, the Misses Stafford, Langran and Cornish. The premises of Mr W. Connett attracted much comment with the model sailing boat outside, which was 'suitably illuminated and looked extremely pretty'.

Axminster Town Band, c.1950.

W.H.B. Knight gave prizes for the best-decorated and illuminated houses. Competition was keen and the display, especially at night, was the best ever seen in Axminster. Sadly *Pulman's Weekly News* did not list the winners.

Adult sports followed the tea (not a wise idea for indigestion sufferers) and there was dancing until 8p.m. when the procession, which numbered approximately 1,700, returned to Trinity Square for more dancing and a firework display.

The inmates of the workhouse were not forgotten although, once more, they were not allowed to join the procession. Instead they got extra fare and joined in the festivities in Trinity Square.

The following evening there were 'old English sports' at The Latches, which were well attended despite the rain. For the curious, these sports included skittling for a live pig (won by C. Neale), walking the greasy pole for a leg of mutton (won by H. Hyde, a well-known Axminster footballer of the time) and cutting off the cock's head (won by Mr Martin).

Out at Kilmington the festivities also began with peals from the bells of the Parish Church. No class distinction here; at 1p.m. all parishioners sat down to a free luncheon in a tent on the cricket field with Colonel Hooper presiding. Revd H. Bowden, Mr R. Bastable, Mr R. Snell, Mr W. Snell and Mr W. Trott supported him. There was also a free tea later in the day and the almost obligatory sports followed. Dancing took place later in the tent to music supplied by Mrs Clist. There was also a bonfire at the cricket field. In charge of all the festivities was a committee with Mr Harry Hurford as secretary and Revd Bastable as treasurer.

Although Edward VIII's coronation in 1937 went ahead, it was George VI who was crowned after the Prince of Wales' abdication in the wake of the Simpson affair.

By coincidence the first carpet made at Axminster for over a century was completed on 14 May of that year at the new factory in Gamberlake. This fitting climax to the coronation week had been brought about by the untiring efforts of Mr Harry Dutfield, the managing director of the company that was formed to revive the industry in the town. *Pulman's Weekly News* reported:

> *The carpet made on Friday was made on one of the four looms by hands brought from Kidderminster. Though it was first intended to only install two looms, a further two were obtained and further ones will be installed by September. At present thousands of pounds worth of machinery has been installed.*

Possibly a golden opportunity was missed here – there is no record that the first carpet was sent to Buckingham Palace as a gift.

Axminster's centenarian, Mrs Mary Sprague, was among the 1,400 people who sat down to tea at the football field after the children's fancy dress and sports had finished. They all sat in what was described as a large marquee. Among the fancy-dress prizewinners were Ivor Chubb, Kathleen Pitman, Barbara McNeil, Marion Cloud, Donald Henley and Ramona Fowler. Winners of the races included a T. (Tim?) Moulding who came first in the sack race and the potato race (?) and a B. Broom was first in the ladies bun-eating competition (shame on you Bertha!).

A winner of a different kind was Mr Williams of Alexandra Road, a sorting clerk at the local Post Office who received the Coronation Medal for 30 years' service.

The news that the Second World War was about to end reached Axminster late in the evening of 7 May 1945 and the children were given two days off school. Quiet at first, Axminster soon began to put out the flags and bunting.

The day began with a Holy Communion at St Mary's. The church was again crowded for a special service that evening. There were also services at the other churches in the town with the American Forces' chaplin, Captain Powell, conducting the one held at the Methodist church where, at the end, the British and the American anthems were sung and the organist played the 'Hallelujah Chorus'.

The church bells were rung intermittently under the captaincy of the 79-year-old Harry Sansom who had been ringing for more than 60 years. In fact, for Mr Sansom and the 83-year-old Jim White, it was the third occasion that they had rung victory peals after British wars. 'Back in the Boer War we used to ring after every big event; I can remember ringing when Mafeking and Ladysmith were relieved,' recalled Mr Sansom. The other ringers on parade were Messrs J.C. Davey, Jack Board, A. Henley, D. Seward, C.E. Tiller, W. Sprague, E. Arnold (Musbury) and W. Stone (Combpyne). In addition, the Axminster Youth Band, under Mr C.E. Turner, played selections in Trinity Square and all the pubs were permitted to remain open until 11p.m. – just one hour extra after five and a half years of the greatest war the world had ever known. The Bench was hardly being generous!

As always, Axminster's celebrations centred on Trinity Square, where spontaneous singing by a large crowd soon started. After a round of popular choruses, everyone joined hands for the singing of 'Auld Lang Syne' as the church clock struck midnight.

Happily, VE Day coincided with the visit of Paulo's Circus and there was a full house for both performances, the first of which was attended by 340 Axminster children whose admission fees had been paid by the Axminster Victory Committee.

By 1977, when Queen Elizabeth II's silver jubilee was celebrated, television had arrived and many people spent much of the day watching the day's events in the comfort of a favourite armchair with ample supplies of food and drink close at hand. For the more energetic the festivities started on the Saturday with a sherry reception followed by a Minster Gala Concert, featuring soloist Isobel Buchanan. On the actual day, Monday 3 June, there was more music, but first a senior citizens' dinner was held followed by a children's ticket-only street party. That evening the music on the Minster Green was provided by Steve Black, Tree Star and Guitar Works – a far cry from celebrations held at the end of the Boer War in 1902.

Kilmington was a trifle more sedate although a Teddy bears' parade through the village and then a Teddy bears' picnic and tea party in the Village Hall sounded interesting. It was there that the children of the village received their jubilee mugs.

Axminster's 1953 coronation celebrations.

Above: *Old folks' party, 1964.*

Above: *Old folks' party, January 1981.*
Left to right: *Jack Sansom (aged 96), Michael Steer (the Mayor), Marie Lacey (carnival queen), Mrs E. Butcher (aged 96).*

Below: *The old folks' party at the Guildhall, 1972.*

Left: *Axminster Conservative Club dinner in Gill's Café in 1952. Local miller Les Morrish is in the middle of the front row.*

Above: *The official opening of Axminster Museum in 1982. The Mayor, Councillor Michael Steer* (left), *and Frank Rowe, Axminster's lord of the manor, are in the stocks.* Also included in the picture are: *Herbert Jeffery, James Rowe, Mr Norton and Jack Newbery.*

Left: *Opening of the new library in South Street in July 1971, by Simon Day, chairman of the Devon County Council Library and Museums Committee. Previously the library was housed in what is now Tesco's Walk.* Left to right: *Lilian Lovatt (town clerk), Mrs Olof, Michael Olof (Axminster representative on the Devon County Council), Simon Day, Fred Smith (chairman, Axminster Parish Council), William Atkinson (branch librarian), Pat Penwarden (vice-chairman, Axminster Parish Council), ?, Mrs Smith.*

Left: *Gerald Hurford, president of Axminster Young Farmers' Club, handing over the board recording their officers between 1933 and 1983 to Herbert Jeffery of Axminster Museum. The club was formed in 1933 and held its first meetings in the Church Rooms in West Street, which has since become the Post Office. The first function they held was a dance attended by several young female shop workers from Edwin Dawkins. The young farmers were not amused because they thought that only farmers should be allowed in.*

Right: *Kilmington silver jubilee parade, 1977.* Geoff Brown (centre) *took time off from acting as scorer for the cricket club to join the procession. The lady with the bicycle is Mrs Laird.*

The dawn of the new millennium was marked in Axminster by the burying of a time capsule at St Mary's Church. Among the items buried were a copy *Pulman's Weekly News* of 24 December 1999, a collection of parish magazines and a photographic record of the businesses in the town. On the big night itself over 1,000 people crowded into Trinity Square, where everyone lit a millennium candle and later watched the firework display.

Kilmington's celebrations began with a torchlight procession that moved from the Village Hall and headed for the Shute Armada Beacon for a singsong around a bonfire. Later, villagers brought their own food and drink to the specially decorated hall for a party. A pig spit proved to be very popular and a gas-fired beacon on the church tower proved to be a great (and safe) attraction. Competing with the beacon was the maroon that was fired from the tower at the last midnight of the twentieth century and 'Auld Lang Syne', which was supposed to end the proceedings, was the signal for the partying to increase in tempo.

There are hopes for more such high days in the future. For example, a source of local pride is the official twinning of Axminster with the Normandy town of Douvres-la-Déliverande, which was signed and sealed on 24 October 1999 after four years of negotiations. A party of 31 people left Axminster for Douvres, a town of some 14,000 souls deep in the heart of the Calvados region, where gifts were exchanged between the two towns. The chairman of the Axminster Twinning Association Committee, Steve Haynes, led the Axminster party and was accompanied by Chris Scott, Erica Dunsmore, Roy Winterburn, Graham Godbeer, Caroline Hillyard and David Capon.

17

HORTICULTURAL AND AGRICULTURAL SOCIETIES

The East Devon and Dorset Agricultural Show was started in 1837. The poster for its third annual show, staged at Axminster on 4 November 1840, is held in Axminster Museum. It was printed by local printer, Mr Willis, and it states that there was a condition that all the cows, heifers, bulls or sheep entered had to be certified – except breeding ewes – not to have been fed on corn, meal, linseed or oil cake or any other food whatsoever except grass, hay and roots. The reason given for this was that 'since the same may respectively have been in the possession of the owner.'

There were also 'Premiums' awarded to the agricultural labourer who had brought up the largest family without parochial aid, and to the labourer and female servant who lived or worked the longest, either on the same farm or with one master, and could bring the best testimonials for honesty, sobriety and general good conduct from their employers.

In a less TV-orientated world small communities such as Axminster enjoyed these events as red-letter days. Indeed, the annual show held by the Axminster Cottage Garden Society was one of the highlights of Axminster's passing days. Its first show on record was in August 1865, on a now-unknown site but, almost certainly, it took place in a field on the edge of town, loaned to the society by a local farmer. Cottagers and gardeners entered separately, the former receiving the higher prizes. (Cottagers were men showing produce from their own gardens, whereas gardeners were showing it from the gardens of the people for whom they worked. Gardeners and labourers of subscribers (members) were allowed to enter only if they grew the entries on their own land. Professional gardeners and nursery owners were invited to send produce but did not receive prizes.) The money prizes were rather good for 1865; the cottagers' first prizes ranging from 1s. (5p in modern money) to 6s. Gardener's prizes did not go above 3s.

The classes included peas in half pecks (7½lbs); broad beans per peck; kidney beans (dwarf or scarlet runners), 50 of each; onions 18 of each type; potatoes per half peck (unlike modern shows where five are submitted on a plate); cherries, gooseberries, raspberries and plums were per pound per entry; apples were nine for each variety and cucumbers came in a brace.

By 1892 the society's name was changed to the

Above: *The 1939 Devon County Show was held on Chard Road where Millwey Rise housing estate stands in 2003. This prizewinning stand of Norrington & Sons of Castle Hill attracted a lot of attention.*

Right: *The judges and stewards of the poultry section of the show held in 1952 in Church Street.*

Officers and committee members of the Axminster Union District Agricultural Association Show in 1911.

Axminster & District Mutual Improvement Society and, two years later, it became the Axminster & District Horticultural and Cottage Garden Society. Two exhibitions were held, the first in August, and the second in November.

The president of the society at that time was Mr W.H.B. Knight, probably a member of the family that built the Catholic church in Lyme Road which replaced the original place of worship built some 30 years earlier in 1830. The vice-presidents included Sir William de la Pole, Bart, Captain Cann, JP, and Mr W.G. King. The treasurer, since at least 1865, was Mr E. Chapple and the secretary Mr J.A. Stevens.

By now honey had been added to the schedule and it had to be shown in either six 1lb jars or three 1lb bottles. The ladies had their own classes for table decoration and bouquets. The entrance fee was 6d. with prizes ranging from 5–10s. Not a bad return if you won.

Obviously such a society would play an important part in any war. Indeed, during the Second World War gardening as a means of producing food was very much encouraged. At the time the society was known as the Axminster & District Allotments Association and its first wartime show was held in 1943. It raised £140 for the Red Cross Agricultural Fund and was the first Victory Garden & Home Produce Show. At that time there were 400 members. The following year all the entries were auctioned after the show by local auctioneer Arthur Gage and keen bidding realised £22; two frame cucumbers on their own were sold for a guinea (£1.05p) each.

For obvious reasons members of the society put in a bulk order for their seed requirements, the potato order being for as much as four tons, and the fertiliser order included 15 tons of Langport Lime.

In 2003, the society continues to flourish as evidenced in the part it plays in the popular two-day Axe Vale Festival of Gardening and Crafts held just outside the town on the road to Kilmington. The event was the brainchild of the late Dave Swarbrick who was looking to introduce a quality floral, gardening and craft exhibition to East Devon, enabling visitors to see the skills of the South West. The first show took place on 24 and 25 June 1995 when around 5,000 people attended to view the stands of 109 exhibitors. Originally any profit was put towards the fund-raising efforts of the Flamingo Pool and a total of £60,000 had been donated by 2002 with other local charities also receiving donations. From the beginning, brothers Dean and Lisle Burrough of Higher and Lower Abbey Farms, have allowed the use of their farm land for the show site and the car parking. Bill Newbery of Hunthay Farm has allowed use of his land for access to the car park. In addition, Axminster Carpets allow the use of their premises for office facilities.

The popularity of the event was underlined by the ninth show, held on 21 and 22 June 2003. A record 16,000 people attended, in ideal weather, and there were around 300 exhibitors.

The champion bullock at the Axminster Union District Agricultural Association Show. It was shown by a Mr Phillips who farmed at Castle Hill Farm between 1910 and 1914.

Left: *The late Dave Swarbrick, the inspiration behind the Axe Vale Festival of Gardening and Crafts.*

Above: *Axe Vale Festival of Gardening and Crafts, 2001. It served as an appetiser for the BBC which was looking for a show to use in its drama series 'Down to Earth' starring Pauline Quirk and Warren Clarke.*

Bottom: *The 1958 annual sheep sale with Fox Hill in the background. The Lea Combe housing estate would be built on the field between Fox Hill and the market.*

18

Axminster Worthies

Dean William Buckland

William Buckland was born in Stoney Lane, Axminster, on 12 March 1784, the eldest son of the Revd Charles Buckland. Educated at Tiverton Grammar School (Blundell's) and at Winchester College, in 1801 he entered Corpus Christi College, Oxford, as a scholar on the Exeter Foundation.

From an early age he showed an interest in geology and attended the mineralogical lectures of Dr Kidd, an eminent geologist. He also made frequent excursions in the neighbourhood of Oxford. It was from these excursions that he formed an extensive collection that is now held in the Oxford Museum.

He took his BA degree in 1804 and, five years later, was elected as a fellow of his college. In 1813 he was appointed to the Chair of Mineralogy and, in 1819, he was made the first Professor of Geology at Oxford. The numerous papers that he contributed to the Geological Society (founded in 1807) had a great influence of the new sciences and helped to enlarge its boundaries. It was during this time that he met the Revd William Daniel Conybeare, a Londoner who was to purchase the living at St Mary's Church in Axminster.

He was elected as a fellow of The Royal Society in 1818 and, in 1847, became a trustee of the British Museum. His life-long devotion to geology led to his returning to Axminster in 1839 when he kept a watching brief on the landslip at Rousdon and Uplyme.

Buckland resigned his fellowship in 1825 to take up the living at Stoke Charity in Hampshire and was appointed Dean of Westminster in 1845 on the recommendation of Sir Robert Peel (he was ordained at Corpus Christi College). He died on 26 August 1856.

John Churchill, Duke of Marlborough

The Churchills first came to Ashe, between Axminster and Musbury, when Elizabeth Drake, the great-granddaughter of John Drake, whose family had held the estate since 1415, married a Dorset knight called Winston Churchill. Oddly enough the Churchills were Royalists and the Drakes Parliamentarians.

The happy couple had a dozen children but only five survived into adolescence. One was Arabella, born 23 February 1647 and baptised at Ashe the following month. She eventually became the favourite mistress of the Duke of York (later James II). Her son, Berwick, followed James into exile in 1688 and fought for France against his uncle, John (also known as Jack) Churchill, First Duke of Marlborough. Arabella died in 1730 having lived under two protectors and in seven reigns (eight if you count William and Mary as two).

John Churchill was born in 1650. There is some confusion over both the date and place. Ashe had been almost completely burnt down during the Civil War, which led some authorities to claim that Churchill was born at Trill, a farmhouse barely a mile away. His baptism was recorded in the parish registers at St Mary's Church, Axminster, 'John, the sonne of Mr Winston Spencer Churchill was baptised at Aish, ye 26 day of Jun.'

RSC
SOUTH - EAST DEVON
Ashe House
Musbury
For Sale by Auction
1972
R. & C. SNELL, Axminster
Axminster Printing Co., Axminster, Devon.

The original page has since been removed, more than likely stolen. A later Winston Leonard Spencer Churchill (1874–1965) mistakenly gives this date as John's birthday in his book *Marlborough*, although later he is less certain and contents himself with saying in his *History of the English-Speaking Peoples* that Marlborough was born in May or June. Even W.G. Hoskins in *Devon* claims that he was born at Trill. The truth can be seen in St Michael's Church in Musbury where a facsimile copy of the entry in that village's parish register is displayed. The date given is 26 May and the place as Musbury. Ashe is in Musbury and Trill is in Axminster.

John Churchill was educated at first in Dublin and later at St Paul's. Like that later Winston Churchill he was never much of a scholar and, also like the great prime minister, he opted for a life in the Army where, by 1667, he had been commissioned in the King's Own Company in Colonel Russell's Regiment of Foot Guards.

He may have been a good soldier but he was never much of a politician and was unable to hide his mistrust of William III (King from 1689 to 1702) whom he suspected, with good reason, of using England to further the interests of the Dutch by waging war against the French. Such thoughts led him to hanker after the return of James II or the succession of Anne. When Anne became Queen in 1702 she created him a Knight of the Garter and elevated him to a Dukedom (Marlborough). The names of his battles roll off the tongue like an ancient litany, Blenheim (1704), Malplaquet (1709) and Ramillies (1706) among many others.

George Pulman.

Sadly, his wife fell out with Queen Anne and the shock waves led to Marlborough's disgrace. He spent his last years in retirement. However, when he died in 1722 he was Duke of Marlborough, Marquis of Blandford, Baron Churchill of Aymouth in Scotland, Prince of the Holy Roman Empire and Knight of the Most Ancient Order of the Garter and still described as England's finest soldier.

William Henry Dutfield

He may have been christened William Henry but the father of Axminster's modern carpet industry was always called Harry.

The son of a Glasgow carpet designer, at the age of 17 he made his first saleable rug on a hand-made loom designed by his father in the attic of their home. It was that small rug that fuelled the inspiration for a product that would, one day, be renowned for its quality around the world.

With very small capital and his home-made looms, Harry Dutfield found premises in an old First World War corn-mill in Kidderminster. He had been educated in this town, at the King Charles Grammar School, after moving south with his family from Scotland. The business enjoyed a flourishing start but suffered a double setback after Harry Dutfield developed appendicitis and fire gutted the building. His insurance cover note expired and he thought that he was ruined – until the then Royal Insurance Company decided to compensate him for his loss. Impressed by this, he remained loyal to the insurance firm for the rest of his life.

When on holiday in the West Country he was surprised to learn that Axminster Carpets were no longer made in Axminster. He quickly founded the modern Axminster Carpets Ltd business, bringing some skilled workers from Kidderminster with him to work in the factory he built at the far end of Woodmead Road. The new firm was a shot in the arm to the local employment market, even if, soon after it opened, the outbreak of the Second World War saw it engaged on war work, including the manufacture of camouflage netting, instead of carpets.

A shrewd businessman, Harry Dutfield overcame the shortage of peacetime yarn by purchasing a mill at Buckfast, which became an instant success. Under his leadership the quality of Axminster carpets became internationally renowned.

Few, if any, of the town's worthies have done more for the people of Axminster than he, especially with regards the many unsung acts of generosity to his adopted home.

George Philip Rigney Pulman

The eldest son of Philip and Ann (née Rigney), George Philip Rigney Pulman was born in Axminster on 21 February 1819. Philip Pulman, the son of a Colyton blacksmith, was a watchmaker who owned a red-brick house on the corner of Lyme Street and George Street that, in 2003, is known as Pulman's House. Mr Barrow Pulman sold the house in 1920 to a Mr Vince.

George Pulman is best known to us in 2003 for *The Book of the Axe* that was initially published in sections in 1844–45 and later as a book. It is both a history of the parishes that flank the river and a piscatorial guide. In all there were four editions and around the 1960s a facsimile edition was published.

He was a man of many talents: an author, a newspaper publisher, a fisherman of some repute and a maker of artificial flies, for which he won a bronze medal at the Great Exhibition of 1851. He also possessed considerable musical ability and was the organist at Axminster's Parish Church by the age of 20.

Left: *Frank Rowe, the auctioneer with a shepherd's crook, at Axminster Sheep Sale in 1956. On average around 3,000 sheep were sold at the annual sale. The area behind the market, where the lorry is parked, is now completely developed.*

When he was 22 he wrote his first book, *Vade-mecum of Fly Fishing for Trout*. In 1848 he moved to Crewkerne, where he lived for 30 years, and where he acquired a printing and stationery business. He still managed to find the time to return to Axminster to play the organ until 1855. On 12 December 1838 he married, at Catistock, Jane Ewens. They had a son and a daughter and, although both married, there were no grandchildren.

There was no low-cost newspaper in the Axe valley at the time although the *Bridport News* was first published in 1855, priced at 1d. All the other news-papers, published at Yeovil, Taunton, Dorchester and Exeter, cost around 4d. In an attempt to fill the void, Pulman first published his *Pulman's Weekly News* in 1857 at a cost of 1½d. An instant success, it was later acquired by the Western Gazette Group and then bought by Tindle Newspapers Ltd of Farnham in Surrey in 1996, at which point it was published in South Street, Axminster, not much more than a stone's throw from the house in which George Pulman was born.

As a result of his failing health, he sold the paper and his printing business in 1878 and retired to Uplyme where he died in 1880. He was buried in Axminster four days later. The obelisk over the family grave is inscribed:

In memory of George Rigby Philip Pulman [sic], *a native of Axminster and author of* The Book of the Axe *and several books of local interest, as well as founder in 1857, and the proprietor and editor for 20 years after-wards of a local paper remarkable for its advocacy and its true independent spirit. He died at Uplyme the 3rd February 1880 and was interred here on the 7th of the same month, aged 60 years. This monument was erected here by many friends who held him in estimation.*

In the 1 January 1901 edition of *Pulman's Weekly News* the last link with the Pulman family was broken with the report of the death of George Pulman's widow, Mrs Pulman. She died at Shepherd's Bush, London, on Christmas Day 1900, at the age of 78. She left a son, Mr W.G. Pulman, a solicitor of Lutterworth, and a married daughter, Mrs H. Franklin of Barnes. Two years after her death, Hermitage House, the family home in Uplyme, was destroyed by fire.

The body of the deceased arrived at Axminster by train at 1.13p.m. and the Revd A. Newman conducted the service in St Mary's Church. Remarkably, the 86-year-old Mr Thomas Webber, the man who played the 'Dead March' in *Saul* when the coffin entered and left the church, had been the organist at the church since 1835 when he took over from none other than George Pulman himself. A nice touch was that Mrs Pulman had been one of his pupils.

Frank Rowe

An Axminster man born and bred, Frank Rowe's profession as an auctioneer probably made his face the most remembered of the last 50 years of the twentieth century in Axminster. An over-used expression when describing a local person is to call him or her 'a character', but in Frank Rowe's case this term was particularly appropriate. He was a man with a ready smile and an even readier joke. However, behind that easy-going façade there was a man who got things done as most of Axminster's organisations, from the carnival to the cricket club, found to their great benefit.

Born at Uphay Farm on 31 March 1922 – the same day that a separator arrived for the dairy – he was the fourth son of Felix and Olive Rowe. He attended school in Axminster before going to the Grammar School in Lyme Regis; he travelled there on the old 'Lyme Billy' on the branch line to the station that was almost opposite the school gates. Later he became a boarder at Ilminster Grammar School.

Although he came from a family of farmers and he spent all his working life among the local agricultural community he never actually became a farmer. When he left school his father gained a position for him with R. & C. Snell, the local auctioneers, where Arthur Gage trained him. The pair became lifelong friends.

As was the case for so many young men, the Second World War interrupted Frank's career. At first he joined the Home Guard and among his many duties was fire-watching from the top of St Mary's tower. He soon volunteered for the Royal Air Force and was posted to South Africa where he was trained as a pilot and became an instructor.

After demob he returned to Axminster and his old job and, on 6 October 1945 he married Marjorie Bright of Coaxden Farm at All Saints' Church. After qualifying as an auctioneer in 1948 he and Leslie Board acquired the business of R. & C. Snell in 1951 when they bought the market, the office in Trinity Square, and the salesroom. Two years later they opened an office in Bridport.

A gamble that paid off was that of converting the Axminster market into a weekly one. Previously it had been held fortnightly and had alternated with the Chard market. Eventually the partnership was dissolved, Leslie Board took over the Chard market, Frank the Axminster and Bridport markets.

Frank Rowe and the Axminster Brownies planting rose bushes in the Abbeyfield garden in Silver Street to commemorate the 50th anniversary of the founding of the Axminster Brownies. Among the Brownies are Shirley Seward, Elizabeth and Lesley Berry, Susan Davies, Frances Wraight, Nicky Crook and Mandy Enticott.

Frank took a keen interest in the life of his native town, particularly that of St Mary's Church where he kept the records, became a member of the PCC and was a sideman. A keen cricketer in his younger days, he gave a lot back to the game and the local club, as a secretary, chairman and president. For many years he was an active supporter of Axminster's carnival, serving as secretary, chairman and president. Among his many other interests was the East Devon Hunt; he organised their annual ball at Allhallows.

He was a founder member of Axminster's Abbeyfield, the very first Abbeyfield in Devon. He also worked for 30 years for the local Cancer Research branch and was its president for a while. Frank was a founder member of Axminster Rotary, a founder member and chairman of Axminster Museum, was involved in buying the Guildhall for the town in 1963 and was a member of its management committee. He was president of the Drama Club, the Operatic Society and was also the lord of the manor of Axminster and, as such, owned the rights to the weekly street market. He was connected with the Horticultural Society, the Royal British Legion and the RAFA.

In fact there was hardly a facet of town life that he was not connected with or interested in. However, that was not the only reason he had so many friends. He was full of fun and generosity, always ready to help. This was reflected when St Mary's Church was so packed for his funeral in 1994 that there were more people outside than inside the church.

Jack Sansom

Probably the only Axminster man to have his name in *The Guinness Book of Records*, Jack Sansom was born in 1885 in a Bristol workhouse. He moved to Churchinford where he began work on a farm at the age of 12.

He came to Axminster in 1909 in search of work and was successful in obtaining a post as a groom for Captain Percy Hardman at Adrian House in Lyme Street. Later he

The oldest fish fryer in the world, Jack Sansom at work on his 100th birthday.

Above: *Jack Sansom outside his fish-and-chip and wet-fish shop in the 1920s.*

Right: *Jack Sansom with son Cecil* (left), *preparing to cut the cake on his 100th birthday, 8 March 1985.*

ran a mineral-water company in North Street before joining the Devon Hussars and serving in Flanders and France. Among the battles in which he fought and survived was the carnage of the Third Battle of Ypres (Passchendaele). Later he moved to the Italian Front where, on the strength of his earlier experience with mineral waters, he worked with a Government-sponsored soft-drinks factory on the Italian-Austrian border.

After the war he returned to Axminster where, in 1926, he started his own wet-fish and fish-and-chip business in South Street, running it until his retirement in 1953 when his sons Ken and Cecil took over. His first fish-frying range was a second-hand one from Bournemouth that cost him £11.

Jack first cooked by coal and soon became a dab hand at judging when the fat was hot enough for the fish or the chips by placing his hand close to the fat. In later high-tec years, when the fish and chips were cooked in thermostatically controlled ranges, Jack was often asked how he judged the heat of the fat in the old days. 'You simply put an elbow in just like Mother did with the baby's bath water', was his reply.

Jack continued working part-time until he was over 100 years old – that was how he came to be included in *The Guinness Book of Records* as 'the oldest fish fryer in the world'. He always insisted on the highest of standards, something he successfully instilled in his two sons, and was a highly respected and hard-working member of Axminster's commercial life.

His great passion was Axminster Town Football Club, which he joined as a committee member in 1927 and in turn became its secretary, chairman, president and patron. He was followed as chairman and president by his younger son Cecil to give 76 years of unbroken family service to the club.

His other sporting interests included the local cricket club and Kilmington Bowls Club, for which he served as captain, secretary and president; he played for them until he was 96 years of age.

A remarkable man with many fine qualities – one of them being that he never bored anyone with rambling stories of bygone days. However, if you genuinely wanted to know about them, he would tell you and reveal his impressive memory. He died in 1986.

Emily Sheppard

Known throughout town as Emmy, Emily Sheppard was born in Axminster. She was one of two daughters of Mr and Mrs Sidney Sheppard, who ran a grocery business at the bottom of Lyme Street. Like her sister Marjorie she remained a spinster. Emmy lived in a house just above the Red Lion in Lyme Street that was immaculately kept by her maid, Miss Elsie Pile.

From there she began her working life as secretary to the Dawkins family when they owned that family store. In time, she purchased the business that she had done so much to promote through her personal charm. She had a real love of wearing large hats, bought through the business, of course.

Emmy was much better known to the world at large, and certainly that outside Axminster, through her life-long association with the carnival for which she served as president for many years. She took a particular interest in the carnival queens, making sure that Dawkins usually provided an entrant, especially in quiet years.

For many years, Emmy Sheppard (right) played a considerable part in the organisation of Axminster's carnival. She is seen here as a young girl with Molly Burrough. They were running a balloon stall at a carnival during the early 1920s.

Thomas Wakley

Thomas Wakley was born and bred in Membury in 1795 (Membury is close enough to Axminster to have no fears of starting an internecine war, so he more than deserves to be included on our list of worthies). The son of a farmer, he became one of the greatest reformers of the medical profession. He was the founder and first editor of *The Lancet*, the eminent medical journal, and was greatly involved in the creation of the medical profession that we know today.

His father was a yeoman of the old school who challenged anyone of his own age to ride a steeplechase on a horse as old as his. There was no challenger – he was 90 and his horse was 33!

Thomas Wakley left Chard School and went to sea. One uncomfortable voyage to India was more than enough for him, so on his return he became an apprentice to an apothecary in Taunton, then to another in Beaminster. He went to study at Guy's and St Thomas' Hospitals in London where he passed his examinations and became a member of the Royal College of Surgeons. Afterwards he walked the 150 miles home to Membury to tell his family of his success.

Instead of going for a quiet life as a surgeon, he devoted his life to fighting the abuses and jobbery that he had found in his chosen profession. It was this that led him to found *The Lancet*; he wanted to publicise his case for change.

Fearless in his criticism, he fought anybody who gained promotion by privilege. He also entered Parliament and became the coroner for Middlesex. His enemies called him a grievance hunter; he was indeed an agitator. For almost 40 years Thomas led the way in dealing with many social ills. His many achievements included the higher standards in hospitals, and the advancement of medical students through their ability and work rather than by promotion through purchase. He was also very prominent in the reform of the Poor Law and with improvements in the treatment of the sick poor. He had to fight for many of his reforms against bitter opposition in the press and Parliament, as well as in the courts.

One of his greatest campaigns was against the adulteration of food in 1851. He published his findings to the horror of the public, as he revealed that, among other things, tea contained black lead, indigo, turmeric and mica, and that unscrupulous traders were buying used tea leaves from catering establishments, drying it, adding chestnut, bay and sloe leaves and selling it as 'fine blended tea'. More than half of the milk samples that he had taken had been diluted with water.

He was the pioneer of all our modern laws for the prevention of adulteration of food and drink and, because of his endeavours, the first Food and Drugs Act was passed in 1860. That year, as a result of failing health, he was advised to live in Madeira where he discovered many fraudulent shipments of pseudo-Madeiran wine. By then he was too ill to fight against this practice and he died on the island in 1862. His body was brought back to London and he was buried at Kensal Green cemetery.

Thomas Nicholas Webber

Thomas Nicholas Webber had been an organist for 68 years when he retired at the age of 88 years; the last 60 years had been spent at Axminster, and, according to *Pulman's Weekly News* published on 24 February 1903, he was England's oldest organist.

He joined the choir at Exeter Cathedral at the age of ten and, after spending eight years as the organist at another church, he moved to Axminster in 1843. Incredibly he was the organist at his first church during the service to celebrate the coronation of Queen Victoria (1837) and at Axminster officiated at the service held for her funeral in 1901. He also played at the services to mark her golden jubilee (1887) and diamond jubilee (1897) at Axminster. For Edward VII's coronation in 1902 he composed an anthem, which was acknowledged by the King himself.

To mark his retirement an address was made and a purse of 50 guineas (£52.50 in modern money) was presented to him by the vicar, the Revd A. Newman, at a gathering kept small in view of Mr Webber's great age.

Mr George Harris, one of Mr Webber's old choirboys, beautifully executed the address, which stated:

> *Presented together with a purse containing 50 guineas to Mr Thomas Nicholas Webber, organist of Axminster Parish Church, by the under-mentioned parishioners and other friends, in token of the high esteem and regard in which he is universally held. This testimonial on his retirement, at the advanced age of 88... from the post he has so worthily held for 60 years, is this spontaneous outcome of the appreciation of the subscribers for his long and devoted service, coupled with their earnest hope that the recipient may long be spared to enjoy the rest and peace he has so well deserved.*

They may have wanted it to be a small, quiet gathering in view of Mr Webber's age, but the words spoken by the local great and good in appreciation of the man took up over 80 lines of small print in the local newspaper. Major W. Forward, as the oldest member of the choir, said a few words and mentioned that when he was a choirboy some 50 years earlier the organ had been on the other side of the church.

Earlier Mr Webber had been the guest at a tea for the choirboys given by Major and Mrs Forward, at which the vicar presented Mr Webber with a silver pencil-case on behalf of the boys.

Visibly overcome with emotion on both occasions, Mr Webber thanked everyone for all their many kind remarks and gifts.

19

SPORT

Axminster RFC, 1908-09.

Below: *Axminster's Wednesday football club. Most members were shop workers who, instead of Saturday afternoons when the town football club played, had their football matches on Wednesdays, when the shops had half days. Judging by the kit this picture was taken in the early 1920s, although the team played until well into the 1930s. The goalkeeper is Bill Stuart, later of the Axminster Inn and Stuart's South Street butchery.*

Axminster Town Football Club

The Axminster Town Association Football Club was born on Friday 14 November 1902, at Moass' New Commercial Hotel in Trinity Square at a meeting, 'at which there was a good attendance'. Mr Cecil Forward presided and would-be members learnt that there was a choice of fields to be had. The club went for one at Secktor *[sic]* Lane but, in the event, this choice fell through and it would be around 20 years before the club moved to Sector Lane where it still plays in 2003. Mr Whittle was appointed captain with Tom McLennan vice-captain. Mr Ward became both the secretary and treasurer and Dr Langran was the first president.

There was some mystery over the club's first colours; that first AGM agreed that they should be green and white but, in the end, the team wore blue and white shirts for the first year, changing to all green in 1904. By 1911 the yellow and black shirts still worn in 2003 were adopted and the team's nickname of Terriers was changed to Tigers.

The first pitch was in a field off Chard Road behind Brookhill, known as Gravelpit Field. It was not all that good, its end-to-end slope often prompting remarks along the lines that teams benefitted 'when the incline was in their favour'.

Axminster's first game was on Saturday 6 December 1902 when they lost 6–0 at home to Exeter Training College. The first ever team was: Curtis, Peate, Jefford, S. Morrish, A. Longman, Taylor, Fred Ball, Pratt, J.M. Whittle, Tom McLennan and S.B. Blamey.

A 5–1 defeat away to Perry Street Lace Works followed when Mr Pratt found his own little niche in the club's hall of fame when he scored Axminster's first ever goal. The first win was by 4–0 at home to Chard Grammar School. They won again five days later, beating Ottery Grammar School 2–0 with goals from Jefford and Woolley. Ward also 'put through an offside goal'.

When Mr Ward, Axminster's first secretary, left the town, Mr W.S. Witt was elected as secretary and treasurer at the AGM in August 1903 at the New Commercial. Dr Langran again consented to be president with William Forward chairman. A second team was run during 1903–04 when anyone who gave 10s.6d. (55p) was made a vice-president and, for some reason, a change was made to green shirts.

Before that AGM, Charles Small, the owner of

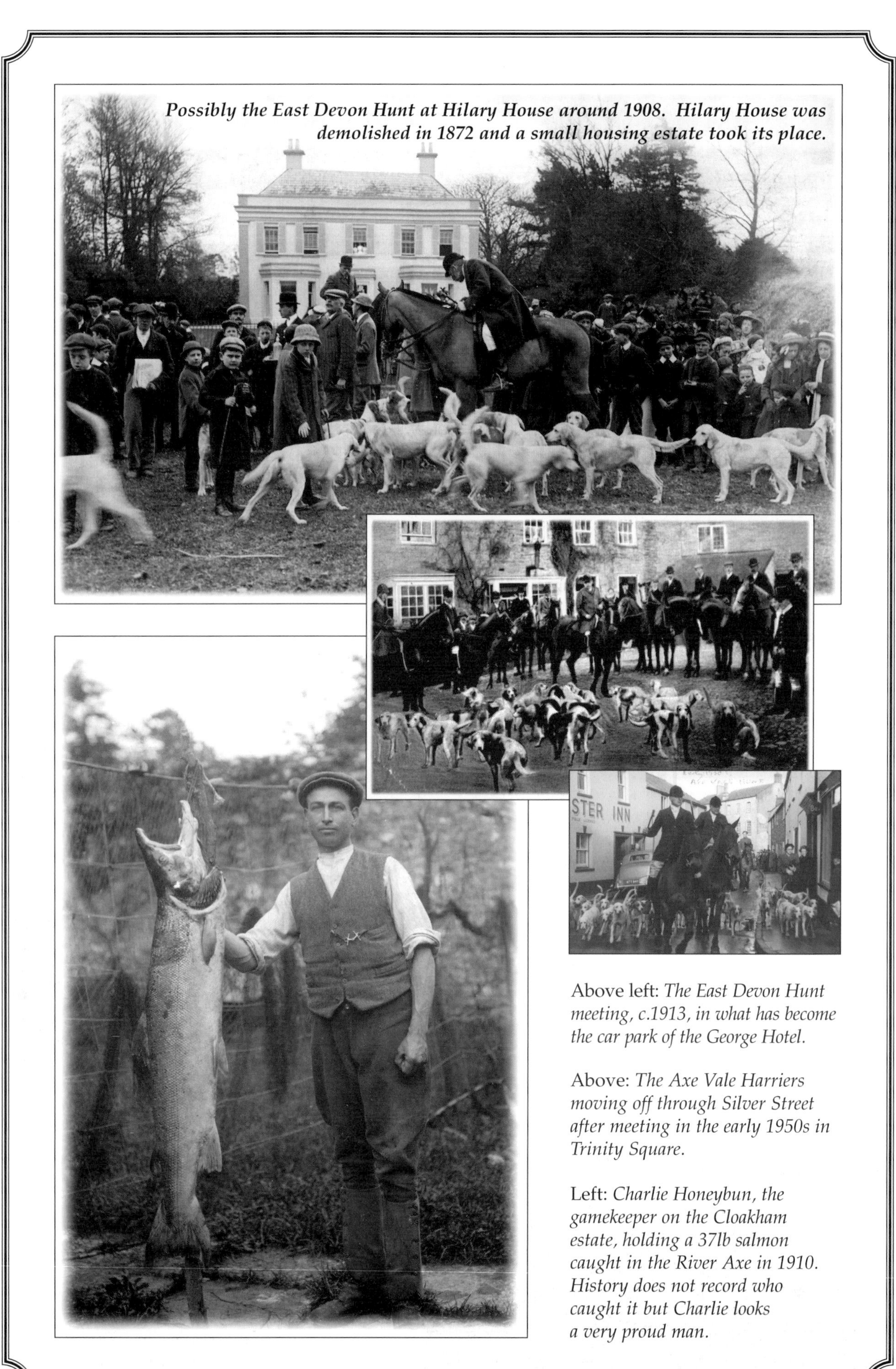

Possibly the East Devon Hunt at Hilary House around 1908. Hilary House was demolished in 1872 and a small housing estate took its place.

Above left: *The East Devon Hunt meeting, c.1913, in what has become the car park of the George Hotel.*

Above: *The Axe Vale Harriers moving off through Silver Street after meeting in the early 1950s in Trinity Square.*

Left: *Charlie Honeybun, the gamekeeper on the Cloakham estate, holding a 37lb salmon caught in the River Axe in 1910. History does not record who caught it but Charlie looks a very proud man.*

Perry Street Lace Works, had called a meeting to discuss the formation of a local league. Giffords (Holyrood Mills), Chard Press, Horton Rovers, Perry Street Lace Works, Combe Wanderers and Axminster Town were asked to attend. A second meeting took place and the Perry Street & District League was formed, its five founding fathers being Perry Street Lace Works, Combe Wanderers, Holyrood Mills, Axminster Town and Horton Rovers, none of which have had 100 years' continual membership.

AXMINSTER TOWN
ASSOCIATION FOOTBALL CLUB
President : MR. D. SCOTT ROWE
Chairman : MR. J. SANSOM

FIXTURES 1955-56

Hon. Secretary :
MR. G. POULTER
Green Lodge, Stoney Lane, Axminster

Hon. Treasurer :
MR. S. A. YEO
National Provincial Bank, Axminster

Colours : Black and Amber Stripes
Ground : Sector Lane

The club's first league win was 1–0 at home to Horton when Goddard headed in a corner by Blamey a minute or so from the end. The team for another historic occasion was: Fred Gay, ? Fowler, Rube Ball, Billy Parr, Tom McLennan, Frank Patterson, ? Blamey, ? Dunn, ? Longman, ? Goddard and ? Whittle.

At first the side struggled in league football, but by 1911–12 had improved sufficiently to win the championship. After the First World War, arguably the best side that Axminster or the Perry Street & District League have ever provided won three titles in a row (1919–20, 1920–21 and 1921–22). Many cups were won as well. However, it was not until after the Second World War that Axminster again had a top-class side. With it they sought admission to senior football with the Devon & Exeter League and Premier status was quickly obtained.

Again the success soon ended and the club returned to the Perry Street & District League. For around 30 years they languished, a slumbering giant never obtaining the position a club of its size deserved, until the beginning of the twenty-first century when a return to the Exeter & District League (in 2003 known as the Devon & Exeter League) was made. The titles of Senior Four and Senior Two were both won and, if optimism is any yardstick, there is more success to follow.

Millwey Rise Football Club

Millwey Rise Football Club was formed in 1958 because the local town club was following a policy of trying to obtain players from all over the area. Such a policy may well have been good for Axminster Town Football Club, but not for Axminster football when local young men were not able to get a game.

The most prominent of Millwey's founding fathers was Bernard Hiscox, a former Axminster Town goalkeeper of some distinction who by then had almost retired from the game and was running the Trout Inn on Chard Road (long-since closed). The pundits called Millwey the seven-day wonder and claimed that the club would not last five minutes. However, the pundits were proved wrong.

It has had its good, bad and indifferent days. Probably its finest hour was when it started life by winning the Perry Street & District Football League's Division Two title in 1958–59. The line-up for the first match, a 2–2 draw at Thorncombe, was: Bernard Hiscox, George Willetts, Cyril Dickson, Dave Mitchell, Henry Trenchard (captain), Dave Thorne, Brian

Below: *Millwey Rise Football Club, late 1960s.* Left to right, back row: *Dave Pike, ?, Bill Hewitt, Derek Seward, Don Chubb;* front: *Mike Facey, Billy Ford, Cedric Vernon, ?, Barry Ives, Alfie Dowell.*

Above: *Millwey Rise Football Club's annual dinner, 1959–60.* Seated at the top table are, left to right: *Percy Downton (secretary), Doug Swaine (Perry Street & District League chairman), Bernard Hiscox (chairman), Charlie Beer (guest) and Aubrey Lee (treasurer).* Others present include: *Tony Turner (a later chairman), Dick Sturch, Edward Cockram and Brian 'Skip' Willey.*

Above: *Millwey Rise Football Club, 1973–74.* Left to right, back row: *Brian Downton, Clive Parkhouse, Ray Tiller, Doug Thompson, John Deaves, Kevin Tratt, Barry Huntley;* front: *Merv Knight, Alfie Dowell, Denis Freeth, Dave Evans, Andrew Badley.*

Below: *The Millwey Rise team won the Tommy Tabberer Cup, 1986–87.* Left to right, back row: *Howard Midworth, Doug Thompson, Alan Beer, Mike Taylor, Mike Hutchings, Colin Moore, Richard Polanek;* front: *Simon Harris, Kevin Turner, Mark Turner, Graham Beer, Neil Meaker.*

Kilmington Football Club, c.1910. Known as 'The Stars' for obvious reasons, they competed in the Perry Street & District League during the 1910–11 season, when they finished second from the bottom. They participated the following year, but withdrew halfway through the season because of their lack of success. The team are pictured here on their ground near George Lane. Later they played off Roman Road and then at Dulcis Farm. Sadly, the club no longer exists in 2003.

Downton, Pete Stevens, Sam Branker, Brian 'Skip' Willey and Dave Hawkins. Appropriately, in view of the years of great service he would go on to give the club both on and off the field, the first ever Millwey Rise goal was scored by Brian 'Percy' Downton.

What followed hardly seems possible today. Millwey Rise won their next 12 games, the scores being: 4–0, 5–1, 9–0, 5–2, 7–1, 7–1, 20–0, 7–1, 5–0, 6–1, 10–2, and 7–2. As well as the league title, the Division Two KO Cup and the Arthur Gage Cup were also won.

Winning their first seven games in the top division, the Millwey Rise success seemed like a fairy tale come true. However, by 1961–62, relegation in successive seasons saw the side down in Division Three. Promotion back to Division Two and then Division One followed. In eight seasons the team experienced promotion three times and relegation three times. Since then they have lived as a middle-order team in the Perry Street & District League, never really setting the world alight again, but neither have they gone under. In the good years, a second team has been run. At the end of the 2002–03 season the Jack Venn Cup was won, Millwey's first cup success since 1988 when they lifted the Tommy Tabberer Cup.

It can be invidious to mention names – someone always gets left out – but Millwey Rise has had more than its fair share of stalwart friends. Stan Trenchard is the first that springs to mind. A more-than-generous president (and his generosity was directed to most sporting aspects of the town), Stan and his wife were a part of the Millwey Rise way of life for a long time.

Kilmington Football Club

Kilmington Football Club was in existence in 1906 as references are made to friendly games with Axminster Reserves in local papers. By 1910–11 they had joined the Perry Street & District League.

Known as The Stars, because they wore a big star on the front of their shirts, a typical team of the time would have been: Dick Pound, Ern Bastable, Ern Newbery, C. Hindmarsh, E. Trott (captain), F. Fowler, C. Browning, Tom Phippen, A. Gush, C. Moulding and C. Smith.

Perry Street & District League Table, 1910–11 Season (Football)

	Played	Won	Drawn	Lost	For	Against	Points
Bodens	16	12	3	1	74	18	27
Holyrood Mills	16	12	2	2	54	12	26
Combe	16	12	2	2	50	18	26
Ilminster St Mary	16	7	2	7	37	27	16
Lyme Rovers	15	4	4	7	31	27	12
Axminster Town	15	6	0	9	22	32	12
Perry Street Works	16	5	2	9	36	34	12
Kilmington	16	4	2	10	18	48	10
Colyton	16	0	0	16	6	116	0

Left: *Kilmington Football Club in the 1980s, just before the club went into abeyance.* Left to right, back row: *Mike Hellier, Tim Boyland, Alan Knight, Martin Johnson, Chris Hopson, Arthur Parsons;* front: *Derek Webb, Chris Hellier, Richard Webb, Graham Knight, Revd Blizzard.*

Right: *The New Inn, Kilmington (date unknown). In 2003, the corrugated building on the right, is the site of the inn's car park. However, it was once the Lace Rooms, where many local people were employed as outworkers repairing machine-made lace, and where Kilmington Football Club changed before and after matches.*

Halfway through the following season, as a result of poor support and playing success, the team left the league and did not return until 1920–21 when it finished mid-table.

No more is known of the club until 1950–51 when it again played in the Perry Street & District League; it finished bottom of the Intermediate Southern Section. Since then it has had varied fortunes, including playing in Division One. Sadly, lack of support led to the club disbanding during the 1980s.

In 1951 the team played on a pitch opposite the New Inn, the players changing in the Lace Rooms in the pub car park. Later they moved to Springhead, then to Roman Road and, finally, Dulcis Farm.

It was at Dulcis that they startled the optic nerves with mauve and yellow shirts and caused visiting players some anxiety when Jimmy Webb's bull grazed contentedly near the touch-line. Jimmy, chairman for many years and a staunch supporter of Kilmington, was known for riding the bull around the field. Jimmy was such a staunch fan that he once ordered a visiting supporter out of the ground (it belonged to him) for swearing. The man went – after demanding his gate money back. Others that must be mentioned include lifelong supporter Aubrey Hutchings, and long-serving chairman Pat Enticott.

Axminster Cricket Club

In 1975 the Axminster Cricket Club celebrated its 125th birthday, but they did so without any proof of the fact whatsoever, although some members had claimed to have seen the year of their formation given in 'a local paper'. A quarter of a century later (2000) the club announced its plans to celebrate its 150th anniversary. However, the club was in fact formed in 1874, so was 101 years old when it celebrated its 125th anniversary. (The error still exists in the 2003 Devon Cricket League handbook.) Consequently the 150th anniversary celebrations were labelled '150 Years of Cricket in Axminster', which was another inaccuracy. There may have been a cricket match played in Axminster in 1850, 1849 or even 1840 but it was not of an organised nature. Rather, and because it was very much a game of the middle and upper classes, they were matches between a team 'got up' for the day against a similar team from, say, Colyford. It would be labelled in the press as Axminster v Colyford. A week or so later a completely different Axminster resident might invite his friends to make up a team to play some acquaintances from Kilmington and that match would earn that game the soubriquet of Axminster v Kilmington. Such games were only reported in the local press when someone bothered to send in the scores, which was not very often. Exhaustive research over many years does not show any Axminster cricket match reports until the 1860s.

The Axminster Cricket Club should have had no doubts as to its age. An 1874 report in *Pulman's Weekly News* reveals that a match against Colyton at Colyford on 11 July of that year was 'the first game of the newly-formed Axminster club.' This was 12 years after the formation of the Lyme Regis (now Uplyme & Lyme Regis) Cricket Club.

Prior to the formation of the club, 'pick-up' matches were probably played in the parks or pitches of the gentry, rather than at North Street, the home of the new club. The cricket club began its life at the rented field in North Street in 1874. Money raised at athletic meetings and other functions enabled the field to be levelled and improved enough to make it 'one of the best in the area... [the]

field was on the small side but [the] surroundings [were] rather pretty.'

In 1875 there was a reference to a tent on the ground but, in 1876, a pavilion was erected through 'the efforts' of a member called Tom Pickering. A Robert Banks is thought to have been the first groundsman. That pavilion, 'neat and commodious' according to the *Chard & Ilminster News*, was erected at a cost of £40 and the club had 'considerable outlay in improving the ground and erecting boundary railings.' One of the early 'stars' was Mr F.S. Cox, the owner-headmaster of Oak House School in Chard Road.

The sports meetings that were held to raise funds were festive occasions, and not only for Axminster. Special trains were laid on from Chard, Lyme Regis, Seaton and Honiton and the whole town would be en fête with even the church being decorated. Usually the 1st Devon Militia Band from Exeter was in attendance and, when it arrived, it 'marched to the ground for sustenance'. They would pass the George Hotel that, along with the New Commercial, had thrown lines of streamers across the road. At the ground there was a large ornamental arch over the entrance that bore a big 'Welcome' on it as well as 'the cricketers arms of a bat, ball and a stump.' As many as 1,000 people would crowd into the cricket ground, each paying 3d. (1½p) for the privilege.

The club prospered for a spell but in 1895 it folded. It was reformed in 1901 and, apart from the war years, has provided cricket for the young men of the town ever since. Its year of pomp came in the Edwardian era when many of its batting records were set up and two-day games played. On the other side of the coin, it was at this time (1911) that Axminster's bowlers had their worst day in the field – Seaton scored 444–4 against them.

Axminster was one of the eight founding fathers of the Exeter & East Devon Cricket League in 1982 (the Exeter part being dropped after one year). The other seven clubs were Alphington, Bradninch, Cullompton, Countess Wear, London & Manchester, Ottery St Mary and Whimple & Whiteways. The following year Honiton RBL joined them.

The Second XIs of Ottery St Mary, Alphington, Whimple & Whiteways, Countess Wear, Cullompton and Honiton RBL formed a second division in 1984, which was enlarged in 1985 by the arrival of Halberton & Sampford Peverell, Kentisbeare and Axminster Second XI.

At first, perhaps sensibly, the league did not insist on all teams playing on the same day and chance had it that North Street staged the first ever East Devon Cricket League game when the London & Manchester club were beaten in Axminster by nine wickets on 24 April 1982.

It is fair to say that Axminster never really played to their full potential in this league. Relegation to Division Two was endured at the end of the 1991 season. Their best years were 1995 and 1996 when they were runners-up, but had the misfortune to compete with a Honiton side that swept away all before them for four years. League games banished many old friends to Sunday games to such an extent that a Sunday XI was formed.

The 1997 move to Devon League cricket saw Axminster go in at the lowest (D Division) level. This was much too low for the strength of the men available; a fact indicated when a nine-man Cricketers team arrived at Cloakham to be beaten by 283 runs after Axminster had opened with 344–4. Matthew Hewer (118) and Paul Miller (146) put on 256 for the second wicket (the 1999 Devon League handbook gives it as M. Hewer and M. Richards). In the return game Cricketers were dismissed for 23 by Mark Richards (6–10) and Phil Spong (4–10) and beaten by ten wickets. Later that year Axminster totalled 347–4 against Yealm. This time Steve Reed (127*) and Mark Richards (115*) added 269 for the fifth wicket.

THE SCORE CARD FOR THE AXMINSTER V COLYTON GAME AT COLYFORD ON 11 JULY 1874, AXMINSTER CRICKET CLUB'S FIRST RECORDED GAME.

Axminster			*Colyton*		
F.C. Cox	*b. Baines*	*83*	*G. Smith*	*c. Brine, b Kyrke*	*14*
Kyrke	*b. Baines*	*23*	*E. Scarborough*	*b. Kyrke*	*0*
R. Langdon	*b. Baines*	*49*	*E. Baines*	*c. S. Cox, b F. Cox*	*10*
H. Cox	*b. E. Scarborough*	*14*	*G. Baines*	*lbw b. Kyrke*	*15*
Brine	*b. Baines*	*0*	*Captain Dick*	*b. F. Cox*	*4*
A.C. Pickering	*b. J. Scarborough*	*1*	*J. Scarborough*	*c. Brice, b F. Cox*	*1*
J.F. Cox	*thrown out Smith*	*6*	*Abrahams*	*not out*	*1*
S. Cox	*b. Baines*	*2*	*Wilton*	*b. Kyrke*	*0*
Stone	*b. Baines*	*6*	*O'Meara*	*b. Kyrke*	*1*
Sillery	*not out*	*0*	*Captain Gooton*	*b. Kyrke*	*0*
Harris	*b. E. Scarborough*	*1*	*Stoke*	*not out*	*0*
		Extras: 24			***Extras: 29***
		Total: 209			***Total: 75–8***

Axminster Cricket Club, 1952.

PRICE THREEPENCE.

AXMINSTER CRICKET CLUB

ATHLETIC SPORTS,

ON WEDNESDAY, AUGUST THE 17TH, 1881.

President.
F. SWABEY, Esq., Coryton Park

Vice Presidents.
CAPTAIN WREY, R.N., J.P. J. I. SCARBROUGH, Esq., J.P. CAPTAIN FORWARD. Dr. BARNES.
W. H. B. KNIGHT, Esq.

Patrons.
Sir H. W. PEEK, Bart, M.P.
Sir J. H. KENNAWAY, Bart, M.P.
Lieut. Col. W. H. WALROND, M.P.
R. M. DAVY, Esq., J.P.
E. L AMES, Esq., J.P.
T. BARNS, Esq., J.P.
W. H. EVANS, Esq., J.P.
CHURCHILL LANGDON, Esq., J.P.
J. R. F. G. TALBOT, Esq., J.P.
W. CHARLESWORTH, Esq.
E. I. SCARBROUGH, Esq.,
Rev. F. SALMON.
Captain DICK.
G. A. SPOTTISWOODE, Esq.
Captain WALSH.
Rev. J. W. HANSON.
J. F. SYMES, Esq.
R. R. HOLLAND, Esq.
J. TANNER, Esq.
J. B. DAVIDSON, Esq.
S. FORWARD, Esq.
T. SELLWOOD, Esq.

Stewards.
(Blue Rosettes.)
The President and Vice Presidents. Mr. W. FORWARD. Mr. J. F. COX. Capt MARTIN, R.N. Mr J. MEWBURN.
Mr. E. CHAPPLE. Mr. WEBBER. Mr. A. PICKERING. Mr. F. PICKERING.

Committee.
(Red and Blue Rosettes (the Club Colours.)
Dr. APPLETON.
Mr. BUCKNOLE.
Mr. CATFORD.
Mr. E. W. FORWARD.
Mr. C. B. GAGE.
Mr. S. GRIFFIN.
Rev. J. W. HANSON.
Mr. JEFFERD.
Mr. C. B. PENNY.
Mr. L. A. PINNEY.
Mr. A. P. REECE.
Mr. J. TURNER.

Referee.
(White and Gold Rosette.)
Mr PICKERING.

Judges.
(White Rosettes.)
Rev. F. SALMON. Mr GERRISH.

Starters.
(Amber Rosettes)
Mr. R. LANGDON. Mr. OAKLEY.

Summoning Stewards.
(Amber and Black Rosette.)
Mr E. W. FORWARD. Mr S. COX.

Announcing Steward.
(Red and White Rosette.)
Mr R. ENGLAND.

Badge Steward.
(Blue and White Rosette.)
Mr L. A. PINNEY.

Clerks of the Course.
Red Rosettes.
Mr C. EWENS. Mr T. D. CHAPPELL.

Handicapper.
Mr. R. H. WICKHAM.

Honorary Secretary.
(Red, White and Blue Rosette.)
MR GEO. R. STEVENS.

Assistant Secretary.
(Red, White and Blue Rosette.)
MR. A. P. REECE.

PROGRAMME OF MUSIC BY THE BAND OF THE FIRST DEVON YEOMANRY.

Under the Conductorship of Mr. BATES.

Grand Parade March	"Balaclava,"	*Millars.*
Overture,	"Invocation A. St Cecile,"	*Lamotte.*
Valse	"Beautiful Ferns,"	*Bathe.*
Selection,	"The Pirates of Penzance,"	*Sullivan.*
Galop,	"Train Poste,"	*Alax.*
	"The Turkish Patrol,"	*Michaelis.*
Overture,	"Fra Diavolo,"	*Auber.*
Valse,	"La Fille du Tambour Major,"	*O Metra.*
Selection,	"Der Freyschutz,"	*Hartman.*
Cavatina	"Gemini di Virgi"	*Donizetti*
Quadrille	National Melodies	*Pinney*
Selection	"Madame Favarte"	*Offenbach*
Valse	"True Love"	*Coote*
Overture	"The Cross of Jerusalem"	*Bleger*
Galop	"Steeplechase"	*Dawson*
Selection	"Les Cloches de Corneville,"	*Planquette,*
Selection	"H. M. S. Pinafore,"	*Sullivan.*

The Prizes will be distributed immediately after the Sports by Mrs. H. KNIGHT.

A Grand display of FIREWORKS by Messrs WILDER, of Birmingham, at 7.45.

Axminster: —Printed by W. Pulman.

Kilmington and Axminster Cricket Clubs during a match at the old Axminster cricket ground in North Street, 1969. Note the old Axe Vale Laundry buildings in the background. Left to right (or at third slip if Phil Spong was bowling), Kilmington: *?, Les Wilkinson, ?, ?, Derek Broom, ?, Mike Collier, Martin Leach, ?, ?, Dudley Hurford (captain);* Axminster: *Phil Spong (captain), Ray Self, Terry Guppy, Mike Chown, Dave Pike, Ian Duckworth, Roger Hurrell, ?, Robert Harris, Roy Thresher, Ronny Seward.*

Score Card for the Axminster v London & Manchester game at North Street on 24 April 1982, Axminster's first league game.

London & Manchester

T. Dewes	*c Hayball, b Spong*	*0*
S. Sandford	*b Batten*	*6*
I. Milton	*c Pike, b Batten*	*7*
M. Bonning-Snook	*b Spong*	*0*
J. Dibstall	*not out*	*14*
J. Young	*run out*	*0*
B. Smith	*b Batten*	*0*
M. Brown	*b Batten*	*3*
R. Morley	*c G Field, b Batten*	*0*
N. Ryan	*b Batten*	*0*
R. Craven	*b Batten*	*0*
	Extras:	***9***
	Total (16 overs):	***39***

Bowling: Spong 8–3–14–2; Batten 8–2–16–7

Axminster

D. Capon	*not out*	*17*
P. Spong	*c Dewes, b Morley*	*5*
R. Moulding	*not out*	*11*
	Extras:	***7***
	Total (10 overs):	***40–1***

Left: *Axminster Cricket Club captain Mark Richards receives the East Devon Cricket League's Division One runners-up shield from Mrs M. Rowe in 1996. This was the second year running that the team finished second to local rivals Honiton.*

Although a second division of the East Devon League was started in 1984, Axminster waited until the following summer to enter their Second XI. The East Devon League amalgamated with the Devon League in 2001.

As far back as 1980 the cricket club's landlords, the Axe Vale Laundry Ltd, had decided not to renew the annual agreement for them to play at the North Street ground where they had played ever since the club was formed in 1874. Several sites for a new field were suggested but, in the end, it was the offer of Mr W.H. Dutfield of Axminster Carpets Ltd, and a former member of the club, that made a field available at Cloakham Lawn off Chard Road.

The discussions that followed with Axminster Carpets Ltd gave support to the idea of trying to create a multi-sports area for Axminster and the Axe valley. There had been discussions in the late 1960s about the two major sports clubs in the town, the football and cricket clubs, getting together at Sector Lane but lack of space had proved the idea a non-starter.

In 1981 the cricket club approached various organisations and businesses in the town and a meeting was arranged at which almost 300 people were present. Plans for the site were presented and a 30-year lease signed between the cricket club and Axminster Carpets Ltd. An appeal for financial support resulted in a donation of £2,000 from the Axminster carnival committee and of £500 from Axminster Inner Wheel.

Following a meeting at the Axe Vale Club members from the cricket and bowls clubs formed what became the Cloakham Lawn Sports Ground Committee and the Cloakham Lawn Sports and Social Club became a reality. One of its first acts was to ask Mr Harry Dutfield to become the club's president. An application was made to obtain charitable status for the project and this was granted in 1988.

Approaches were made to East Devon District Council, the Sports Council (South West Region) and Axminster Town Council to secure grants and loans to assist with phase one of the scheme. Generous donations were made including one from Axminster Town Football Club of £2,000. Advice was sought from the Sports Turf Research Institute for ploughing and grading the field, installing drainage and laying and forming the cricket table and outfield. Phase one also included the provision of an all-weather cricket wicket (partly grant-aided by the Lords Taverners), a car park and an equipment store.

The first cricket match took place at Cloakham Lawn on Saturday 27 April 1988. The following day Ian MacDonald scored the first century on the new ground. Oddly enough he had also scored the last century on the cricket club's old ground in North Street. During this first season the main building was still under construction and the cricketers had to share the groundsman's shed for both changing and the provision of teas.

An impressive presentation of the suggested second phrase, the construction of an indoor bowling centre had been made to the East Devon District Council in 1987 and a second open evening was made at the Guildhall in March. The East Devon District Council offered a grant of £45,000 and an interest-free loan for the same amount and there was further support from the Axminster Town Council and the Sports Council. In order to finance the proposals much fund-raising was necessary. The generosity of the public in Axminster was also much in evidence, so the project went ahead.

The quotation from Pearce (South West) of Taunton was accepted for the main building, which would house three indoor bowling rinks, a bar and changing rooms. The completion date was scheduled for October 1988 and the president officially opened the Harry Dutfield Bowls Hall in December of that year.

Following a period of consolidation the management committee decided to improve the facilities in order to enable them to be enjoyed by a wider section of the community. The main proposals of phase three were to provide an outdoor bowls rink, cricket practice nets, a multi-sport club area for tennis and five-a-side football, plus the relocation of the artificial wicket. The cost to complete phase three was £250,000. Support was successfully sought from the newly created Lottery Fund and work began on the project in early 1996. The bowling club was formed in April and the multi-sports area later in the summer. An offer of further monetary support from Axminster Carpets Ltd has led to hopes of a home for Axminster RFC, a skateboarding area and a BMX track.

Kilmington Cricket Club

Kilmington cricket club is in possession of minute books that date from 1903 and scores, more or less, from 1912. Few village cricket clubs can match this and, in Kilmington's case, a missing score can be filled in by reference to the files of two local papers, either the *Chard & Ilminster News* or *Pulman's Weekly News*. Before 1903, however, a Stygian darkness, through which only the briefest glimmer of occasional light penetrates, covers the doings of the club and no record exists of the year in which the club was formed.

The earliest reference to the club discovered so far is of a game at Rousdon on 4 July 1879, which was reported in *Pulman's Weekly News* at the time. Modern cricketers, used to a game ending once the team batting second has either passed their opponents' score or been bowled out in the attempt, may find it strange but, until the outbreak of the Second World War and occasionally beyond, it was normal for a team to bat on once they had passed their opponents' score and, time permitting, sometimes a third, and even fourth, innings was played.

There were four innings in that game at Rousdon, who were patronised by the Peek family and had a pitch in the grounds of Rousdon Manor (later Allhallows School). The home side scored 88, Kilmington replied with 48, out of which their skipper William Snell made 11 and batsman Jack Newbery 17; half a dozen of the Kilmington side failed to score. Rousdon followed with 90 in their second innings and then dismissed Kilmington for 38 runs, 15 of which were extras. No bowling figures survive, but William Snell took five wickets and Mr Farnham four.

For many years local newspapers often ignored who took the wickets, let alone for how many runs. However, we know that the first Kilmington team was: W. Snell, T. Wood, W. Hussey, R. Farnham, T. Snell, E. Dare, Revd Southam, J. Newbery, C. Bartlett, F. Ando and T. Broomfield.

Later that year, 'on the Kilmington ground', Rousdon scored 94 with R. Farnham and J. Snell taking three wickets each. Kilmington were dismissed for 25 and had five more ducks on their side including C. Wakely who was 'thrown-out by Oldridge for 0.' Kilmington were beaten by 42 runs when Oldridge bowled them out for 27 runs in their second innings. There were another five ducks with eight extras.

After that there is only the briefest reference to any cricket in the village for the remainder of the nineteenth century. In 1883 Axminster Second XI won by four runs at Kilmington after the home side

Above: *A working party on the new cricket field at Cloakham Lawn in 1988.* Left to right: *Les Haynes, Peter Hayball, Steve Downton, Andrew Moulding, Andy Cross, Bert Pike, Dave Capon.*

Above right: *The main building of the Cloakham Lawn Sports and Social Club nears completion in 1988.*

Right: *Work on the outdoor bowls green at Cloakham Lawn in 1996.*

had opened with 130. Axminster's Jack Love took seven wickets. In 1889 there is a reference to the club in the parish magazine for June:

> *The cricket season has come round again, and this year the committee hope to be able to give the smaller boys a separate pitch to themselves on which they can practice at the same time that other members are playing. We hope to arrange some matches for this season, due notice of which will be given in the parish magazine. Mr Snell has kindly permitted the club to have the use of his field opposite the church as in former years.*
>
> *C. Boucher, Hon. Sec.*

The scores of three games that summer were given in the parish magazine. On 27 July Oak House School, Axminster, scored 39 despite what must have been accurate bowling from A. Sanisbury (possibly a printing error which should have read 'Salisbury') who clean-bowled nine batsmen; Jack Newbery bowled the other batsman. Kilmington made 39 but lost by seven runs when, after the school made 49 in their second innings, they were dismissed for 42. In another game Kilmington beat the Gentlemen of Coryton by 10 wickets. They made 45 and, after dismissing the Gents for 18 and 28, won on 2–0.

Apart from a trip to Dalwood when Kilmington were dismissed for 19 runs, exhaustive research has failed to find any other mention of the club until 1901 when the name of Boucher is again mentioned as secretary and Harry Hurford is mentioned as being on the committee along with William Snell, A. Snell, E. Newbery and J. Newbery. Even checking the fixtures of other clubs is no help. Quite a few village teams in the Chard area had their matches well covered by the *Chard & Ilminster News* but Kilmington was in *Pulman's Weekly News* country and at that time the publication paid scant attention to local cricket other than that of Seaton and Axminster.

Kilmington's ground was, as far as we know, the field immediately below the cricket field that is used in 2003, although some games had been played across the road in a field behind St Giles' Church. Both fields opposite the church were part of the Kilmington Farm estate. William Snell was probably captain throughout the 1880s and 1890s and it is highly likely that Mr C. Boucher was the club's first secretary until his retirement in 1903 when Harry Hurford began his stint in this position. Both men also acted as treasurer but the financial transactions of the club would not become a burden until well after the Second World War. There was the occasional function to raise cash, as £2.15s.3d. (£2.76) from a dance in 1906 suggests, but that seems to have been when extra funds were needed and, certainly by the start of the twentieth century, the club relied in the main on subscriptions. These ranged from the chairman's (Mr E.C. Hope-Hall) £1 down to individual players who paid 1s. (5p) each.

In 1904 the total expenditure was £3.18s.9d., of which only £0.17s.9d. was spent on equipment of any kind (three balls and a score-book). However, there was an interesting entry of 'To boys for finding ball, one shilling'. As a cricket ball cost between 1s. and 4s., we suspect this was for the whole season rather than finding one ball, which would hardly justify such a reward.

The club paid 10s. a year to Mr E. Hurford to 'look after and take charge of the goods of the club on practice nights and see that they were safely stored away.' Probably some players owned their own kit, but it is hard not to feel that a pair of batting gloves that were purchased in 1908 was worn in turn by most members.

There were teas, often provided as an act of generosity by a patron. In Kilmington's early games it was Mrs Hope-Hall's name that was usually

The official opening of the new cricket club pavilion at Kilmington, c.1910. It was a gift from Arthur Hitchcock **(second from the right).** *Those present include Jack and Jim Newbery, Revd J.H.H. Copleston, Colonel Hooper, James and Jack Sanders, George Warren and Ern Bastable.*

mentioned in this respect. That said, some teas had to be provided by the club and players – in 1909, Mr A. Snell proposed that cards should be provided to the effect that 'the sum of 4d. would be made by all persons having tea with the exception of the visiting team.' In the 1904 accounts 1s.10d. was paid out for bread (5d.), tea (1s.) and sugar (5d.) in May, along with payments of 1s. for butter and 5d. for milk. In June 1s.8d. was paid for similar items. The payments were made to KVS (presumably Kilmington Village Stores).

Teas caused considerable comment in the minute books and were considered important enough for a sub-committee of Mrs William Snell, Mrs Newbery, Miss Salter and Mrs Hitchcock to be formed to deal with them. Mr French, the village baker whose shop was next to the chapel, however, made some teas, on a commercial basis.

An entry for 6s. for 'Adams to All Saints' on 30 July 1909 could only be for the hire of a brake to an away game, but it is the only time that such an entry appears. With so many farming members in the club, it is hard not to feel that Kilmington cricketers were self-sufficient in the equine department.

Happily there was little in the way of a major outlay to be met. At the end of the 1908 season the move had been made to the club's new home (where it is still based in 2003), although the new pitch needed relaying and claying. Members gratefully accepted an offer from their captain, who never seemed to receive any rent, for a horse and cart to carry the material from his orchard. In such a rural village there would be no shortage of men to do the work. Mr Snell allowed the club to trim the hedges as necessary and to shroud (lop?) the walnut trees that once stood beside the ground. It was a different matter when it was felt necessary to place a fence inside the hedge that faced the road. It cost £7.16s.10d., money the club did not have – indeed they were in debt to the tune of 1s.10d. at the time – and members had to pledge the cash. Revd J. Harris pledged £3, Harry Hurford £1, and seven other members 10s. each. The money pledged was repaid to the members concerned between April 1908 and May 1909. Why that fence was needed was never made plain in the minute book; perhaps there were gaps in the hedge that allowed passing livestock to wander in.

It is interesting to note that the 1s.10d. (11p) debt reported by Harry Hurford at the 1909 AGM had only moved up to 14s.4d. (£1.73) profit 42 years later when he presented his last accounts in 1951. In between, funds had stood as high as £10 on occasion.

What of the early players? Head and shoulders above everyone else was J.G. 'Jack' Newbery, a bowler of great repute and no mean slouch with the bat. It is not known when he first turned out Kilmington, but he was the Jack Newbery who played in the 1879 game at Rousdon. This meant that his playing career saw him play into his eighties, during the 1930s. He became captain and was universally respected as a hard but fair opponent. Jack is one of the colourful characters of Kilmington, not least because he always sported a black waistcoat when playing, and his spaniel, which accompanied him everywhere, was unrivalled when it came to finding lost balls (which would have saved the club paying boys for performing that duty).

If the late Sidney Gowing (one of the first Spar Ramblers tourists) is to be believed Jack Newbery also wore a watch with the waistcoat. In 1975, mulling over the Spar Ramblers' early tours, Sidney remembered:

> *But some incidents remain in the memory: the old gentleman who, in one Devon village* [Kilmington], *bowled, and very accurately, in a waistcoat: and how having tempted some rash batsman into an injudicious sweep, he would grin broadly and pull an enormous hunter from his waistcoat pocket – as though deciding whether he had time to bowl the remainder out before milking time.*

There were often four Newberys on the side and, allowing for a mix-up in the initials from time to time, around seven or eight of the clan appears in Kilmington's Edwardian score-books. Teaming up with Jack on occasion to destroy many an opposing side was his son Jim (R.J. Newbery), who bowled underhand with telling affect and who must have been one of the last exponents of the now-forgotten art, which he was still utilising in the very early 1930s. There was an E. Newbery who, as far as we have been able to trace, was another of Jack's sons who died early after becoming the only man in the club's history to take nine wickets in an innings twice. He had 9–20 against Charmouth in 1907 and 9–26 against Mr C.D. Lansley's XI four years later. The only Kilmington player to have bettered E. Newbery's return is Revd J.H.H. Copleston who took 9–11 at Charmouth in 1909.

Ernest George Bastaple was the son of the Baptist pastor of Kilmington and Loughwood who had fallen in love with baking through watching it at French's bakery near the chapel in Kilmington. He learnt that trade and ended up as a highly successful baker at Berry Stores in Colyton. E.G. was the first of Kilmington's wicket-keeping batsmen and a very good one at that! He was a dour batsman given to fighting it out of the worst of wickets long after most others had decided discretion and the pavilion were the better part of valour.

The star of the early sides was the Revd J.H.H. Copleston, curate-in-charge at Kilmington between 1908–11 and a member of a family that supplied Offwell's rectors for around 200 years. J.H.H. probably looked upon the Sabbath and his duties on that day as an intrusion into what would otherwise have been a seven-day cricketing week. It was said that he had thought up an excuse for the Bishop to allow him to play on Sundays but never had the courage to try it out. He appears in the score-books of almost every local club in the area, his main club being Seaton.

When he came to Kilmington he served as a chairman, captain and a committee member between 1906 and his departure to Widworthy in 1916. That was close enough to allow him to still play for Kilmington from time to time and bring his own XI there for games.

J.H.H. Copleston was a fine bowler who came in with a bounding stride to fling the ball straight at the wicket, basing his action on the sensible theory that if you missed he hit. A whole crop of wickets each season showed that it was a theory based on fact. In addition, he made enough runs to make even the cricketers of 2003 raise the odd eyebrow. His not-out 152 against Mr Hope-Hall's XI in 1910 has only been bettered by two Kilmington batsmen, Pete Davis and Julian Page, both of whom have done so twice. As captain he would always gather his team in the pavilion before the game for a prayer, telling them, 'If you win say nothing, if you lose say less'. He insisted on leading them out on to the field in an orderly fashion and woe betide the man who, once he was out, changed before the end of the game.

Those early games were frequently low-scoring affairs, but scoring did improve in the years immediately before the First World War. A more noticeable development in the local game, certainly since the 1970s, has been the interest shown in ground maintenance, and this had led to better conditions for batsmen and run scoring. Having said that, it appears that Edwardian Kilmington looked after their ground as much as possible, as evidenced by their spending the considerable sum of £9.15s.3d. on a water-ballast roller. Even then, for Kilmington and all other local village sides, the bowler was to the batsmen what the English archers were to the French at Agincourt, Crécy and Poitiers.

All Saints, Axminster Second XI, Chardstock, Colyford, Dalwood, Hawkchurch and Upottery – that was about the extent of Kilmington's horizon. It was a horizon dictated by the distance the club were prepared to travel, the strength of the teams they were prepared to take on and the cost of travelling. Cash, and the raising of it, took up a lot of the committee's time and long deliberations always took place before the purchase of any bats, balls or pads. They used (or bought) two or three balls a season which were frequently, along with bats, sent back to the suppliers, Messrs Meddam & Lewis, for repair. In 1907, at a time when most players paid a 1s. subscription, a new half-a-crown was introduced for outside members. At the same time the 4d. charge for tea was reconfirmed. The cash book was always carefully kept by Harry Hurford, every penny carefully accounted for.

The year 1908 is always accepted as the time of the move to the new ground, a fact seemingly borne out by the new fencing required. It is interesting to note, therefore, that the minute book makes no mention of

Kilmington cricket club before their East Devon Cricket League debut against Newton St Cyres on 4 May 1966. Left to right, back row: *Mike Wallis, David Cook, Simon Church, Edward Greathead, Simon Lambert, Geoff Brown (scorer), Ralph Cook, Ashley Cook, David Lavender (secretary), Mark Jenkins, Ian Watson, David Capon;* front: *Hal Cook, Keith Rockett, Chris Bolton (chairman), Martin Huscroft, Harry Pape (president), John Lavender, James Kirkcaldie. Their record for the first three seasons was unique:*

		Played	Won	Drawn	Lost	Points
1996	*Division Four*	18	12	6	0	300
1997	*Division Three*	18	11	7	0	295
1998	*Division Two*	18	9	9	0	264

Left: *Kilmington Cricket Club, c.1980.* Left to right, back row: *Harry Pape (umpire), Brian Gage, John Lavender, Mike Marsh, James Kirkcaldie, Chris Bolton, Geoff Brown (scorer);* front: *Chris Marshal, Mike Collier, Tony Rockett, Brice Cornelius, Denis Hutchings, Bill Bagwell.*

Right: *Kilmington's old Village Hall in the corner of the cricket field. The new hall, built on the other side of the road, is in the background.*

the fact, although a vote of thanks was passed to Mr Hitchcock at the AGM at the Old Inn on 2 April 1909 for 'his intention of supplying the club with a pavilion.'

It is perhaps pertinent to discuss Mr Hitchcock at this point. A gentleman of known generosity, he lived at Betty's Ground at Haddon Corner. He was described shortly after his death in 1931, at a ceremony in the pavilion at which his portrait, a gift of his sisters, the Misses Hitchcock from Paignton, was unveiled as a memorial, as the man who:

> *... purchased the field upward of 20 years before and laid it out as a cricket field and also built a commodious pavilion and provided a bowling green beside the cricket field.*

Generous he was without doubt, but it is hard to avoid the feeling that he liked his own way and got it where the cricket club was concerned. Before 1926, when the word president appears in the minute books for the first time, it is difficult to state for certain if Mr Hitchcock, or anyone else, held this title. The only mention made is that he (and others) 'took the chair'. After 1926, a chairman was not elected but a senior member of the committee took the chair on the occasions when the president was absent. Elijah Wakely was chairman during the war years and immediately afterwards (1941–47) when the position of president became vacant. Since then, with a succession of presidents who, more often than not, were active rather than figureheads, the position or use of the term chairman again fell into disuse until the election of Chris Bolton in 1990.

Secretary Harry Hurford was not prepared to whistle Mr Hitchcock's tune indefinitely and, when at variance with him over the building of the Village Hall in the corner of the cricket field opposite the pavilion, he resigned. Mr Hitchcock had wanted the Village Hall to be the same wooden design as the pavilion, whereas Harry, who could lay his hands on a good supply of stone on offer from a burnt-down building in the neighbourhood, suggested stone for the bottom half. He was overruled by Mr Hitchcock. The folly in not building in stone would be proved over and over again in the years to come but, in the meantime, Arthur Tucker, Mr Hitchcock's handyman, succeeded Harry Hurford as secretary. Harry stayed on the committee, however, and was soon acting as secretary again.

Whatever the rift that occurred, it was soon healed and, in 1929, shortly before his death, Mr Hitchcock not only wrote saying that the ground was theirs on the usual conditions, but went on to say he would meet all their outstanding liabilities (they were 18s.3d. in debt at the time), would put £10 in their funds, would pay all rates, tithes and taxes, including Income Tax assessed against the club and have the Atco mower overhauled and repaired at a cost of £6.2s.6d. He also invited members of both teams, the umpires and scorers to accept his hospitality during the season for their teas at all home matches whether played in the afternoon or evening. He added that it was quite understood that if any visitor wished to pay for him or herself they were quite at liberty to do so. He added:

> *Though I have no intention of imposing any condition in this matter, it is certainly my wish that the enjoyment of this ground should be, first and foremost, for the residents of Kilmington.*

One occasion when neither side accepted his generous offer came in 1930 when Kilmington were wined and dined at the George Hotel in Axminster by Spar Ramblers.

Mr Hitchcock, as mentioned earlier, became the first real president of the club and remained so until his death in 1931. The club, pavilion and the ground are lasting testimonials to his generosity to both the cricket club and the village.

William Snell's long association with the club ended in 1912 when he left the district. Members had played on his field for so many years without so much as a suggestion of rent in the accounts book, and he had been a more-than-useful player and captain. Although he must have been getting on a bit at the time, he turned out for one last game before his departure. The dismissal of Kilmington's last man for a single after the game had already been won hardly attracted much comment at the time but the entry in the score-book may be of interest today, 'J. Lavender bowled W. White'. It was the father of Jack Lavender, club secretary from 1952–94.

In 1924 a scorer is first mentioned by name when Miss Edie Cook was appointed at the tender age of 11. She would do the job on and off until she was 50. She was born to the job. Her father, Harry Cook, had been the manager at Bidwell's Brush Factory at the foot of Castle Hill in Axminster and had moved to run his own brush factory next to the chapel in Kilmington. After playing for the club he acted as umpire in the 1920s and 1930s. Transport for away games was no problem for Edie; she travelled on the pillion of Elijah Wakely's motorcycle. He was her boyfriend and later her husband. Bill Hurford travelled the same way on Arthur Tucker's motorcycle. Mr Bastaple could take six players in his big Studebaker and took them to away games for which he received only a nominal sum for petrol. Not all the team could get in his car of course, and a Model T Ford belonging to Jim Symonds was press-ganged into use. It enjoyed the name of The Yellow Peril. In 1924, when Mr Bastable was unable to drive, Harry Hurford was instructed to obtain a charabanc for away games.

The cricketers and the bowling club have existed side-by-side and done so more or less amicably. (Sadly the formation of a bowling club at Cloakham Lawn in Axminster, from where many of the Kilmington club's players came, led to Kilmington starting the 2000 season without the warming background clatter of woods hitting woods.) There was, however, friction with the tennis players in the early 1920s when tennis games began to interfere with the cricketers. A strict set of times was laid down: tennis was allowed on Tuesday and Thursday evenings and Wednesday afternoon until 6p.m. It was also permitted on Saturdays and Bank Holidays if there was no cricket match on at the time.

It took a world war to stop Kilmington playing cricket but, once that had ended, one of East Devon's most popular village clubs was back at what it did best – playing cricket in the true sense of the game, and playing it to a much higher standard than one would expect from a village side.

Not even their entry into the East Devon League in 1996 changed their outlook, although they won the Division Four title at the first attempt and followed by winning Division Three (1997), Division Two (1998) and Division One (2000). They like to win, but one suspects that the post-match pint in the Old Inn tastes just as good if they win or lose.

Harry Hurford with wife Rhoda May (née Vessey) and their daughter May in 1922.

Jack Lavender with Kilmington Cricket Club's minute book in which he had written the minutes of their meetings for 42 years (1952–94) as their secretary.

The presentation of commemorative mugs on Kilmington cricket field for Queen Elizabeth II's silver jubilee (1977) by Bruce Beckingsale, the chairman of Kilmington Parish Council.

Postscript

First a quick look at the past. Axminster has a varied and interesting past, from Roman times to the present day. Sadly, with the passage of time, it lost its identity as a major Devon town through a variety of reasons. The outbreak of foot-and-mouth disease, which struck Devon so hard in 2001, has all but killed off the local livestock market – the feature that gave old Axminster its identity as a market town. Axminster must find a new identity. It is up to us to fight for it.

I am setting out my case for a vibrant town that must include a complete age range of people living here. We have the infrastructure; we have a rail-head, a Cottage Hospital that is second to none, a comprehensive school that is going from strength to strength. We also have a superb indoor heated swimming-pool and a hydrotherapy pool as well as sports centres and are looking forward to a brand-new sports hall. We have an excellent variety of primary schools and a good mixture of clubs and societies who can be contacted via the library website. And, although most people will laugh when I say it – until they need one – there is even a chiropodist in town.

As to the regeneration, we have had at last some movement on the Webster's Garage site that should bring in extra shops and commercial facilities in the centre of the town, as well as housing.

The traffic problems that occur in our Saxon town should, we hope, be solved by a north–south road link between Chard Road and Lyme Road using grade-three land, which will mean that there will be no loss of prime agricultural land.

As Axminster looks forward to its expansion opportunities it is vital that some of the new housing is provided for rent and for low-cost sale so that our young people can remain here.

Our industrial estate at Weycroft, for which I fought years ago as a county councillor, goes from strength to strength. Our town is home to a number of wide-ranging industries from small textile work-shops to internationally renowned firms such as Axminster Carpets and Axminster Power Tools.

My final pipe dream is to see young people from the continent joining our young people to learn together, so widening the horizons of both.

Douglas Hull, Axminster Town Mayor, July 2003.

Right: *1st Axminster Girl Guides, c. 1924.* Left to right, back row: *Maude Honeybun, Amy Humphrey, Annie Burrows, ?, Delia Richards, ?, Dolly Sweetland, Mary Tuck;* middle: *Sylvia Bass, Alice Henley, Lieutenant Saunders, Captain Lansley, Miss Atkins, Queenie Wakley, ?;* front: *?, ?, Bubbles Musgrave.*

Left: *The 'milk parade' at Axminster Scout camp, 1922.* Left to right: *Bill Manley, Peter Collier, ?, ?, Freddie Shaw, Bernie Goddard, Douglas Avery, Jimmy Hayball, Laurie Daniels, Robert Daniels, Frank Parker, Norman Snell, ? Trivett, Bill Bulled, Sammy Wench (scoutmaster), Frank Manley, 'Pa' Burt (assistant scoutmaster), ?, Jack Goddard, Vincent Robinson, ?, Arthur Snell.*

Bibliography

Bracken, C.W.*

Bryne, Colonel A.H., *Battlefields of England.**

Chard & Ilminster News, Chard (later Taunton), Various issues, 1880–2000.

Cornish, Robert, *Kilmington Church Wardens' Accounts MDLVV—MDCVIII*, William Pollard & Co. Ltd, Exeter, 1901.

Cornish, Robert, notes on the *Axminster Church Wardens Accounts*, 1896, now in the Devon County Records Office.

Davidson, James, *History of Axminster*, London, 1836.

Davidson, James, *History of Newenham Abbey*, London, 1843.

Denison, *Chronicles of the Coach.*

Gosling, Gerald, *A Tiger's Tale, The History of Axminster Town Football Club 1902–2002*, Axminster Printing Company, 2003.

Grimley, Roger, *The Rambler Remembered, the Story of Stan Wakley*, Devon Omnibus Collection.

Hadfield, Charles, *The Canals of South West England*, David & Charles, Newton Abbot, 1967.

Hoskins, W.G., *Devon*, David & Charles, Newton Abbot, 1977.

Pulman, George, *The Book of the Axe.*

Pulman's Weekly News, Yeovil (Axminster in 2003), Various issues, 1880–2002.

Sutton, C.M., *Axminster Hospital 1886–1986*, Axminster Printing Company, 1986.

Swete, John, *Tour of Devon.**

Watts, H.C., *Book of Axminster*, Snell, Axminster, 1902.

Wilkin, Major W.H., *Notes on Axminster Church and the Vicars Since 1602*, Southwoods Ltd, Exeter, 1921.

Pulman's Weekly News.

Messrs. R & C. Snell, Axminster. Yeovil, June 1st 1920

To the Western Gazette and Pulman's Weekly News Newspapers & Printing & Publishing Co., Ltd.

Pulman's Weekly News is the Leading Agricultural Paper in the West of England, and Circulates in Somerset, Dorset, and Devon. Published Monday afternoon for Tuesday

Cheques should be made payable to Western Gazette &c. Co., Ltd., and all letters addressed "Manager," Pulman's Weekly News, Yeovil.

Official Advertisements for Somerset, Dorset, and Devon appear in Pulman's Weekly News.

The Company cannot acknowledge any Receipts unless given on their Official Adhesive Forms.

1920 To Advertising in Pulman's Weekly News:

Property "Bell Hotel" 8 ... 5 5

INVOICE.

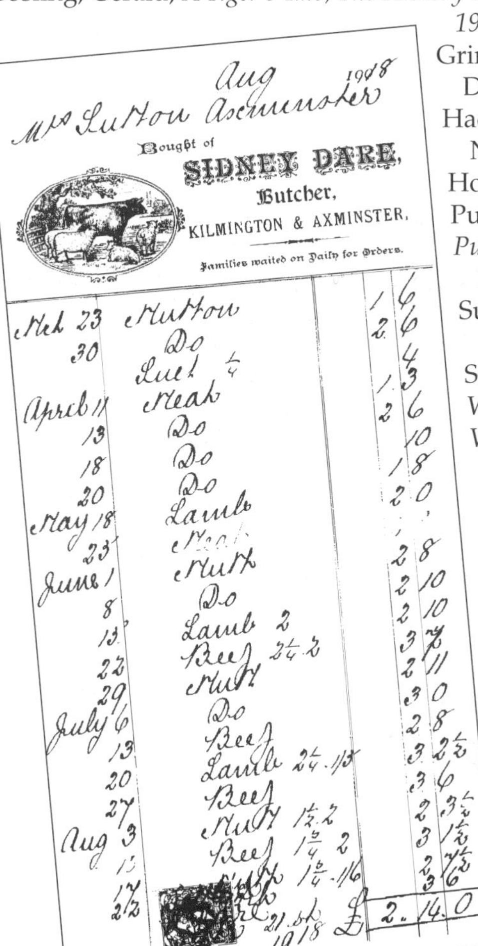

Mrs Sutton Axminster Aug 1918

Bought of SIDNEY DARE, Butcher, KILMINGTON & AXMINSTER.

Families waited on Daily for Orders.

Looking at Axminster, c.1900 from Membury Road.

*Taken from press reports, and no further details are available.

SUBSCRIBERS

Adams-Hutchings
Mrs M.J. Ambrose, Axminster, Devon
A.R. Anning
The Apsey Family, Chardstock
A.J. Bagwell
Amy C. Baker, Hawkchurch, Devon
Jackie Bennett, Yukon, Oklahoma, USA
Mr and Mrs N. Berry, Kilmington, Devon
Jane Bostock
Gill and Simon Boston
Carole C. Botley, Axminster
Diana L. Botley, Axminster
Mark Boyland, Axminster, Devon
Joy Broadbridge, Axminster
Mr Leslie R. Broom
Susan Brown (née Kendall), Axminster
Kenneth Browne, Axminster, Devon
John and Jean Bucknall
Brigid A. Bull, Axminster
Martin J. Bulled, Hucclecote, Gloucester
William Bulled, Hucclecote, Gloucester
Bill and Jan Burrough, Hawkchurch, Devon
K.J. Burrow, Bucks Cross, Devon
Deborah Carmichael, Katoomba, NSW, Australia
Charles Chick, Axminster, Devon
John D. Church, Kilmington
The Coath Family, Millbrook, Axminster, Devon
Mr Ernie Coles, Axminster, Devon
Mrs J.M. Conachie, Winsham, Somerset
John Cook, Kilmington, Axminster
Roy and Mal Cook, Rivendell, Dalwood, Axminster
W.C. Cousens, Axminster
Jean M. Cox, Wolverhampton
Peter Davis, formerly Boxfield Road, Axminster
E.M. Dibble, Smallridge, Axminster, Devon
Paul C.W. Dimon, Axminster, Devon
Brian P. Downton, Millwey Rise
Steve and Eileen Downton, Axminster, Devon
Roger T. Durrant, Axminster, Devon
Malcolm Dyer, Shute, Devonshire
John E. Ebdon, Smallridge, Axminster
Brian Edwards, Axminster, Devon
The Rt Hon. Sir Peter Emery
Mrs Heather Evans (née Forsey), Hastings
Eveleigh, Axminster
Tony and Jenny Fells, Axminster, Devon
Margaret R. Foden, Axminster, Devon
Jennifer P. Ford, Shute, Axminster, Devon
Fred French, Axminster, Devon
Kenneth John Gapper
Mr Reginald Gardner, Raymonds Hill, Devon
Christopher Gardner, Axminster
Michael Gledstone, Axminster, Devon
William F. Goddard, Axminster, Devon
Bazil Walter Gosling, Kilmington, Devon
Roger E. Gould, Axminster, Devon
Bob and Wendy Graham
Mr and Mrs R.J. Harris, Churchill, Axminster
Mrs Lesley K. Harwood (née Restorick), Crewkerne
Hawkchurch History Society
Elizabeth A. Hayball, Axminster, Devon
David Hayne, Axminster
Steve Haynes and Paula Hutchings, Axminster, Devon
Mr W.D. Hepworth, Membury
Mr Terence R. Herbert, Axminster, Devon
Rachael M.S. Hill, Kilmington, Devon
Mr M.W. Hill, Kilmington, Devonshire
Mrs Emma Hill (née Love), Seager's Cottage, Axminster
Frank Hooper, Axminster
Margaret and Eric Howes, Sector Lane, Axminster
Douglas R.H. Hull (Cllr) Mayor, Axminster
Dawn A. Hunt, Axminster, Devon

J. Hurford
Mr and Mrs J.T. Hussey
David J. Jeffery, London SE1
Bill Johnson, Axminster, Devon
Cedric and Veronica Johnson, Axminster
Joan Jones (née Braddick), Axminster, Devon
Julie Kendall-Ridout, Bournemouth
Mr R.W. Kerslake, Kilmington, Devon
Cecil F.G. Knight, Colyford, Devon
Brian W. Lavender, Kilmington
Lindley and Sue
Gillian M. Long, Chardstock, Devon
Mr Gilbert N. Love, Gamberlake, Axminster
Mrs Norma-Ann Love, South Street, Axminster
Mr Simon M. Love, Applegarth, Axminster
Mr Jamie R. Love, Honeysuckle Cottage, Axminster
Christopher J. Love Esq., Tudor Cottage, Axminster
David J. Lucas, Axminster, Devon
Mr Malcolm MacDonald, Axminster Carpets employee for 38 years
Drs D. and R. Mackenzie, Hawkchurch, Devon
Mrs E. Maeer, Axminster
Keith and Stella Marks, South Chard
Mrs Carolyn J. Marks (née Restorick), Crewkerne
Barbara Marshall (née Tolman), Ohio, USA
Pamela Massey, Axminster, Devon
Mr Paul Maughan, Axminster
Ian C. McLennan, Guernsey, Channel Islands
Robert C. McLennan, Ripon, North Yorkshire
Roy T. McLennan, Axminster, Devon
Mr Christopher E. Miller, Axminster
Susan Moore, Kilmington, Devon
Bev and Tony Moore, Axminster, Devon
Bill Moore, Shute, Devon
Mrs G. Morley, South Woodham Ferrers, Essex
Mr R. Newberry, Maidstone, Kent
Geoffrey E. Newton, Axminster, Devon
Ken G. Norman, Charmouth, Dorset
John K. Norman, Yorkshire
Chris and B. Painton, Dulcis Farm, Kilmington
Chris and Romy Parker-Sales, Axminster, Devon
Vera Parsons
Gillian Perham
Robert and Karen Pethybridge, Kilmington
David Pike, Chard, Somerset
Bob and Freda Pitfield, Hawkchurch
John and Anne Playford, Westwater, Devon
Robert Powell, Axminster, Devon
Mr Stanley Powell
Ron and Liz Purvey, Axminster, Devon
Christine M. Putt, Axminster, Devo
Peter and Vi Pym, Axminster, Devon
Mr Roger and Melanie Pym, Dalwood, Axminster, Devon
Mrs Dorothy Quick, Axminster, Devon
Colin Reece, Loveridge, Hawkchurch
Mr Charles W.G. Restorick, Misterton
Mr Geoffrey F. Restorick, Misterton
George William Restorick, Braydon, Wiltshire
Ray and Penny Rhodes, Axminster, Devon
Alan William Roberts, Longacre, Tytherleigh
Ms Margaret F. Rosling, Axminster
Mrs Mollie Rowe, Axminster, Devon
James Rowe, Lord of Axminster
Mrs Vivienne A. Rowe (née Restorick), Misterton
George Geoffrey Rugg, Axminster
Mrs Gladys Russell (née Trivett)
John and Margaret Ryan, Axminster, Devon
Kenneth G. Sansom, Axminster, Devon
Ellen E.A. Scott, Axminster
Paul Antony Scott, Lewknor, Oxfordshire
Julian and Helen Shaw, Kilmington, Devon
Bill Short, Alston, Axminster
J. and C. Sweetland, Stanwell, Middlesex

Community Histories

The Book of Addiscombe • Canning and Clyde Road Residents Association and Friends
The Book of Addiscombe, Vol. II • Canning and Clyde Road Residents Association and Friends
The Book of Axminster with Kilmington • L. Berry and G. Gosling
The Book of Bampton • Caroline Seward
The Book of Barnstaple • Avril Stone
The Book of Barnstaple, Vol. II • Avril Stone
The Book of The Bedwyns • Bedwyn History Society
The Book of Bickington • Stuart Hands
Blandford Forum: A Millennium Portrait • Blandford Forum Town Council
The Book of Bramford • Bramford Local History Group
The Book of Breage & Germoe • Stephen Polglase
The Book of Bridestowe • D. Richard Cann
The Book of Bridport • Rodney Legg
The Book of Brixham • Frank Pearce
The Book of Buckfastleigh • Sandra Coleman
The Book of Buckland Monachorum & Yelverton • Pauline Hamilton-Leggett
The Book of Carharrack • Carharrack Old Cornwall Society
The Book of Carshalton • Stella Wilks and Gordon Rookledge
The Parish Book of Cerne Abbas • Vivian and Patricia Vale
The Book of Chagford • Iain Rice
The Book of Chapel-en-le-Frith • Mike Smith
The Book of Chittlehamholt with Warkleigh & Satterleigh • Richard Lethbridge
The Book of Chittlehampton • Various
The Book of Colney Heath • Bryan Lilley
The Book of Constantine • Moore and Trethowan
The Book of Cornwood & Lutton • Compiled by the People of the Parish
The Book of Creech St Michael • June Small
The Book of Cullompton • Compiled by the People of the Parish
The Book of Dawlish • Frank Pearce
The Book of Dulverton, Brushford, Bury & Exebridge • Dulverton and District Civic Society
The Book of Dunster • Hilary Binding
The Book of Edale • Gordon Miller
The Ellacombe Book • Sydney R. Langmead
The Book of Exmouth • W.H. Pascoe
The Book of Grampound with Creed • Bane and Oliver
The Book of Hayling Island & Langstone • Peter Rogers
The Book of Helston • Jenkin with Carter
The Book of Hemyock • Clist and Dracott
The Book of Herne Hill • Patricia Jenkyns
The Book of Hethersett • Hethersett Society Research Group
The Book of High Bickington • Avril Stone
The Book of Ilsington • Dick Wills
The Book of Kingskerswell • Carsewella Local History Group
The Book of Lamerton • Ann Cole and Friends
Lanner, A Cornish Mining Parish • Sharron Schwartz and Roger Parker
The Book of Leigh & Bransford • Malcolm Scott
The Book of Litcham with Lexham & Mileham • Litcham Historical and Amenity Society
The Book of Loddiswell • Loddiswell Parish History Group
The New Book of Lostwithiel • Barbara Fraser
The Book of Lulworth • Rodney Legg
The Book of Lustleigh • Joe Crowdy
The Book of Lyme Regis • Rodney Legg
The Book of Manaton • Compiled by the People of the Parish
The Book of Markyate • Markyate Local History Society
The Book of Mawnan • Mawnan Local History Group
The Book of Meavy • Pauline Hemery
The Book of Minehead with Alcombe • Binding and Stevens
The Book of Morchard Bishop • Jeff Kingaby
The Book of Newdigate • John Callcut
The Book of Nidderdale • Nidderdale Museum Society
The Book of Northlew with Ashbury • Northlew History Group
The Book of North Newton • J.C. and K.C. Robins
The Book of North Tawton • Baker, Hoare and Shields
The Book of Nynehead • Nynehead & District History Society
The Book of Okehampton • R. and U. Radford
The Book of Paignton • Frank Pearce
The Book of Penge, Anerley & Crystal Palace • Peter Abbott
The Book of Peter Tavy with Cudlipptown • Peter Tavy Heritage Group
The Book of Pimperne • Jean Coull
The Book of Plymtree • Tony Eames
The Book of Porlock • Dennis Corner
Postbridge – The Heart of Dartmoor • Reg Bellamy
The Book of Priddy • Albert Thompson
The Book of Princetown • Dr Gardner-Thorpe
The Book of Rattery • By the People of the Parish
The Book of St Day • Joseph Mills and Paul Annear
The Book of Sampford Courtenay with Honeychurch • Stephanie Pouya
The Book of Sculthorpe • Gary Windeler
The Book of Seaton • Ted Gosling
The Book of Sidmouth • Ted Gosling and Sheila Luxton
The Book of Silverton • Silverton Local History Society
The Book of South Molton • Jonathan Edmunds
The Book of South Stoke with Midford • Edited by Robert Parfitt
South Tawton & South Zeal with Sticklepath • R. and U. Radford
The Book of Sparkwell with Hemerdon & Lee Mill • Pam James
The Book of Staverton • Pete Lavis
The Book of Stithians • Stithians Parish History Group
The Book of Stogumber, Monksilver, Nettlecombe & Elworthy • Maurice and Joyce Chidgey
The Book of Studland • Rodney Legg
The Book of Swanage • Rodney Legg
The Book of Tavistock • Gerry Woodcock
The Book of Thorley • Sylvia McDonald and Bill Hardy
The Book of Torbay • Frank Pearce
The Book of Watchet • Compiled by David Banks
The Book of West Huntspill • By the People of the Parish
Widecombe-in-the-Moor • Stephen Woods
Widecombe – Uncle Tom Cobley & All • Stephen Woods
The Book of Williton • Michael Williams
The Book of Witheridge • Peter and Freda Tout and John Usmar
The Book of Withycombe • Chris Boyles
Woodbury: The Twentieth Century Revisited • Roger Stokes
The Book of Woolmer Green • Compiled by the People of the Parish

For details of any of the above titles or if you are interested in writing your own history, please contact: Commissioning Editor Community Histories, Halsgrove House, Lower Moor Way, Tiverton Business Park, Tiverton, Devon EX16 6SS, England; email: naomic@halsgrove.com

In order to include as many historical photographs as possible in this volume, a printed index is not included. However, the Devon titles in the Community History Series are indexed by Genuki. For further information and indexes to various volumes in the series, please visit: http://www.cs.ncl.ac.uk/genuki/DEV/indexingproject.html